WAITING TO INHALE

Cannabis Legalization and the Fight for Racial Justice

AKWASI OWUSU-BEMPAH AND TAHIRA REHMATULLAH

The MIT Press
Cambridge, Massachusetts
London, England

The MIT Press would like to thank the anonymous peer reviewers who provided comments on drafts of this book. The generous work of academic experts is essential for establishing the authority and quality of our publications. We acknowledge with gratitude the contributions of these otherwise uncredited readers.

This book was set in Adobe Garamond and Berthold Akzidenz Grotesk by Jen Jackowitz. Printed and bound in the United States of America.

Library of Congress Cataloging-in-Publication Data is available.

ISBN: 978-0-262-04768-5

10 9 8 7 6 5 4 3 2 1

WAITING TO INHALE

Contents

Introduction

Throughout this book, the tales of those whose lives have been damaged by the War on Drugs are told by the victims themselves. Likewise, we let those working toward a more equitable era of legalized cannabis tell their own stories. We will also share our own stories in our voice from time to time, indicating to the reader whose tale is being told. Enjoy.

TAHIRA

At first glance, it didn't seem like Akwasi and I had much in common. I grew up in small-town Ohio, a quaint community in an area deemed the "Rust Belt" of America. As much as I was determined to move away to the big city someday, in hindsight, it was a lovely place to call home. The kind of place where I never carried house keys because we never locked our door. I was the middle daughter of Muslim immigrants from Pakistan. My father was the orthopedic surgeon in town, and my mother stayed home with us. Like most kids, I played sports (terribly), participated in a dozen after-school activities, and aimlessly roamed the town with my friends. Unlike most kids, I attended Friday prayers at our mosque an hour away and spent summers in Pakistan. I landed at The Ohio State University for undergrad, which led to jobs in finance and, eventually, a master's in business administration (MBA) at Yale.

Eight years ago, while still at Yale, my younger sister and I received a text from my mom asking if we knew where to get marijuana. Was this a test?! We were too old to be grounded for the wrong answer (I think?), but my parents' sense of humor had not quite crossed the barriers to make such jokes. Turns out it was my mother's attempt to bring some much-needed comfort to her father, my grandfather, suffering from stage 4 lung cancer. She was looking for alternative treatments and kept coming across cannabis in her Google searches. The seemingly simple request led me down a rabbit hole of research, revealing an oddly political, confusingly racist history about a flower that could ease suffering. It was a plant that could change lives, in many instances for the better. So why had it also ruined so many?

AKWASI

As a kid I wanted to be a cop. My neighbor was a retired law enforcer who glamorized the job. The gun, the badge, and the fast car all appealed to me as a young boy who had moved to Canada from a British city where the police walked the beat wearing funny hats. Chasing bad guys would be fun, I thought. My view of policing had been skewed from watching *Police Academy* and *Beverly Hills Cop* too many times. My criminal justice education taught me what I had known but tried to ignore all along—too often, the bad guys were not bad at all. And, sadly, some of the good guys really wore dark hats. So instead of becoming a cop, I decided to research the police and became a professor. I found the complex relationship between law enforcement, racism, and drug laws playing out on the streets of North America daily to be both maddening and fascinating.

In the spring of 2018, at a cannabis policy symposium at Montreal's McGill University, I crossed paths with Tahira. We bonded, and not just because we both had names that no one could pronounce. I spoke on the first day of the conference, laying out the various ways that cannabis laws have harmed racial minorities in Canada and outlined a number of measures for redress that could be incorporated into legalization.

TAHIRA

I was one of only two speakers on the business side of the conference. When I listened to what Akwasi had to say, I heard so many similarities to what I planned to present the following day. Good for me that I found a kindred and equally feisty spirit who wanted to right the wrongs that continued to unfold before us. Bad for me that he spoke before I did. Wanting to not seem like a total plagiarist, I stayed up all night rewriting my presentation.

I was living proof that cannabis businesspeople were not all white men with MBAs looking to simply cash in on a new industry. Not all MBAs were white men at all, or the enemy, in this brave new world of weed. Indeed, here I was, having discovered cannabis because my mom was looking for solutions to a distressing family situation. I did, however, come to the world of cannabis with a business perspective sculpted by Ohio State, Yale, and time spent in finance. I found that the cannabis industry mirrored the business world in general where there were few women or minorities in leadership roles. There really was no template in cannabis. It had quickly become populated by white men, and I wanted to represent a different perspective.

For those of us who have a stake in the industry, particularly people of color, there is a lingering responsibility to push for inclusion and ensure we are not reinforcing the prohibitive practices of other industries. We know we must bridge the gap in hiring practices, funding, and resources. Yet sometimes we feel we are still not sufficiently empowered to make decisions that will lead to the changes we absolutely need. But just because there aren't easy fixes should not deter us from continually having these conversations.

We run the risk of leaving behind the many minorities who paid the price—past and present—for being affiliated with what has increasingly become a legal industry. Every shiny new dispensary makes us forget the plant's racially charged history because cannabis is, more than anything, about social justice. Cannabis is a curious product. It can be used not only to persecute the unprotected classes but also to economically empower those same populations. Cannabis can change the world. In fact, it already has. It changes the way in which we innovate and how we operate, and it will continue to do so. But how do we help those who came before us? How do we help those who continue to pay the price under prohibition?

AKWASI

I did not intend to study drug policy as part of my work on racism and criminal justice, but it became clear very quickly that no such research could be thorough without including drugs, and especially cannabis. Black, Brown, and Indigenous people in Canada are overrepresented in cannabis arrests, while the white population is underrepresented in every major city. Economically marginalized Canadians, Black, and Indigenous people are more likely to live in cramped apartments, meaning they are often forced onto the streets to use cannabis. The nature of policing drives up arrest rates, particularly the stop-and-search practices that we have seen in many Canadian cities, where merely being a person of color on the street in a particular neighborhood means questioning—harassment, if you are the one being questioned—from the police. The same is true across North America, and we cannot deal with the racism obvious in cannabis arrests until we deal with systemic racism in policing more generally. Too often, cannabis acts as a gateway drug, a gateway into the unrelenting grip of the criminal justice system for members of our most marginalized populations.

For me, the theoretical became reality weeks after I moved to Indiana University Bloomington to begin my academic career, and the streets of Ferguson, Missouri, became nightly battlegrounds following the police shooting of an unarmed young Black man, Michael Brown, in 2014, prompting unrest that spread across the country. That is where we come from. This is where we think we should be going.

Cannabis legalization has been a mainstream topic across North America and the world for several years. We knew we needed to combine our voices and perspectives to do something more to shed light on the evolution of cannabis legalization and the future we need for the industry to truly thrive in a just way. A year after our first meeting, we found ourselves both presenting at another event, this time the Economist's Cannabis Summit. Over drinks after the conference, we cooked up the idea of writing a book together that would cover these themes and wed Tahira's professional experiences in the cannabis industry with my related academic and advocacy work. We agreed that our combined view, shaped by real-life experience, was novel, much needed, and could have a significant impact on the direction that legalization takes in jurisdictions considering the policy shift.

As this project has evolved, so has the world.

TAHIRA

Two years after our meeting at McGill, a pandemic has swept the globe, disproportionately attacking Black and other racial minority communities. George Floyd's death under the knee of a white police officer on an unassuming street in Minneapolis has been watched the world over, sending protesters into the streets once again—many outside my own window in New York City. Demonstrators were flushed out of Lafayette Square by federal troops firing flash grenades and tear gas in front of the White House, and peaceful protest and confrontation have played out from New York to Portland, London to Hong Kong, and Rome to Rio de Janeiro.

Defunding the police became more than just a slogan, and Black Lives Matter was stenciled on Pennsylvania Avenue in the shadow of Capitol Hill. Colin Kaepernick is no longer an outlier. Professional athletes—carrying gloves, wearing skates, awaiting a National Basketball Association tipoff—kneel during anthems to protest police treatment of Black people and wear slogans on their backs demanding racial justice. Central to all of this is the racist application of cannabis laws.

Knowing the landscape as we do, our key challenge was to ensure that the book was neither too academic nor too technical and that it would have broad appeal and broad relevance. Instead of relying solely on academic research or business case studies, we decided on a different approach—one that would tell the stories of the people actually affected by the War on Drugs, that would capture the viewpoints of the activists and the lawmakers involved in legalization efforts, and that would highlight the good and the bad from the business side of the equation. Our goal is to help others understand the baffling history of cannabis, realize the vast potential for its current legalization, and democratize its future.

Before we continue, a couple of housekeeping explanations. Throughout this book, we use the words "marijuana" or "marihuana" based on their use and spelling in historical context, as it was used by others at that time. All other references are to cannabis—the name of the plant that produces the substances used for medicinal and recreational purposes. "Cannabis" is in common usage, while "marijuana/marihuana" was popularized by Harry Anslinger, the first director of the US Federal Bureau of Narcotics, whose life we examine in this book. Anslinger used "marihuana" to highlight its use by Mexican immigrants, and the term is rooted in racism. Second, we refer throughout this book to the War on Drugs. The term was coined by US president Richard Nixon half a century ago, but, as we point out, the actual war on Black, Brown, Indigenous, and all racial minorities dates back more than a century, even if it did not have an official endorsement from the Oval Office.

AKWASI

We are not solely writing for Black, Indigenous, Hispanic, and other marginalized groups. You know only too well the racism of cannabis laws. But we are not writing solely for a white audience either. We are writing for all who seek knowledge and justice. We are living in tumultuous times. To us, that means justice is at hand. We hope this book lives up to the goals we have set for ourselves, for our criminal justice system, and for the industry.

Akwasi Owusu-Bempah
Tahira Rehmatullah

1 LONGEST WAR

The War on Drugs. It is part of our culture and has been for generations. It is the name we have had imposed on us by government and media, to invoke a modern-day racist shame with roots that date back more than a century. It conjures images of government and law enforcement leaders passionately working to eradicate the narcotic plague that limits the potential of our youth and allows our once-vibrant communities to wither away under the burden of drug use and addiction. Many of us have memories of this war, but our experience with it—if we had a meaningful experience at all—is a product of our perception, one forged from our social status, our income, and the color of our skin.

If you are Black, Brown, or Indigenous, you are still trying to survive this war. If you are white, more often than not, you will forever dodge its draft. The war has been waged with some of the most trite slogans an ad exec could assemble:

Just Say No
Get High on Life, Not on Drugs
Drugs: You Use, You Lose
Be the Best You Can Be—Be Drug-Free

The journey to legalize cannabis is too often littered with folklore. From the antics of Cheech and Chong in *Up in Smoke*, Dave Chapelle in *Half Baked*, and Seth Rogen in *Pineapple Express*, to the sounds of Bob Marley, Jimi Hendrix, Snoop Dogg, and Dr. Dre, popular culture has long celebrated and made light of people who like to get high. This merely masks the truth of war, one that, on the periphery, features moral suasion, shame, and threats but, for far too many, also deploys the real artillery of conflict, including automatic weapons and batons, bullhorns and battering rams, military vehicles, and illegal street checks.

The War on Drugs, even as it burrowed deep into our cultural fabric, is nothing more than linguistic sleight-of-hand. Drugs are an excuse for hostilities, but the real target is the class of North American society born under siege. Make no mistake, there is a war—but it is ridiculously one-sided. This war is waged on those who live in our most marginalized inner-city neighborhoods, transformed into urban battlefields by those who cloak themselves in morality while terrorizing and oppressing the racial minorities among us. We may have all heard of this war anecdotally, but far too many live it. Driving while Black or Hispanic? Hopefully not with weed in the car—a simple traffic stop could end in arrest and imprisonment, or worse. How about our young people? Not the privileged frat kids funneling beers and smoking blunts at their parties, but the poorer kids, forced out of their cramped apartments to escape the watchful eyes of their parents. That same activity, the passing of a joint among friends, could quickly leave one's hopes for a better future crushed under the weight of a police officer's boot. An illegal street check, undertaken for no reason other than the economic state of the neighborhood, will become a cannabis pat down in the blink of an eye.

This is a shocking era of racism and persecution, and it has played out worldwide. It will forever be a stain on our collective history. It has never gone away, but today it is captured on phones, and the video evidence means the world can no longer just look elsewhere or pretend we do not see it. It is no longer possible for the police to cook up a story and claim justification for abuse and excessive force without fear that they will end up making the news. We now watch it on Twitter, TikTok, and YouTube and come to our own conclusions.

The arguments we make in this book are not theoretical or made in the abstract. They are rooted in the real-life experiences of those who have paid a steep price for a misguided and futile campaign to criminalize society's most vulnerable.

AKWASI

I have witnessed arrests of poor Black kids for trivial amounts of weed, and I know only too well the devastation those arrests bring to families and communities. I have visited prisons teeming with those serving time for selling quantities of cannabis so insignificant that players in the legalized industry today would laugh at the amount. We have both been deeply engaged in cannabis activism and been frustrated as governments attempt to implement new policy without restoring the damage done by bad, racist legislation.

TAHIRA

I have spent ample time in boardrooms with the new breed of drug dealer, the affluent white male cannabis executive, whose experience with its distribution and appreciation of it could not be further removed from the people targeted in the War on Drugs. I have watched as modern-day cannabis businesses, preaching the power of the plant, have systemically shut the door on the participation of those who would bring the most knowledge and heart to the table. We come to this issue from different upbringings and perspectives. A random phone call from a former Yale classmate in the wake of my grandfather's death led to me being asked to make the jump to the legal cannabis world. A blessing from my Pakistani parents certainly wasn't expected, but because of their belief in natural remedies, my family viewed cannabis through a slightly different prism, and that blessing was surprisingly given, a risk was taken, and a rise in the cannabis industry followed. Somehow, *I* have become a modern-day drug dealer.

But with my sprint up the business ladder came an ever-increasing concern for those left behind and a determination to diversify this suddenly lucrative industry that attracted those who came from privilege, not the Black and Brown people who have paid the price for a racist period of criminalization. Where are the people of color in this industry? Where are the women? Why were they being shut out yet again?

AKWASI

As a kid from Leicester, England, I found I had an interest in race and policing that could not be satisfied by a government post. Criminal justice and the treatment of Black people—and the ubiquitous use of cannabis by police to harass and oppress kids who looked like me—became my passion. My voice has only grown louder in this time of racial reckoning in North America. Tahira and I come from different backgrounds, yet we have much in common. We are two people of color who are unmoved in our conviction that it is time to end this inexcusable cycle of racism and make good on long-standing societal debts. This is our call for a new approach to cannabis legalization, and it is based not only on our experience and expertise but also in the knowledge that either of us could have become another casualty of the War on Drugs.

Today, we stand on the precipice of a cultural and social revolution. In 2021, adult-use cannabis has been legalized in Uruguay and Canada, the first G7 nation to do so. Mexico has decriminalized and is awaiting Senate approval of a bill to fully legalize sales, making it the world's largest legal cannabis market. Jamaica has decriminalized and legalized cannabis use for religious purposes. Legalization and decriminalization efforts in Europe have made the most progress in the smaller nations of Malta and Luxembourg, but regulations regarding sales and consumption have not been uniform. All eyes will be on the new government in Germany as well as Switzerland where leaders have announced their plans to legalize and regulate cannabis, but the legislative paths in both countries remain unclear. South Africa and the one-time Soviet Republic of Georgia have legalized personal use but not retail sales. Georgia is the first formerly Communist country to legalize cannabis. The Australian Capital Territory, which includes Canberra, has legalized possession, although it is illegal in the rest of the country, and a legalization referendum in New Zealand failed by less than two percentage points, or 67,662 votes out of 2.9 million cast in late 2020.[1]

More significantly, by the summer of that year, cannabis was legal in eighteen US states and the District of Columbia, and, although predicting the whims of state legislatures and ballot initiatives is risky business, momentum for legalization was building across the country. Some thirty-six states allowed some type of access to medicinal cannabis, and there were fewer states that had not legalized either recreational or medicinal cannabis than had given a green light to recreational adult-use. It is impossible to minimize the importance of this revolution, even if so many of us feel it is long overdue and lament the collateral damage on the road to legalization. We know there is so much more ahead to bring justice and a level playing field to the cannabis industry.

A ceasefire may not be imminent, but the trend clearly indicates a lessening of cannabis hostilities in the not-too-distant future. However, that does not mean that, as the War on Drugs wanes, there are not new casualties each and every day, and it certainly doesn't mean that the casualties littered across our society in years past have suddenly been given a new life. The real enemy here, according to those waging the war, has always been "the Other": the Mexican migrant fleeing war in the early twentieth century, the Black jazz musician of New Orleans in the 1920s, the Chinese immigrant viewed with suspicion on Canada's West Coast, the Indigenous youth already reeling from a childhood of deprivation and trying to adapt to life in the city. They are the threats to the entrenched white way of life. The Other inspires fear, not only because they are different, but because they are seen as a threat to white privilege and well-being.

Richard Nixon added another category of enemy combatant—the hippies, whose counterculture lifestyle and opposition to the Vietnam War displayed open hostility to his corrupt presidency. The one constant over the decades has been the relentless fire raining down on the economically disadvantaged in our society. It has long been this way, dating back almost a century to the shrill warnings of Harry Anslinger. The first head of the US Federal Bureau of Narcotics sought to alarm a country about "marihuana" with baseless tales of cannabis-fueled hysteria and the inevitable atrocities that would follow. His was a ceaseless campaign of fear, a tried-and-true tactic that would endure through the final days of the Donald

Trump administration, when Americans were told that the Black Lives Matter movement was the home of the "radical Left" who would burn down American cities and threaten white suburban comfort. Fear has always been the weapon of choice of those whose comfort and entitlement are threatened. That fear has been baked into the DNA of white people in North America and beyond who cling to that sense of entitlement.

North of the border, around the same time that Anslinger's beliefs were gaining traction in the United States, Emily Murphy, once featured on the Canadian $50 bill and celebrated as an early feminist icon, was linking the "Negro menace" to cannabis use in her writings. As a side gig, she dabbled in eugenics. Once the defamatory foundation built by influential racists had been constructed, it could not be torn down for decades, and the association between minorities and drug-crazed cannabis use lived on. Even the most casual observer should have been able to see this for what it was—a caricature of the Other whose "differences" threatened to impose on that comfortable, white way of life.

This war has featured a disproportionate and costly show of force that is meant not just to intimidate but also to keep entire neighborhoods and communities in constant distress. It has ruined lives and torn apart families, disenfranchised and incarcerated countless people, and ensured that the marginalized among us remain beneath the privileged. It has killed dreams and extinguished futures, split brothers from sisters, mothers from fathers, parents from children. It has ended livelihoods, mobility, and hope. It has also been the most spectacular social and policy failure of our time. During much of this war, science had already crushed the myth that cannabis was a gateway to harder drug use.[2] Science was pushed to the curb, dismissed, or ignored by successive governments globally, and we have all paid an awful price for that.

The War on Drugs costs taxpayers billions of dollars each year on policing, courts, and corrections. In the United States, the American Civil Liberties Union (ACLU) pegged the price tag for arresting, trying, and tossing those convicted of simple cannabis possession behind bars at $3.61 billion in 2010.[3] With a willingness to hit taxpayers with such an enormous bill—and the taxpayers' willingness to pay that bill—cannabis law enforcement became a major growth industry. In the first decade of this century, there were more than 8 million cannabis arrests in the United States. Almost nine out of every ten arrests were for possession—ninety-one possession arrests each day in Chicago, for example, and a cannabis arrest every thirty-seven seconds nationwide between 2001 and 2010. Simple cannabis possession accounted for nearly half (46 percent) of all drug arrests in the United States in 2010.[4] And the young, arguably those with the most to lose, were disproportionately targeted. In 2010, more than six in ten of those arrested in the United States for possession were under the age of twenty-five, and one-third were teenagers or preteens.[5]

Throughout history, the United States has set the pace for disparaging and incarcerating cannabis users. It was a leading force in the global push at the United Nations in 1961—Anslinger's hand again—for incarceration and zero tolerance for cannabis traffickers and penalties for users. It set the standard for drug laws in Canada, the United Kingdom, West Germany, and elsewhere, and, ultimately, as many as 180 jurisdictions signed on to the 1961 Single Convention on Narcotic Drugs.[6]

This is where this road has led us: US prisons are sadly populated with people who have spent a large part of their adult lives incarcerated for an offense that would be legal today. Wendy Sawyer and Peter Wagner of the nonpartisan Prison Policy Initiative reported in 2020 that 2.3 million Americans were incarcerated at the local, state, or federal level, and one in five was locked up for a nonviolent drug offense. They also found more than a million drug possession arrests being made each year, through 2018 (including, but not limited to, cannabis possession).[7] The ACLU, analyzing the same statistics, reports that one in three Black boys born in the United States today will end up in prison at one point in his lifetime. For Latino boys, the figure is one in six; for white boys, one in seventeen.[8] According to the Last Prisoner Project, a nonprofit coalition of cannabis leaders who believe legalization demands justice for those left behind, more than 40,000 Americans are behind bars for cannabis-related offenses, even as the move to legalization continues across the country.

Many of the stories are painfully familiar. These are stories of Black kids who too often lack adult male guidance, who are unable to cope with challenges that are unknown to white adolescents, who lack the maturity to make proper decisions, and end up drifting into a world where quick money beats hitting the books. They are told repeatedly that they will never make it, that they aren't good enough, and many of them are made to feel from a young age that certain rungs on the ladder are out of reach. School seems like a waste of time; teachers are either uninterested in helping what they see to be a lost cause or lack the resources to do so. They know the statistics. Maybe the kid dreams of being an athlete or a musician because the daily grind is getting them nowhere, and they can see the money, the fame, the swagger. And then, one night . . .

If they enter the justice system, they find Anslinger's old zero tolerance has merged with three-strikes laws or immovable and harsh habitual offender laws. In some cases, weapons are marginally involved—ironically, in an America where white gun ownership is often equated with patriotism and celebrated by its president. In most cases, these crimes do not include violence. But they are often committed by young Black men who cannot escape their confining neighborhoods and never got to that next rung on the ladder. Michael Thompson never got out of Flint, Michigan. Thompson's life changed on December 19, 1994, when a man in his hometown approached him to buy three pounds of cannabis.

The sale was arranged for $4,200, but, unknown to Thompson, the man seeking the cannabis had flipped and was working with the Flint Area Narcotics Group, trying to avoid a lengthy sentence himself after his home had been raided by authorities the previous month. Undercover police gave the informant the $4,200, which was delivered to Thompson, but he said he couldn't do the deal at his home and had to head to a "safe house" and that he "would take care" of the informant at his place later. Police tailed Thompson to that safe house, a condo owned by Bethany Gayden, then followed him to the informant's home where Thompson made good on his promise, honking his horn to summon his customer to the street. The informant went out to the car and, on Thompson's direction, picked up a grocery bag from the car's passenger side, took it into his home, saw that it was filled with cannabis, and turned it over to police. A police search of Gayden's home found scales, a duffle bag stuffed with cannabis, and another stuffed with cash. But they found no guns. When they stopped Thompson to arrest him, they searched his car and found no cannabis and, again, no guns.

It is worth remembering that today adult-use cannabis is legal in Michigan and that cannabis entrepreneurs, largely white, are making big money doing what Thompson was doing in 1994. They are doing it in shiny stores, not quietly delivering it in their cars, and the quantities of legal cannabis changing hands are much, much larger. Gun ownership is also celebrated in Michigan, and the world watched as "very good people," according to Donald Trump, stormed the state legislature brandishing automatic weapons in the spring of 2020 demanding Governor Gretchen Whitmer reopen the state during a deadly pandemic. The guns were flaunted by a militia that called the demonstration an "American Patriot Rally." But it was Thompson's guns that were the determining factor in the forty-to-sixty-year sentence that he ultimately received. What guns, you might ask. There were none found in his friend's home or in his car, so there were no guns involved in the cannabis sale.

But the police searched Thompson's home at midnight that night, three hours after they arrested him, and they found guns. They had to prove a "nexus"—that is, a connection between the guns and the trafficking of cannabis. They had to determine that Thompson knowingly carried a gun in the commission of the trafficking crime. Police found a .357 between the mattresses of the bed in the master bedroom and a .32 caliber gun in the master bedroom closet. There were other guns in a locked closet on the second floor of the home. Thompson's wife Bridgit said she owned the .357 that was found on her side of the bed, and she told police the .32 was a gift from Thompson to his father who ultimately gave it back to her. She also told police she owned the guns in the locked closet.

The Michigan Court of Appeals accepted the fact that there were guns in the Thompson home when the informant and he had discussed the cannabis sale, even though the controlled substance and a firearm were never actually possessed at the same time. But the court ruled: "One who possesses a firearm while collecting payment for a controlled substance that will soon be delivered in exchange for that payment can be convicted of possession of a firearm during the commission of a felony even though the controlled substance and the firearm are never actually possessed at the same time."[9] In other words, guns on the premises during the transaction meant the use of a firearm in the act of a crime, even if that gun was nowhere nearby.

Thompson had previous felonies, and he was not allowed to have guns in his home. Yes, he had guns, but this was a nonviolent offense by a man with absolutely no history of violence. It did not matter. Michigan's habitual offender law kicked in, and he was sentenced to forty to sixty years in a Michigan prison. He languished there for more than twenty-five years, fearing that without clemency he would likely die there. He knew he was not eligible for parole until April 29, 2038. Michigan Attorney General Dana Nessel, in appealing to Whitmer in 2020 to free Thompson, said his sentence was the product of a time in Michigan when harsh drug laws mandated such disproportionate sentences. As Nessel said, thankfully, that time had passed. Such sentences in Michigan are now reserved for offenses such as second-degree murder or rape, not for selling cannabis while several guns (described in court as antiques) are locked in a room upstairs. "Sentences of this length for selling marijuana are simply unheard of, even when accompanied by firearms offenses," Nessel wrote. "Given that recreational and medicinal marijuana is now legal in Michigan, allowing Mr. Thompson to continue serving the very draconian sentence in this case is even more distasteful."[10]

Thompson remained in penitentiary as his seventieth birthday neared and COVID-19 swept through the institution. Both his parents and his son died while he was stuck behind bars. Even though Thompson has been described as a "model prisoner," he was handcuffed when he was allowed to attend his mother's funeral. Ultimately, a lengthy and concerted campaign for his release was successful, and he finally won his freedom in early 2021. He will tell his story himself in a later chapter.

Corvain Cooper of Los Angeles was serving a life sentence in Louisiana, far from family members who could not afford the travel costs to visit him. Without presidential clemency, Cooper would have spent the rest of his life behind bars for a nonviolent crime in North Carolina, which applied the three-strikes law to a man convicted of money laundering, tax evasion, and conspiracy to distribute a ton of cannabis from California to North Carolina. That is a lot of cannabis, but Cooper was never actually caught trafficking that amount. In fact, that amount was a mathematical conclusion that police arrived at strictly on evidence that included phone records and the testimony of associates. He faced no firearms charges.

Cooper is a proud man, and that pride may have gravely hurt him. He refused to plead out, pointing to his relative poverty as proof he was no ringleader and relying on evidence that he had neither threatened nor used violence against anyone. He was convicted nonetheless, but there was certainly hope for comparative lenience. He was to be sentenced at a time when the Barack Obama administration had directed district attorneys to refrain from seeking enhanced sentences for nonviolent offenses. The penitentiaries were already filled with too many people who did not deserve to be there. But North Carolina saw things differently, and Cooper received a life sentence for a nonviolent cannabis offense just four months before adult-use cannabis was legalized in Washington and Colorado.

We will revisit Cooper's case later in this book, but the state where he was incarcerated, Louisiana, figures prominently in any study of disproportionate sentencing of Black people who have come into conflict with the law. Louisiana has the nation's highest incarceration rate and the greatest proportion of inmates in penitentiaries for nonviolent crimes in the United States. The state prison in Angola is the country's largest maximum-security institution and just happens to be built on the grounds of a former plantation where enslaved people were also held captive. In Louisiana, you can be sentenced to life for attempting to steal hedge clippers—that's right: attempting to steal hedge clippers.

The case of Fair Wayne Bryant attracted international attention after five white justices on the Louisiana Supreme Court rejected the Black man's appeal, pointing to the state's habitual offenders law. In reality, it is a twenty-first-century iteration of the "pig laws" that were a product of Reconstruction in the US South, a means of continuing to enslave Black people after the abolition of slavery. Those laws derived their name from a popular form of robbery in its day—the theft of farm animals—usually swine. Essentially, the laws' aim was simple—if Black people could not be enslaved, they could be incarcerated. In 1979, Bryant was convicted of attempted armed robbery and sentenced to ten years of hard labor. His other offenses were for possession of stolen goods, burglary, and check forgery—nonviolent crimes stemming from poverty.

When Bryant was convicted of trying to steal hedge clippers, he had four previous felony convictions, allowing a court to sentence him to life without parole under the habitual offenders law. A recent study found that 72.8 percent of Louisiana inmates serving life sentences and 83.4 percent of those serving life sentences for habitual offenses were Black.[11] According to the US Census, Black people make up 32.8 percent of Louisiana's population, but according to the Vera Institute of Justice, a Brooklyn-based organization that advocates for a more equitable US justice system, they make up 67 percent of the state's prison population.[12] Bryant's incarceration had cost Louisiana taxpayers more than $500,000 by 2020 before he was finally paroled in October of that year. Regardless of this stunning judicial overkill, it is a ridiculous price tag for taxpayers to protect the citizens of Louisiana from a man seeking hedge clippers by unlawful means.

Derek Harris's story is an equally troubling saga. Harris had served his country honorably in the Gulf War, but when he returned home, he developed a substance use problem, and his country was not there for him. He did not get the help he needed from the Veterans Administration, either unable or unwilling to be there for this Black vet from the small town of Abbeville, Louisiana. When you look at his photo in full military uniform, the Stars and Stripes fluttering in the background, you see a proud, resolute young soldier with his life ahead of him. But he was not the same after he returned from war. On October 2, 2008, Harris, an unemployed vet with a drug problem, was at home minding his business, when he received a knock at the door from a man looking to buy some weed. Harris obliged, selling the man 0.69 grams of cannabis for thirty dollars, a tiny transaction that would give Harris some money to help feed his addiction. Harris was no drug kingpin. There were no scales or packaging paraphernalia in his home, and he sold the stranger the equivalent of about two joints.

The man who knocked on Harris's door was an undercover cop in Vermilion Parish who had approached a juvenile on the street and asked him if he knew where he could buy some weed. The boy led the undercover cop to Harris, the boyfriend of the boy's mother. It was a case of police entrapment:

everyone knew the identity of the boy who brought the police to his home, and everyone in the small town knew Harris was with the boy's mother. Harris, too, had a largely nonviolent record, including distribution of cocaine, simple burglary, theft with a value between $300 and $500, two counts of simple robbery (classified as crimes of violence), and then his distribution of marijuana conviction. He was sentenced to six years for a 1997 burglary, but he had done his time and was fifteen years clear of any violence and, according to legal counsel who handled his appeal, was dealing with mental illness brought on by drug addiction rather than any underlying habitual criminality. Then he answered the door. For two joints, Harris was sentenced to life in prison. He was the hapless victim on two counts. First victimized by an incompetent public defender who did not challenge the sentence, argue entrapment, or even convey a potential plea deal to Harris. And second by the judge, Durwood Conque, who tried to administer a shorter sentence but ultimately decided he had no choice under Louisiana's habitual offender law, when pushed by the prosecution, but to sentence him to life. "I mean you were not a drug kingpin selling bales of marijuana to school children on the school ground," the trial judge said. "That's not the kind of thing that we're looking at here." But he sentenced Harris to life, nonetheless.

The sentence was imposed in 2012 and upheld by the white judges on the Louisiana Court of Appeals a year later. Judge Sylvia Cooks, the lone Black woman on the appeals court, had a different view: "I believe it is unconscionable to impose a life-sentence-without-benefit upon this defendant who served his country on the field of battle and returned home to find his country offered him no help for his drug addiction problem. . . . It is an incomprehensible, needless, tragic waste of a human life for the sake of slavish adherence to the technicalities of law. It is bereft of fundamental fairness, and absent any measure of balance between imposition of the most severe punishment short of death with the gravity and culpability of the offense."[13]

With the intervention of the Promise of Justice nonprofit in Louisiana, the life sentence was challenged, and Harris was granted a new hearing. Finally, in August 2020, after spending nine years behind bars, Harris was freed by a Louisiana court. He headed to Kentucky to be with his brother Antoine and his family. The celebration was muted, however, as it was nine lost years for a young man who had a drug problem and should have been a candidate for rehab—not prison. "Supporting Derek did not end with overturning his egregious life sentence and it did not end the day he walked out of Angola," his lawyer, Cormac Boyle, said in a statement to media. "Righting the harms done to a person through incarceration includes supporting their health, housing, and adjustment to their long-deserved freedom; we need all the help we can get."[14] Still, Harris can count himself lucky; others have paid with their lives in the War on Drugs, victims of the unchecked militarization of police.

The name Breonna Taylor is now forever immortalized in the ever-growing litany of innocent Black people whose lives have been cut short by the police. Taylor was a twenty-six-year-old emergency room technician in Louisville, Kentucky, when her life ended in a barrage of police bullets in March 2020. Seven officers arrived at her home executing a "no-knock" warrant to enter in search of drugs. Three officers, Jonathan Mattingly, Brett Hankison, and Myles Cosgrove, fired a total of thirty-two rounds throughout her apartment. Taylor was struck six times, and she died in the hallway. Her boyfriend, Kenneth Walker, heard pounding on the door but did not hear anyone announce they were police, as police claimed, before they began using a battering ram to force their way into her apartment. Walker, fearing an intruder, fired one shot in response and struck Mattingly in the leg as the front door of the apartment was coming off its hinges.

The tragic details of her death are well known, but Taylor's killing puts the focus on two other facets of the War on Drugs. "No-knock warrants" are a key element of a 1990s-era Department of Defense program known as the 1033, created by Bill Clinton as a key component of his particular War on Drugs. Under that program from 1996 to 2014, the ACLU found that the US government transferred $4.3 billion worth of military equipment to local police forces. It was then reined in by Barack Obama, following images of police in military vehicles in Ferguson, Missouri, that shocked the country. In 2017, the Trump administration rolled back the Obama restraints, and that figure had topped $7 billion in transfers to more than 8,000 local law enforcement agencies by 2020, according to the agency overseeing the 1033 project, the Defense Logistics Agency.[15] This funding included the transfer of mine-resistant ambush-protected (MRAP) vehicles built to withstand armor-piercing roadside bombs. The militarization of the police went hand in hand with shock-and-awe SWAT teams carrying out drug search warrants. The ACLU study found that 68 percent of those warrants targeted Black Americans.

If the results were not so deadly, some of the tales of the arming of North American police would be comical. The Ohio State University campus police accepted delivery of an MRAP (Mine-Resistant Ambush Protected) vehicle in 2013. The town of Keene, New Hampshire, received a ballistic engineered armored response counterattack truck (BearCat) from the Department of Homeland Security, at a cost of $286,000, presumably to protect its pumpkin festival from terrorist attacks. There is nothing funny, however, when an armored SWAT team comes storming through your door in the middle of the night because there might be cannabis in your house. And when they come to the wrong house, the outcome, as we know, can be all the more tragic.

According to a lawsuit filed against the Louisville Metro Police, SWAT teams in July 2019 raided a home after marching down the street in military fashion, shooting objects through the window before bashing down the door with weapons drawn. The lawsuit alleges that they handcuffed the terrified man hired to paint the vacant house, along with his girlfriend and her ten-year-old daughter. The property was vacant because police had already stormed the house in a drug raid and seized the man they were looking for. He was in custody when they raided the empty house a second time. In a separate suit, a Black Louisville couple, Ashlea Burr and Mario Daugherty, say they were getting their children, aged thirteen and fourteen, ready for school when Louisville SWAT officers smashed down their front door in October 2018, using explosive devices and holding the family at gunpoint. Officers had claimed they smelled cannabis coming from inside the house and suspected an illegal grow-op. Wrong house. No cannabis was found.

In an unredacted video of the police raid obtained by *Vice News*, one of the daughters tumbles down the stairs in fear as armored police point guns at her. Another can be heard screaming in panic and trying to run down the alley to get to her grandmother's house before a heavily armed SWAT officer tells her to get on the ground and demands to know if she has any guns, "anything that can hurt me?" "I'm fourteen," the weeping girl replies. Reports in Kentucky identified five officers who smashed their way into the home of Daugherty and Burr as officers who took part in the raid that killed Taylor. The tragic tale of Taylor has a sidebar, showing how the War on Drugs can also be used to gentrify neighborhoods. In this case, according to a lawsuit brought by her family, Taylor's ex-boyfriend, whose alleged drug dealing brought police mistakenly to Taylor's door, was aggressively targeted because he rented a house in a West Louisville neighborhood that the city wanted bulldozed so developers could move in with expensive real estate and retail outlets. In this case, a drug arrest was a method of expropriation.[16] The City of Louisville pushed back hard on the lawsuit claim.

The night Taylor died, at 12:40 a.m., the police used their no-knock warrant to bash down her door in the most terrorizing fashion with no announcement of who they were, according to Walker and neighbors. The main suspect they were seeking lived ten miles from Taylor's home, but they did have a warrant to enter Taylor's home because they believed the suspect, a former boyfriend, was using the apartment to receive drugs. He wasn't. They could not have been more misguided. Taylor had ended that relationship, and no drugs were found in her home. She had no criminal record and was in bed watching a movie with her partner, who also had no record. The same night they killed Taylor, Louisville police found cocaine, cannabis, and cash at the home of her ex-boyfriend, about ten miles away.

In Toronto's Graffiti Alley off downtown Queen Street, a portrait of twenty-eight-year-old Jamal Francique has been painted on a wall in memory of the man shot in the back of the head by police in Mississauga, a Toronto suburb, during a drug investigation in January 2020. He was put on life support and died two days after the shooting. Initially, his family asked that his name not be released, but their minds were changed by the George Floyd murder and the subsequent outpouring of protests and passion across North America, and, in June of the year of his death, they held a vigil for the man described by his sister as "perfection in progress."

The Peel Regional police, just west of Toronto, say Francique was under surveillance and had breached the terms of his probation by visiting his girlfriend. Police spotted him sitting in his blue Acura TSX. Under police threat, Francique is alleged to have driven his vehicle in the direction of the police. Multiple shots were fired at Francique, and one photo shows an officer kicking at him as he lay on the asphalt beside the driver's side door of his vehicle. A lawyer for the family alleged that the police did not attend to Francique for twenty-five minutes as he sat bleeding at the wheel of his disabled vehicle that he had driven into a pole. They also allege that they took him to a hospital more than thirty minutes from the scene of the shooting instead of a much closer hospital. He had no weapon. He was not posing a threat to anyone that evening. His death was sadly unremarkable in Toronto and the surrounding area.

A 2018 Ontario Human Rights Commission report entitled *A Collective Impact* found that Black people were twenty times more likely than white people to be shot dead by police in Canada's largest city. The study found that, in seven of the ten deadly police shootings from 2013 to 2017, the victim was a Black man. A separate study by the Canadian Broadcasting Corporation found that, in 36.5 percent of the fifty-two deadly Toronto police shootings from 2000 to 2017, the victims were Black men or boys, a rate four times higher than their share of the population. In its follow-up report, *A Disparate Impact*, released in August 2020, the commission found that, even though Black people comprised 8.8 percent of Toronto's population, between 2013 and 2017, they represented 37.6 percent of all cannabis charges (4.3 times higher than their representation in the population would predict). This despite the fact that Black people use cannabis at similar rates to white people. Overall, Black people in Toronto represented more than 32 percent of all arrests of nine low-level offenses examined by the Human Rights Commission, an arrest rate that is 3.9 times higher than it is for a white person in the city. Black Torontonians were more likely to be tasered, pepper-sprayed, beaten up, or charged with obstruction of justice than any other segment of the population, the report found.[17] It concluded: "It is clear from both *A Collective Impact* and *A Disparate Impact* that the time for debate about whether systemic racism or anti-Black racial bias exists within the Toronto Police Service is over."[18]

It has long been a fallacy that the often-deadly intersection between policing, cannabis, and race is largely a US epidemic. Canada, where the national police force was created to move Indigenous peoples off their land to make room for white settlers, has a history that puts the lie to the belief that systemic racism in policing is a phenomenon restricted to south of the border.[19] Canada has always been perceived as more progressive on cannabis laws than its southern neighbor, and its government was debating legalized cannabis while Nixon was telling Americans it was their most dangerous enemy. However, successive Canadian governments have spent years jumping back from the brink of common sense—mainly because of US pressure. By 2014, the final full year of the rule of Conservative prime minister Stephen Harper, Canada was spending CDN $2 billion annually in chasing drug arrests and on court and incarceration costs—more than the country spent on Indigenous health services, veteran healthcare, health research, and public health programs combined. The Conservatives, by that point, had already known for some time that this approach was unsustainable and needed to stop or, at least, be greatly modified.

In the United States, in the decade ending in 2010, Black people were 3.73 times more likely than white people to be busted for cannabis. That year, there were 192 white people arrested for cannabis violations per 100,000 people. There were 716 arrests per 100,000 people for the same violations among Black people.[20] More distressingly, when the ACLU updated its study seven years later, little had changed, despite a number of states having subsequently legalized adult cannabis use. In its updated April 2020 report entitled *A Tale of Two Countries: Racially Targeted Arrests in the Era of Marijuana Reform*, the ACLU found that, while cannabis arrests were down 18 percent since 2010, there had still been 6.1 million arrests over the ensuing eight years, with almost 700,000 cannabis arrests in 2018 alone. Cannabis arrests made up 43 percent of all drug arrests over that period, and nine in ten of those arrests were for possession.

The ACLU found that a Black person is 3.64 times more likely to be arrested for cannabis possession than a white person, even though, again, cannabis use was similar for members of both races, with lifetime cannabis use only slightly higher for whites. In 2018, 567 Black people per 100,000 people were arrested for cannabis possession, compared to 156 white people per 100,000. In Montana, if you were Black, you were 9.62 times more likely to be arrested for cannabis possession than your white friend, and since Montana is 89 percent white and less than 1 percent Black, you would have a lot of white friends. Kentucky was close behind with Black people arrested 9.36 times more often than whites. In Illinois, West Virginia, and Iowa, Black citizens were arrested for cannabis possession more than seven times more often than whites, according to the ACLU data.

In thirty-one states, racial disparities were larger in 2018 than in 2010; in eighteen states, racial disparities were narrower than in 2010. (In typical Florida fashion, that state refused to provide data.) US racial disparities remain consistent across the country, from the rusting urban centers of the Northeast, to the snow-white heartland of the Midwest, to the sprawling Latino diaspora of the West Coast. While Black and other racial minorities were being seized on North America's streets, their white contemporaries were lighting up after dinner parties, unaffected and ignored by the police. White kids in detached homes or downtown condos are not forced onto the streets from overcrowded apartments, and police rarely break down the doors in white suburban neighborhoods. Immunity for white cannabis users spreads even to those who were arrested and were often able to hire the lawyers needed to ensure young lives were not derailed by a minor indiscretion.

For example, Canadian prime minister Justin Trudeau has admitted that his family intervened to have possession charges against his late brother dropped. As he was moving to legalize cannabis in Canada, Trudeau came clean about the luxury of white privilege in Canadian society, particularly when that white privilege rests with his father, a former prime minister with the best of all possible connections. Trudeau revealed the anecdote to highlight how Canadians of color and others without the financial means did not have that recourse to spare themselves a conviction. He also admitted to smoking cannabis himself while he was a sitting member of Parliament. Whites are largely protected by the right to walk the streets without drawing police attention as well as access to good lawyers if they run afoul of the law. The venue for the War on Drugs was too often the neighborhoods of Black and other marginalized North Americans, the lowest of the low-hanging fruit for law enforcement agencies.

Canadian statistics tell the same story as the United States, and Toronto was not alone.[21] A study by one of my colleagues in the Durham region, just east of Toronto, came to a similar conclusion. Black boys found with cannabis were charged by Durham police 38 percent of the time, versus 22 percent for white boys. The study, "Youthful Discretion" by Kanika Samuels-Wortley, found that Black youth, who made up 6 percent of the region's population, accounted for 14 percent of all arrests for cannabis possession and petty thefts, and were charged 19 percent of the time. White youth were charged only 16 percent of the time for the same offenses.[22]

Some of my own work with *Vice News* paints a similar picture. In the prairie city of Regina, Indigenous people were nearly nine times more likely to be arrested for cannabis possession than white people between 2015 and mid-2017, according to police statistics obtained under Canada's freedom of information legislation. In the East Coast city of Halifax during the same time frame, Black people were more than five times more likely to be arrested for possessing cannabis than whites.[23] Vancouver, a West Coast city with a "pot-friendly" vibe, was decidedly not Indigenous friendly when it came to cannabis possession arrests in 2015, according to our research. Only 2.5 percent of the city's population identify as Indigenous, but Vancouver police revealed that 17 percent of cannabis possession charges that year were against Indigenous people.[24]

When we look at the factors that impede advancement for Black people in North America, the arrest rate for simple cannabis possession rises near the top of any list. A conviction for cannabis possession can cost you your job or bar your reentry to the workforce. It can prevent you from driving a car, but the costs to mobility can be even greater: it can tether you to your home, exclude you from international travel, or prevent emigration to other countries that might offer better life prospects. It can affect applications for student aid, deny you custody of your children, or disqualify you from public housing.[25]

We know from a University of Pennsylvania study that, since the days of free love and "smoking up," Haight-Ashbury, and peace signs of the 1960s and '70s to the official fiftieth anniversary of the War on Drugs in 2021, the United States spent more than $1 trillion on the war. The results, from a 1990–2010 snapshot alone: "A 53 percent increase in drug arrests. A 188 percent increase in the number of people arrested for cannabis offenses. A 52 percent increase in the number of people in American state prisons serving drug sentences."[26] The latter statistic continues to amaze, no matter how many times it is repeated. A country with less than 5 percent of the world's population warehouses 25 percent of the world's prisoners. Too many are prisoners of war from the War on Drugs. There are too many Michael Thompsons and Corvain Coopers.

This war has had a succession of generals but no one to take a step back and examine the overall success of the campaign. If Nixon was the original field leader, his efforts were continued to varying degrees by Jimmy Carter, Ronald Reagan, both Bushes, Bill Clinton, Barack Obama, Donald Trump, and Joe Biden. Years after leaving office, Carter, the most conflicted of modern-day US presidents when it came to prosecuting cannabis crime, had his late-in-the-day epiphany. As president, Carter proved more moderate on penalties for nonviolent drug use. He advocated for the decriminalization of possession of less than an ounce of cannabis and told Americans that the penalty for possession of any drug should be no more onerous than any damage done by recreational use of the drug itself. But on the fortieth anniversary of Nixon's declaration that drug use was America's "public enemy number one," Carter went further, becoming the first US president to publicly declare the War on Drugs a failure. In a 2011 op-ed in the *New York Times*, he chronicled the explosion in the number of incarcerated Americans, which had jumped from 500,000 when he left office in 1980 to nearly 2.3 million by the end of 2009; 743 prisoners for every 100,000 Americans, seven times the rate of Europe. Carter noted that rates of incarceration for nonviolent drug offenses were twelve times higher than when he left office: "Not only has this excessive punishment destroyed the lives of millions of young people and their families (disproportionately minorities), but it is wreaking havoc on state and local budgets."[27]

Yet the war continued, virtually unabated through the Obama years and the ascension of Trump, whose first attorney general, Jeff Sessions of

Alabama, tried to turn back the clock by decades. "We have too much tolerance for drug use psychologically, politically, morally," Sessions told a crime conference in Virginia shortly after Trump's inauguration. "We need to say, as Nancy Reagan said, 'Just say no.' Don't do it. There's no excuse for this. It's not recreational. It can be destructive and it consistently is destructive. Lives are at stake and we're not going to worry about being fashionable."[28] The former attorney general clearly felt that righting almost a century of injustice was merely "fashionable," perhaps a passing mode like baggy jeans and Starter jackets. In his remarks, Sessions also appeared to equate heroin and cannabis use.

Sessions may be remembered for many things, most notably his months acting as Trump's punching bag on Twitter, but, before his political career imploded, he was a dangerous advocate of old school drug warfare. Sessions moved to undo an Obama initiative—the Cole Memorandum—which allowed states to deal with cannabis reform on their own, unencumbered by federal laws. Sessions instead ordered that directive overturned and told federal prosecutors to move in and disrupt drug commerce, which he believed was tied to organized crime and fueling a "drug crisis" in America.

But here is the counterpoint, what keeps us going in our belief that the views of Sessions and his kind will be relegated to the history books: in 2019, twenty-seven Democrats sought the party's 2020 presidential nomination, and twenty-one of them supported the legalization of cannabis. Another five would leave it up to individual states, with only former Vice President Joe Biden, now the country's forty-sixth president, clinging to the decriminalization policy perch. Biden, however, would not intervene in the paths chosen by individual states. His vice president, Kamala Harris, has changed her cannabis views in a decade, leading a push against legalization in California as a state prosecutor in 2010, but becoming the Senate sponsor of the Marijuana Opportunity Reinvestment and Expungement Act in Congress in 2019.[29]

This bill passed the House of Representatives in December 2020—and an almost identical bill passed the same chamber again in 2022—leaving it still far short of becoming law but marking a racial watershed nonetheless. It would expunge federal nonviolent cannabis convictions and provide funding for states to expunge their records. It would remove the drug from the

Nixon-era Controlled Substances Act, levy a 5 percent tax on cannabis sales to be poured back into communities ravaged by cannabis criminalization, and provide small business grants to Black, Indigenous, and people of color (BIPOC) applicants shut out of the burgeoning market. Democrats framed their support of the bill as a measure to end years of cannabis racism. "We are recognizing that there is a long-time war on civil rights that was instituted by the Nixon administration," said Jerrold Nadler, the New York Democrat who sponsored the bill in the House, "and we're eliminating it."[30] In sponsoring the bill, Harris told her Senate colleagues that records needed to be expunged so millions of Americans could get on with their lives.

TAHIRA

Biden may be pushed to hold his decriminalization view because of the success in the primaries of two of the most progressive but failed candidates for the Democratic nomination, Senators Bernie Sanders and Elizabeth Warren, who are leading advocates for the expungement of existing criminal records for cannabis use. Sanders believes that ending institutional racism in the United States means legalizing cannabis, something he promised to do by executive order within one hundred days had he become president. His is also a leading voice among US political leaders who advocate funneling legalized cannabis revenue back into devastated communities. Sanders asked why, in 2020, Americans could still be arrested for smoking cannabis when not a single Wall Street "crook" was jailed for their role in the 2008 economic meltdown. It is an excellent question.

And, as he says (and as I have seen firsthand), white men are reaping millions of dollars in revenues from legalized cannabis while Black people are getting shut out of the industry, being denied credit, and still getting swept up and jailed in states where it remains illegal. Various figures are cited by different sources, but Black ownership in the legal cannabis market sits in single digits. The most-cited survey, a 2017 study by *Marijuana Business Daily*, pegged white ownership at 81 percent and Black ownership at 4 percent. Another landmark study, Leafly's *The Seeds of Change*, reported that, by June 2021, the US legalized cannabis industry was worth $18.3 billion and employed 321,000 Americans. But only 2 percent of the country's estimated 30,000 cannabis companies were Black-owned, even though the Black population in the United States was 14 percent.[31]

Biden has continued to back decriminalization over legalization but has had to push back against a tide within his own party. The former vice president would expunge past convictions, move cannabis to a Schedule 2 drug federally, legalize it for medicinal purposes, and leave states to set their own course. In the United States today, cannabis is still a Schedule 1 drug, along with heroin, meaning that, in the government's eyes, it has a high risk of abuse while providing no medicinal value (despite all evidence to the contrary). Cocaine and methamphetamine are Schedule 2, meaning that they are classified as less likely to be abused than cannabis. Despite signs of an unstoppable societal shift, by the summer of 2022, one could still be arrested for simple possession in thirty-one American states, and thousands were still being arrested each day.[32] Rather than see that as a reason to be discouraged, we see it as an incentive to double down on our efforts.

It is impossible to deny that a social revolution is gaining steam and that the best efforts of those who want to return to an earlier era will not be able to turn this train around. This revolution comes with a historic responsibility for payback and justice. The scope of this payback cannot be underestimated because it will mean a level of redress that sufficiently acknowledges over a century of injustice. US jurisdictions have already headed down this progressive path, and we will share their efforts with you.

AKWASI

My work with the not-for-profit organization Cannabis Amnesty reveals how critical it is for cannabis records to be expunged. Pardons and other half measures that leave the leg work to the individual with the criminal record will not suffice. The onus is on the state to right its wrongs, not to punt the responsibility to the person with the record who, already burned by the justice system, would be left to navigate an unfamiliar, unforgiving, and intimidating bureaucratic maze. Artificial intelligence programs that do the work seamlessly and efficiently are now being used with no financial burden on the citizen. This began in San Francisco in 2018 and has since been adopted in other California jurisdictions as well as Illinois. We explore the future of these programs and their value later in this book. Justice also means that those scooped up on the battlefield and robbed of their futures must be provided with the opportunity to benefit from riches that will accrue from legalized cannabis. We believe that they need to move to the head of the line. The profits from legal cannabis should not be restricted to the wealthy and well-connected business class.

TAHIRA

The barriers for Black people and others are real. The cost of a cannabis business license can be prohibitively steep, and, in the ultimate irony, some jurisdictions ban anyone with a criminal record from obtaining that license. Anyone unjustly criminalized for a nonviolent drug offense faces double jeopardy by being denied a slice of the legal pie. In some US states, room in this industry is already being carved out in legislation. At the local level, Black city councilors are moving unilaterally to ensure Black people own and run adult-use cannabis stores in their majority BIPOC wards. Cities like Portland and Oakland are making room for Black entrepreneurs, not only restoring some semblance of justice but also coming to the realization of what most of the corporate world already knows—namely, that diversity is simply good for business.

There are also moves to divert revenues from legal cannabis sales back into communities ravaged by this ugly war. These funds can be used to rebuild and allow these communities to prosper while giving residents their lives back. It can give them more. It can give them the pride of ownership and entrepreneurship and revitalize the most disadvantaged parts of North American cities. There are progressives out there, in places like California, Illinois, Washington State, and Massachusetts. They will need others pushing with them because history has taught quite starkly that any march into the light means overcoming countless detours along the way. Canada led in legalization, but it lags in the steps that must be taken to advance cannabis justice. That is a lack of vision that can be remedied by efforts to bring this question onto the international stage.

The potential revenue that could be used to undo past wrongs cannot be overstated. According to a 2018 study by New Frontier Data, a cannabis analytics firm, a cannabis industry legalized in all fifty states would create $132 billion in federal tax revenue in the eight-year period it studied through 2025. It also estimated that 1.1 million new jobs would be created by the end of the same period.[33] Illinois, for example, set aside $12 million for financial assistance to eligible start-ups in what it calls equity funding. The state estimated that its legal cannabis program could generate sales of $224 million by 2022, and this estimate has already proved conservative. It raked in $11 million in the first week of legal sales at the beginning of 2020.

Illinois is planning a $20 million low-interest loan program for social equity applicants—defined as a business with at least 51 percent ownership or control by those who have been arrested or convicted of cannabis offenses. Any business that is 51 percent owned or controlled by residents who have lived in neighborhoods that have suffered during the cannabis wars are also eligible. But Illinois has faced tough growing pains with its social equity efforts slowed by litigation and disputes over the administration of a points system. We will offer more details on the Illinois problems in a later chapter, but this state is not alone with its uneven equity roll out.

In the spring of 2021, former New York Governor Andrew Cuomo finally signed a bill legalizing recreational cannabis in the state with ambitious social equity goals. Cuomo said the bill would "right the wrongs of the past" and estimated legalized cannabis would create more than 60,000 new jobs, spur $3.5 billion in economic activity, and generate $300 million in annual tax revenue when fully implemented. According to another New Frontier Data analysis from 2020, New York legalization would swell state revenues by at least $2.4 billion by 2025.[34] But, a few months later, Cuomo was gone, felled by a sexual harassment scandal, and the state's first retail outlet was not expected until 2023.

Voters in neighboring New Jersey approved legalized adult-use cannabis in a ballot initiative in November 2020. They were joined by Arizona,

Montana, and South Dakota residents, which became the first state to simultaneously allow access to recreational and medicinal cannabis (although its recreational legalization was facing challenges). In Arizona, where the cannabis proposition garnered more "yes" votes than votes cast for either Trump or Biden, those convicted of previous cannabis offenses can petition to have convictions expunged. Space is also set aside in the legal business for those damaged by the War on Drugs under a social equity program. New Mexico, Virginia, and Connecticut passed legalization bills in the first half of 2021.

Dinosaurs of the drug war still roam this continent and beyond, but their time is coming to an end. We hope to hasten their demise with forward-looking proposals while creating momentum for those initiatives that have wound their way through legislative labyrinths and those still stuck in the bottleneck of law-making. History hands us windows of opportunity, but they come infrequently and are often squandered. This is one of those windows, and we believe this opportunity will be embraced.

2 PROHIBITION AND RACISM

In the late nineteenth century, the central Pennsylvania community of Altoona, with its burgeoning rail industry and promise of prosperity, became a place for European immigrants to lay down roots. Home to the Pennsylvania Railroad, it had become a key hub, where heavy locomotives maintained in the town were switched for the more challenging journey across the Allegheny Mountains. Its population had doubled to 20,000 over a mere decade, and it looked like a potential island of stability for a Swiss-born barber named Robert Anslinger and his German-born wife, Rosa Christiana, who made the journey to a quiet town from bustling New York in search of one of those jobs. As legend has it, the town had taken its name from the German town of Altona.

There was optimism, an expectation of better days ahead, cemented with the establishment of the new Electric Passenger Railway Company, which constructed the ultramodern Altoona and Logan Valley line. This was just what the Anslingers had envisioned with seven children in tow and the eighth on the way. Harry, the Anslingers' eighth child, was born in 1892, and as he approached adolescence, it was expected that he would follow his father in the railroad trade, which is exactly what happened. By the age of fourteen, he was working on the railroads at night after attending school during the day. But young Harry had more ambition than his father and felt the need to move beyond the restrictive confines of a small dot on the Pennsylvania landscape. Harry had his eye on something bigger.

That ambition would eventually lead to an era of oppressive, racist cannabis laws that were built on an imaginative foundation of untruths and fantasy, scare tactics, and race-baiting, fueled by a complicit press and a deeply ingrained and suddenly threatened sense of white privilege in the United States. Although we are reaching back nearly a century, we see the remnants of that era on our streets today. The targets are the same; the hysterical print news stories have merely been replaced by the shouters on Fox News, and the results mirror those of years past. The same people of color who were in Harry Anslinger's sights a hundred years ago are still being disproportionately targeted by cannabis legislation in the twenty-first century.

The Anslinger era is wrapped in mythology and some stories that are surely fictional. There has been an effort among his backers to scrub part of his legacy clean, to remind scholars that he was a product of the attitudes of his time. They point to his Second World War achievement when he was praised for having sufficient foresight to stockpile some three hundred tons of opium for the use of American soldiers in battle, as well as his work against organized crime, particularly the Mafia. It would be wrong to lay the era of cannabis prohibition solely at the feet of Harry Anslinger. But it would be equally misguided to point to anyone with a fraction of the power and the influence during these times as this single-minded, anti-drug crusader.

There are historians who believe Anslinger has been caricatured and unfairly demonized over the years by pro-cannabis crusaders who overlook his dexterity in navigating the bureaucracy, his tenacity in fighting crime, and his honest beliefs about the dangers of cannabis. In looking back on his life, other historians believe much of Anslinger's zeal was crafted by pressure from his political bosses and members of Congress and that he was, most of all, loyal to his superiors. But his years of instilling fear in the masses, his heavy-handedness, and his zealotry make it difficult to find much in the man.

He was a precocious child, but one memory that he carried from the age of twelve shaped his obsession with cannabis and narcotics later in life. As Anslinger tells it in his 1961 book, entitled, with his typical lack of subtlety, *The Murderers: The Shocking Stories of the Narcotics Gangs*, he could not shake the memory of the bloodcurdling screams of a neighbor in morphine withdrawal as he was sent on an urgent mission to a drug store to purchase more of the narcotic to feed her addiction. He remembered how the screams stopped when he returned with the drug, and he remembered the ease with which a twelve-year-old purchased the drug. Embellished or not, this memory from adolescence clearly had an impact on the young Anslinger.

As a young man, he took a break from his railroad job to attend Penn State University, spending his off hours as a substitute piano player in a local theater to earn spare cash; he spent summers as a landscaper. It was then that he intervened on behalf of an Italian immigrant coworker who had been badly beaten in a dispute over protection money with a practitioner of the so-called Black Hand, an extortion tactic that threatened harm or even death if payments were not made by the target. The Black Hand was a specialty of the Italian Mafia, but it had found its way to US shores at the dawn of the twentieth century. Anslinger said he had threatened to kill his coworker's nemesis, but we cannot determine whether this story is true or part of an embroidered autobiography, and even his backers concede that this tale of Anslinger's heroism may have been fictional. "Anslinger understood the power of a good narrative, whether it was exaggerated or not," wrote Michael Weinreb in his 2018 *Penn Stater Magazine* article entitled "The Complicated Legacy of Harry Anslinger."[1] Regardless, it was a convenient jumping-off point for his anti-Mafia work later in his career.

After leaving Penn State, he became a detective for the railway, winning a promotion to captain after saving the railway $50,000 with his diligent work on a negligence lawsuit. His work so impressed his superiors that, when his superintendent was assigned to the state capital of Harrisburg to oversee the state police, Anslinger was chosen to oversee the reorganization of a department of some 2,500 personnel. However, war had broken out, and the twenty-five-year-old Anslinger wanted to serve his country. Turned down twice for the regular forces because of a boyhood eye injury, he volunteered at the Ordnance Department, moving up the ranks and eventually applying to the US State Department, where his knowledge of German and his improving Dutch led him quickly to its senior ranks during the First World War.

Eventually, he landed in the Bahamas in the 1920s, where he worked against Bahamian rumrunners who were getting rich by overwhelming hapless US treasury agents during Prohibition and flooding the thirsty US market. His success there led to a reduction of alcohol smuggling from other ports, including Newfoundland, Nova Scotia, and British Columbia, and eventually landed him a senior post in the newly created Narcotic Controls unit. As the 1920s drew to a close, Prohibition was on its last leg, and the Prohibition Bureau was rife with corruption and dispirited agents who had landed once-plum posts through a thinly veiled system of patronage. In 1930, a congressman from Anslinger's home state of Pennsylvania introduced a bill creating a separate bureau of narcotics enforcement. The Narcotics Division of the Prohibition Bureau continually tested greater depths of corruption, fraud, padding reports, collaboration with gangs, and drug use within. Anslinger was a natural choice to lead the bureau, but it was the endorsement of Andrew Mellon, secretary of the treasurer (and related to Anslinger by marriage) that tipped Congress in his favor. At the age of thirty-eight, Anslinger had been appointed to the job, earning $9,000 per year. His self-actualized mandate to demonize and criminalize cannabis and other drugs was in motion.[2]

Harry Anslinger was to become the unchallenged architect of an enduring era of reefer madness in the United States as he piled lies upon baseless theories. He had a hypnotic effect on a US Congress too easily swayed by tales of cannabis atrocities. He had the trust of five US presidents under whom he served, and he eventually won an audience of global leaders. Before Anslinger rose to power, cannabis prohibition had long been a subject of international debate, often couched in racist caricatures. It was the subject of competing scientific views dating back centuries when it was largely limited to medicinal, spiritual, and religious uses. Although much cannabis control legislation was sparked by ignorance and fear, fueled by hysterical media coverage, there were earlier scientific studies that stood the test of time. One such study was the 1894–95 Indian Hemp Drugs Commission Report. The commission was formed not because of cannabis fears in India but, instead, because there were concerns from British legislators that "ganga" users were filling the insane asylums of India. It produced seven volumes and concluded: "[Regarding] the alleged mental effects of the drugs, the Commission has come to the conclusion that the moderate use of hemp drugs produces no injurious effects on the mind." The drug did not lead to crime or violence, it concluded, adding that widespread prohibition might simply lead to the use of other, more dangerous stimulants. It was widely ignored.[3]

Cannabis had its day in the late nineteenth century as a legal pain reliever sold at local pharmacies and was marketed as a cure-all for everything from joint pain to cramps and from nausea to fatigue. It was sold to mothers who used it to soothe the gums of their babies and to Queen Victoria of England to ease her menstrual cramps.[4] It was, in fact, the pharmaceutical industry that was the target of the 1914 Harrison Act, which heavily regulated and taxed opiates (but did not give police power to arrest or seize), eventually diminishing, then virtually eliminating, any advantage for America's pharmacists, who had to label all ingredients in any such products they were offering to their suffering customers.[5]

The first successful attempt at international drug control came when the League of Nations met at the International Opium Conference in The Hague in 1911. Its convention, which twelve nations signed, banned cocaine and heroin and raised the danger of opium smoking. It was US pressure (even though it was not a member of the League of Nations) that led to the Second International Opium Convention of 1925, which set the parameters of cannabis prohibition.[6] The drive for cannabis prohibition came largely from Egypt, particularly that country's delegation head, Dr. Muhammed El Guindy, who brandished a report from Dr. John Warnock, the medical director of Cairo's Hospital for the Insane.[7] Both men believed that the use of hemp and hashish had to be ended in the colonies before they made their way to European and US capitals. Specifically, they were focused on the "Oriental mentality" that made that race vulnerable to cannabis addiction, and they made the link between cannabis use and insanity and violence.

It would take years of subcommittee work before the convention was formalized. But, by 1934, when it finally took effect, efforts to contain the cannabis menace to the problem of "Orientalism" had failed, as it began appearing in North America. Another scapegoat was needed. As head of the US Narcotics Bureau, Anslinger may have initially been under pressure from his superiors and some members of Congress to take a hard line on marijuana, but he did not appear to require much encouragement. He did not design criminalization—sixteen states had already outlawed it by the time he was elevated to the narcotics job, and more than thirty had taken the step before his seminal 1937 legislation.

Anslinger was regularly accused of ignoring science or empirical evidence that did not further his goals. He was a master of inciting moral panic among white people in America who feared for their children's safety at the hands of drug-crazed Mexicans or hopped-up Black men intent on sexual relations with their women. "Most marijuana smokers are Negroes, Hispanics, jazz musicians, and entertainers," Anslinger told Congress during his tax act testimony: "Their satanic music is driven by marijuana, and marijuana smoking by white women makes them want to seek sexual relations with Negroes, entertainers, and others. It is a drug that causes insanity, criminality, and death—the most violence-causing drug in the history of mankind."[8]

Fear was his currency of choice, as in this first paragraph from his 1937 *Marijuana: Assassin of Youth*: "Not long ago the body of a young girl lay crushed on the sidewalk after a plunge from a Chicago apartment window. Everyone called it suicide, but actually it was murder. The killer was a narcotic known to America as marijuana, and to history as hashish. Used in the form of cigarettes, it is comparatively new to the United States and as a coiled rattlesnake."[9] In Anslinger's world, marihuana—the spelling he used to remind the public that specifically Mexican immigrants were to be feared—was a fast track to the insane asylum. Anslinger was said to have told a meeting of the Narcotics Bureau that a month's use would render one's brain a "storehouse of horrid specters." It was a message repeated on the editorial pages of the *San Francisco Chronicle*.[10]

Even before he embarked on his own campaign of horror stories, Anslinger had lots of material to work with in the Mexican media, dating back decades. One published tale told of the cannabis-crazed local who attempted to dismember an innocent passerby, before turning on himself and chomping away at his arms in a valiant but futile attempt to eat himself. When US news services began establishing Mexican bureaus, they merely translated such fables and sent them back to the United States for American audiences. As early as 1905, the *Los Angeles Times* was relying on the *Mexican Herald* to warn its readers that marihuana was being used by low-class Mexicans and those serving prison terms and that "people who smoke marihuana finally lose their mind and never recover it . . . their brains dry up and they die, most of the time suddenly."[11] On July 6, 1927, a Mexico City dispatch on page 10 of the *New York Times* informed readers: "Mexican Family Go Insane, Five Said to Have Been Stricken by Eating Marihuana."[12]

Anslinger sometimes relied on racist tropes, although some contemporaries insist that he was not a racist himself but a product of his time. While he received very little pushback at home, he had his detractors on the global scene, and he was often mocked. Thomas Wentworth Russell, the head of Egypt's Central Narcotics Intelligence Bureau, responded to Anslinger by characterizing heavy users of hashish as more likely to lapse into a state of "jovial idiocy" than "homicidal insanity."[13] Anslinger's signature legislative victory was the Marihuana Tax Act of 1937, but by then more than thirty states had already passed some version of anti-marihuana legislation.[14] There were conflicting studies on the harms of marihuana, but there were certainly some scientific reports that backed Anslinger's contention that the plant was extremely dangerous.

There were also responsible studies available for legislators countering what they were hearing from Anslinger and reading in the popular press, but they were ignored. In 1925, the US Army, concerned about cannabis use in the Panama Canal Zone, convened a commission that included Canal Zone officials and military representatives. It found the power of the drug to be greatly exaggerated and dismissed earlier studies that said it could cause insanity. The Canal Zone study was notable because it did laboratory experiments on cannabis-smoking subjects. No such research was ever done by the US Surgeon General, Congress, or any state that had passed anti-marihuana legislation.

Now locked and loaded with his Marihuana Tax Act as the law of the land, Anslinger may have been frustrated by a lack of targets for his anti-cannabis zeal. There had been no "marihuana problem" before the act was passed, and one did not suddenly materialize with its passing. By and large, the laws were not aimed at the drug but at those who used it, particularly the Mexicans fleeing political upheaval and making their way to the United States and the Black populations along the Gulf Coast where it had found favor in the brothels and jazz clubs of New Orleans. Anslinger was tapping into a historical trend. Musicians have always been part of counterculture and have instilled fear in whites, particularly overwrought parents. We all remember the lyrics that sparked "parental advisories" on albums in the 1980s (Prince sang about masturbation!), the rap and hip-hop artists who wrote songs about violence and life on the streets (many in fact rapping about their own experiences with the War on Drugs), or the "acid rock" era of the 1960s and 1970s (what was Iron Butterfly on, anyway?). Music that appealed to the young spooked the old. And so it was in the 1920s, but the fear was rooted in the use of "marihuana."

Black jazz musicians popularized cannabis use. Some of the best-known celebrities of the genre ended up in Anslinger's files, including Charlie Parker, Duke Wellington, Count Basie, Cab Calloway, and his favorite target, Billie Holiday. Even before passage of the Marihuana Tax Act, Louis Armstrong, by his own recollection, spent nine nights in a California jail after being caught smoking a joint in 1930. Long before Donald Trump coined his media enemies as purveyors of "fake news," there was fakery in the news media that would shake the foundations of the craft if practiced today. It was an era in which newspaper proprietors hatched stories to suit their own self-interest, irrespective of the facts. A constant in the media coverage was the danger posed by cannabis-crazed Negroes, particularly the sexual threat they posed to white women.

The *American Mercury*, a US literary magazine founded in 1924 by H. L. Mencken, described for its readers one "story" of reefer madness involving a Negro who "(was) brought to a New York hospital because he had run after and threatened two women in the street while under the influence of reefers; he said he had seen in his reefer-dream 'a bunch of naked wimmin,' some of 'em in bed, black and white together, like dey was expectin' men."[15] The country's "yellow" press of the era was doing its part to racially stereotype marihuana users. The era of "yellow journalism" took root in the late nineteenth century and featured sensationalized news stories that sparked fear or appealed to base emotions but were often fabricated. It gained its name during a newspaper war between press barons William Randolph Hearst and Joseph Pulitzer, which also included a battle over a Pulitzer cartoon strip featuring a "yellow kid" dressed entirely in that color.

Still, this wasn't enough for Anslinger, who began spreading his own propaganda. He loved to repeat the story of Victor Licata, a twenty-one-year-old Florida man who awoke one morning, grabbed an axe and killed his parents and siblings, leaving his home, in Anslinger's best tabloid description, "a human slaughterhouse."[16] This quiet, young, previously sane man, Anslinger told Congress, had become crazed by six months of smoking marijuana cigarettes. Aided and abetted by a complicit media, this story sprouted deep roots in the American sensibility even though doctors who studied Licata found no evidence of cannabis use, and the word "marijuana" never appeared in any clinical reports on the young man's insanity. Anslinger entertained members of the Congressional Ways and Means Committee with tales of drug-crazed adolescents killing Chicago cops, a fifteen-year-old who had gone mad from marijuana use, and drug-crazed jazz musicians wreaking all manner of depraved havoc.[17]

In 1936, a propaganda film entitled *Reefer Madness*, originally entitled *Tell Your Children*, was released. Many of us have seen it and laughed wildly, perhaps while smoking a joint. It is filled with exploitative images of young white kids becoming hooked on cannabis, leading to vehicular homicide, attempted rape, murder—and some terrible piano playing. It became a source of tasteless joy for generations, but it was a source of fear seven decades ago. As Anslinger told Congress in the wake of the film's release: "Opium has all of the good of Dr. Jekyll and all the evil of Mr. Hyde. This drug [marijuana] is entirely the monster Hyde, the harmful effect of which cannot be measured."[18]

But Anslinger was a slacker compared to the mysterious Mr. Munch, a fabulist he recruited to amplify his tales of marihuana mayhem. In his crusade to enact his 1937 Marihuana Tax Act, Anslinger enlisted the help of James C. Munch, a professor of philosophy at Philadelphia's Temple University who had tested marihuana on dogs and became one of the most legendary demonizers of the drug. When lightly pressed by a congressman on his dog experiments, Munch dismissed the question, saying that the effects he had seen were hard to characterize because he was not a dog psychologist. The federal bill passed easily, and Anslinger made Munch the "official Expert of the Federal Bureau of Narcotics on Marihuana," a title he held for a quarter century, despite his penchant for uttering some of the most bizarre statements ever heard about cannabis.

In 1938, he was called to testify about the effects of marihuana in a New Jersey murder trial in which two women, allegedly under the influence of cannabis, killed a bus driver in a robbery that netted them what would be considered pocket change, even in that era. Later in the year, he also testified in the trial of a twenty-one-year-old man who was one of six defendants who murdered a police detective. In both cases, Munch told fantastical tales of his own experience with a "marihuana cigarette," which involved living in an ink bottle for two hundred years, flying out of the bottle, and flying around the world twice. New York media reported on the snickering in the courtroom the first time he told the tale, but he drew the ire of Anslinger with his April 7, 1938, testimony in the case of the murdered cop: "After the first one I puffed," he said. "I thought I had wings. Great blue wings—and I was flying all around the world. After the second one, I was depressed. I thought I had spent 200 years at the bottom of an ink bottle."[19]

But he was just getting warmed up. During another court appearance, Munch testified that he had felt he could walk across the ocean or jump from New York to the Panama Canal. Another time, he had become a bat and flown away. Eventually, the inevitable happened—Munch was way too far out there for even Anslinger, and savvy defense lawyers began using the "Munch defense," citing marihuana as a drug that caused uncontrollable violence in its users, and they began winning acquittals for clients who were "crazed" on marihuana. Anslinger cut ties with Munch, but the Temple University philosopher and purveyor of studies of cannabis-created canine angst retained his grand expert title until 1962.

The Marihuana Tax Act was initially sold as a revenue bill, restricting the possession and sale of marijuana through the purchase of a tax stamp. But the real goal was prohibition. Until the 1937 act, marihuana could still be prescribed and sold at pharmacies. Anslinger's bill was to stand as law until its repeal more than three decades later. Hearst and Anslinger worked together to promote the racist scare, with Hearst working hard on prohibition, calling marijuana a "short cut to the lunatic asylum."[20] This gave the anti-cannabis crusader room in all his papers to publish a series of articles suggesting that exposure to marihuana led innocent white girls to seek sex with Negroes.

The August 1937 passage of Anslinger's bill was a historic moment in the saga of prohibition. Marihuana use was already associated with the recent influx of Mexican migrants who fled following the 1910 revolution and were caricatured by Americans as lazy and dirty. It was argued that marihuana use was behind their shiftlessness and lack of personal hygiene, and a move to drive them back over the border was couched in the panic over the potential spread of marihuana use. As Eric Schlosser wrote in *Atlantic Magazine* in 1994, prejudice against the new arrivals extended to their intoxicant of choice, and Texas police spread rumors of Mexican arrivals distributing "killer weed" to Texas schoolchildren.[21]

Similarly, Black Americans in the south were said to be crazed by marihuana, raising the horrifying specter of frenzied Black men raping the innocent white women of America and unleashing criminal mayhem in their white communities. Anslinger, himself, read from a file of his newspaper clippings at the congressional hearings: "Colored students at Univ. of Minn. partying with female (white) students smoking and getting their sympathy with stories of racial persecution. Result: pregnancy."[22] In the year following the passage of the Marihuana Tax Act, Black people were arrested for marihuana use three times more often than whites, while Mexicans were nine times more likely to be arrested for the same charge.

Though often cited, statistics are unreliable, and the sample size is small. It is worth noting that a 1938 Marihuana Conference chaired by Anslinger included testimony from Walter Bromberg, the senior psychiatrist at New York's Department of Hospitals. Bromberg reported a study on 67 persons arrested for marihuana offenses that year included "23 Negroes, 20 Puerto Ricans (some of whom are considered to be racial mixtures), 2 Mexicans, and one Negro and Indian mixture." Bromberg pointed out that he had seen no evidence that marihuana use led to murder, rape, or sexual depravity. Anslinger told him he knew of two cases where the link between sex crimes and marihuana use could be "proved," and he later spoke of a young Canadian teen who went into "marihuana withdrawal" while remanded in jail.[23]

The first charges and convictions under the act targeted two men. A Denver man of Mexican heritage was sentenced to eighteen months for possession. The other was a serial criminal found in a Denver flophouse with four pounds of cannabis who was sentenced to four years at Leavenworth Prison for selling what was now popularly known as marijuana. Anslinger, seeing the propaganda value of a trafficking conviction, attended the trial of the grifter, Samuel Caldwell. Following the Second World War, Anslinger worked to persuade legislators to implement mandatory incarceration terms for the possession of any illegal drug, claiming marijuana led directly to the use of heroin.[24] The federal Boggs Act of 1951 and the 1956 Narcotics Control Act introduced ever-harsher penalties for the possession of cannabis, with the former requiring two-to-five years of imprisonment for the first offense. Marijuana trafficking technically carried a potential death penalty. The doors of America's jail cells were flung open, and, today, the United States is acknowledged to have the highest per capita incarceration rate in the world.

North of the border in Canada, a similar prohibition trajectory was playing out, also rooted in racism and initially meant to deal with white unease in Vancouver. On September 7, 1907, the white supremacist Asiatic Exclusion League, alarmed by the fact that Chinese immigrants recruited to build the country's national railroad had remained in the country and now threatened jobs of white Canadians, held a protest rally that got out of hand. A mob of more than 10,000 turned on the enclaves of Chinese and Japanese immigrants in the city, tossing them into the Vancouver Harbor and smashing every immigrant-owned window they could find.[25] A deputy minister was sent to investigate, but this was no ordinary bureaucrat. William Lyon Mackenzie King, who would one day become prime minister, was shocked to learn that legal opium manufacturers were seeking government compensation. He informed his political superiors that opium was becoming popular with white Canadians, including youth. To be indifferent to the growth of such an evil as opium use in Canada, he said, "would be inconsistent with those principles of morality which ought to govern the conduct of a Christian nation."[26] A year later, government legislation banning the manufacture, sale, or import of opium for any reason other than medicinal purposes passed quickly and without debate. There could be no doubt about the intent of the law. It was a measure designed to economically suppress the Chinese population.

Anslinger's ideological counterpart in Canada, Emily Murphy, was gaining a name as an early feminist and magistrate who fought to win equal status for women under the British North America Act.[27] She undeniably pioneered women's rights in Canada, and she served as the first president of the Canadian Women's Press Club, vice president of the National Council of Women, and the first president of the Federated Women's Institutes of Canada. For that, she has been honored as one of the country's Famous Five Suffragettes, immortalized in bronze on the grounds of the Parliament Buildings in Ottawa and once featured on the back of the Canadian fifty-dollar bill.

Murphy also spent much of her life preaching a philosophy that was a counterweight to her early feminist bona fides. Hers was also a life of white supremacy, support for eugenics, and a racist view of rampant drug use, including marijuana. She was writing about a largely unknown substance when she connected marijuana with the fear of the "Negro menace" in her 1922 book, *The Black Candle*. She wrote the book under the name Judge Emily F. Murphy, a.k.a. "Janey Canuck." In it, she boasted of her knowledge of cannabis derived from her days as a magistrate in Edmonton, acknowledging that its use and danger was little known in either Canada or the United States. But she was a match for Anslinger when she sought to sound the alarm to white Canadians. To make her case, she quoted the chief of police in Los Angeles, Charles A. Jones, explaining this potential plague:

> Persons using this narcotic smoke the dried leaves of the plant, which has the effect of driving them completely insane. Addicts to this drug while under its influence, are immune to pain, and could be severely injured without having any realization of their condition. While in this condition they become raving maniacs and are liable to kill or indulge in any form of violence to other persons, using the most savage methods of cruelty without, as said before, any sense of moral responsibility.[28]

Murphy devoted most of her missive to dire warnings of the social cost of cocaine, heroin, morphine, and opium addiction, particularly among the deplorable "Chinamen" and the addicted Negroes shuffling aimlessly with the hollowed-out zombie eyes of the opium addict. Young girls allowed anywhere without chaperones ran the risk of becoming "cocainomaniacs," she wrote. Marihuana and "hash heesh" were dealt with in one compact chapter, but it was a chapter that compensated for its brevity with heavy doses of hype and sensationalism. She quoted a Mr. Hamilton Fyfe, writing in something called *The Real Mexico*, who reported that Mexicans on marihuana "madden themselves" and proceed to do whatever is uppermost in their minds, then went on to tell this sad tale: "At El Paso, a paeon (laborer) came across the international bridge firing a rifle at all and sundry. Much talk about the Americans and a dose of Marihuana had decided him [*sic*] to invade the United States by himself. The bridge-keeper quickly put a bullet into the poor wretch."[29]

Murphy dedicated much of her later life to warning about drug-crazed maniacs, mainly Chinese and Black immigrants, who she felt were preparing to run amok over the proper white Canadian settlers, killing, raping, and pillaging in the most barbaric and bloodthirsty manner imaginable: "There was nothing but mayhem and murder awaiting our innocent citizens. We were talking about things that had never before been seen or imagined. Drug abuse threatened the very foundation of civilization and might necessitate returning the Chinese to their homeland," she argued in a series of magazine articles that preceded her book.[30] Murphy had become quite a prolific writer, but her ravings were gaining little or no traction in traditional Canadian newspapers. Still, historians tie much of the decision to criminalize cannabis in Canada to *The Black Candle*, even with scant evidence to back such theories. There is also much debate as to whether anyone in government was actually paying much attention to her writings.

Canada added marijuana to its list of prohibitive substances in 1923, some fourteen years earlier than the United States, and the reasoning remains a mystery. The motivation of legislators is usually dismissed as "obscure" in official historical accounts, and the cannabis addition to the list was approved without a word of recorded debate in the House of Commons. Instead, the addition of cannabis to a restricted list was conveyed to members of Parliament in a single sentence from the health minister of the day, and there is no record of the decision being covered in the media. Murphy's influence has been discounted by Canadian historian Catherine Carstairs, who has concluded that government bureaucrats did not view her as a serious and trustworthy authority, although her magazine articles induced some anti-marihuana panic in Canada.[31] King, who had been shocked by the West Coast opium trade fifteen years earlier, was now the prime minister. Still, Canadian historians found no evidence that experience shaped drug prohibition while he led the country, and there is not a single reference to cannabis in his detailed diaries.

The lack of parliamentary debate mirrored the lack of debate in the country. Cannabis was simply not on the radar—there were no references to it in the mass media at the time—and no one was raising red flags over the cannabis menace, Murphy's determination notwithstanding. In their book *Panic and Indifference: The Politics of Canada's Drug Laws*, acknowledged to be the most exhaustive study of Canadian drug policy history, authors P. J. Giffen, Shirley Jane Endicott, and Sylvia Boorman conclude that the inclusion of marijuana on a list of prohibited drugs in 1923 "remains a mystery," a solution looking for a problem.[32] The first seizure of a cannabis joint did not occur in Canada for another nine years.[33]

During the 1940s and 1950s, there was no marijuana controversy in either country. Few arrests were recorded. Joints were smoked, but quietly, in tightly confined substrata of society. Anslinger was still determined to globalize his campaign. In 1961, he helped declare worldwide war with help from the United Nations Single Convention on Narcotic Drugs, with its central tenets of prohibition, harsh penalties, and zero tolerance.[34] Cannabis was restricted to limited medical and scientific research. For the first time, cannabis was added to the list of globally controlled drugs, embedded firmly in the UN treaty, which demanded that the use of nonmedical cannabis be discontinued as soon as possible. Cannabis became a Schedule 1 drug, categorizing it along with the world's most addictive and dangerous narcotics.

But the volatile 1960s were dawning. This was a decade of racial conflict, political assassinations, urban unrest, antiwar demonstrations, Kent State, flower power, and, ultimately, Richard Nixon. It was also the era of Lester Grinspoon, Raymond P. Shafer, and Lowell Eggemeier, names less well known but nevertheless vital to the history of prohibition and the long road to legalization. Nixon came to power in 1968 amid a disastrous US war in southeast Asia and street demonstrations that had forced his predecessor, Lyndon Johnson, to decline another term. The year before, Detroit was the site of the worst riot in US history, five days of pitched battles that left 43 dead, nearly 2,000 injured, and an estimated 2,000 buildings burned and destroyed. The United States of Richard Nixon had, in many ways, devolved into war between the president and two separate and determined adversaries—Black people and antiwar demonstrators, known generically by the Nixon White House as the "hippies."

Nixon launched his infamous War on Drugs. Suspicions that this declaration of no-holds-barred hostilities was really a political vendetta rooted in race and lifestyle were starkly confirmed, years later, by his Watergate coconspirator John Ehrlichman. "The Nixon campaign in 1968, and the Nixon White House after that, had two enemies: the antiwar left and black people," Ehrlichman told writer Dan Baum in an interview published in *Harper's* some twenty-two years after he had interviewed Nixon's chief domestic adviser. Baum unearthed the quote from the late Ehrlichman from notes he had taken during a 1994 interview, and his story was featured on the cover of the magazine's April 2016 issue. "You understand what I'm saying? We knew we couldn't make it illegal to be either against the war or black, but by getting the public to associate the hippies with marijuana and blacks with heroin and then criminalizing both heavily, we could disrupt those communities," Ehrlichman said. "We could arrest their leaders, raid their homes, break up their meetings, and vilify them night after night on the evening news. Did we know we were lying about the drugs? Of course we did."[35]

Never before, even in the darkest days of Anslinger-inspired racism, was the heavy hand of the state used so blatantly in disruption and discrimination in the name of drug control.[36] Here was an example of cannabis being used as an easy excuse to use harmless drug possession for larger disruptive purposes, something that was still being used on the streets of Donald Trump's America in 2020. As early as 1969, Nixon, citing perhaps inflated statistics showing tens of thousands of heroin addicts on New York streets and a national crime rate that had jumped 100 percent since the end of the Eisenhower administration, was foreshadowing what would become an obsession. It was all happening against an international backdrop that was signaling changing attitudes. The UK Advisory Committee on Drug Dependence had already concluded that long-term cannabis consumption had no ill effects. The Netherlands, concluding that the use of harder drugs was the result of pushers on the streets, was moving to the decriminalization of cannabis possession, and, shortly thereafter, an Australian Senate committee would recommend that criminal penalties be removed for personal possession or use. Closer to home, Canada was about to embark on the Le Dain Commission.

Nixon himself would set up a committee helmed by Raymond P. Shafer while steadfastly reaffirming his opposition to decriminalization. In 1970, he signed the Comprehensive Drug Abuse and Prevention Act, which brought all existing controlled substance acts under one legislative umbrella.[37] It also made them all consistent with Anslinger's 1961 UN treaty. Focusing on such a crisis allowed Nixon to target the long-haired hippies he so detested and who, in turn, detested him and his administration, so steeped in corruption that Nixon would ultimately be forced to resign. The official declaration of war came at a June 17, 1971, press conference. "America's public enemy number one in the United States is drug abuse. In order to fight and defeat this enemy, it is necessary to wage a new, all-out offensive," Nixon said. "Fundamentally, it is essential for the American people to be alerted to this danger, to recognize that it is a danger that will not pass with the passing of the war in Vietnam which has brought to our attention the fact that a number of young Americans have become addicts as they serve abroad, whether in Vietnam, or Europe, or other places. Because the problem existed before we became involved in Vietnam; it will continue to exist afterwards."[38]

The true enemy in Nixon's war was not the drug itself but the hippies and Black Americans who were using and distributing cannabis. Like the war in Vietnam, this war at home led to ballooning costs, both in steadily climbing policing expenditures and in the militarization of law enforcement. The streets of US inner cities were seemingly becoming as perilous as the jungles of southeast Asia. Nixon created the Drug Enforcement Administration (DEA) in 1973, providing it with a budget of $75 million and 1,470 agents.

The budget and number of agents doubled in the first two years, and, by 2021, the DEA had a budget of more than $3 billion and more than 9,800 employees, including 4,469 agents.[39]

Nixon believed in his war but seemed to be ceding popular ground as the US nightly newscasts routinely led with more American deaths in Vietnam and dispiriting military prognoses. He called on his constituents for support, dubbing them "the great silent majority." As Trump faced increased street protests in 2020—his "unhinged, left-wing mobs"—he declared "the great silent majority is stronger than ever."[40] But the two men had radically different outcomes with their claim that the majority of silent law-abiding Americans backed get-tough messages from the White House. Nixon received a huge jump in popularity, and his silent majority speech was one of the triumphs of his first term; Trump delivered his message at a rally in Tulsa, Oklahoma, mocked for its sparse attendance. Nixon, buoyed by his bump in popularity, soldiered on with renewed vigor, but he did not count on friendly fire in his War on Drugs, and he was not prepared to dodge some incoming in the form of science, research, and ultimately literature.

Lester Grinspoon was an unlikely turncoat in battle. Grinspoon, a Harvard psychiatry professor who died in June 2020, spent decades working at the Massachusetts Mental Health Center in Boston, where he was in the 1960s as cannabis use increased. Perhaps more accurately it can be said that cannabis use was exploding. As an acknowledged Ivy League academic, Grinspoon moved in circles where other academic elites smoked cannabis, most especially his good friend, Carl Sagan, then an unknown Harvard colleague, years before he became an internationally known astronomer. Grinspoon, in a number of interviews, said he was concerned of the potential danger to Sagan's health because of his heavy cannabis smoking.[41] As a result, Grinspoon set out to write a definitive treatise on the perils of marijuana, the better to save an entire generation—and his friend—bent on destroying themselves. But as he continued his research, Grinspoon began to suspect that government officials were scamming the electorate. His research continued to push him away from the widely held view of marijuana as a dangerous gateway drug that led to psychosis and ruined lives, and he realized his silence made him complicit in a War on Drugs that was persecuting young Black people and other youth.

He published his findings in the *Journal of Psychiatry*, and when colleagues told him he needed a wider audience for his findings, he published *Marihuana Reconsidered* in 1971. It became a landmark study of the effects of cannabis and an international bestseller with its cover challenge: "Before we put all our children in jail, let's take an adult look at marihuana." In deconstructing a number of myths around cannabis use, Grinspoon also pointed out the inherent racism in marijuana criminal prosecutions. Cannabis use had long been seen as the domain of "Negroes," Mexicans, and Puerto Ricans, he wrote, but it was now becoming more widely used in white circles, and it was likely covert racism that was behind most of the severe penalties in southern states with the largest Black populations. For example, in Georgia at that time, the sentence for a first offense of trafficking to a minor was life in prison. A second offense meant the death penalty. In Louisiana, a first trafficking offense meant the death penalty, but a provision allowed a jury to show clemency and recommend a lesser sentence ranging from thirty-three years to life. Grinspoon pointed out that in Louisiana a twenty-one-year-old man providing pot to his twenty-year-old girlfriend could be legally executed.

Grinspoon questioned harsh, draconian, and ultimately ineffective anti-cannabis laws. Cannabis use did not lead to heroin addiction as Anslinger and his followers claimed, Grinspoon wrote, pointing out that cannabis use also did not lead to crime, sexual debauchery, or any antisocial behavior. It was essentially a crime without a victim, he concluded. Further, he argued that smoking a cigarette or drinking alcohol represented more significant harm to your health than smoking a joint. Given the prevalence of cannabis use in the late 1960s, Grinspoon believed that if the United States continued to arrest people, it would soon overwhelm the court system, and juries would include those who had smoked cannabis themselves. They would be unlikely to convict others for something they had done. "A more rational approach to the problem of smoking of marihuana would include legalization of the use of marihuana," Grinspoon wrote, "regulation of its distribution and the development of sound educational programs about it. . . . By legalization is meant the freedom for people of a certain age, say 18, (to smoke cannabis) of a predetermined potency." Penalties would be limited to those who brought others into danger, such as driving under the influence of cannabis,

Grinspoon argued: "Such legalization would immediately put an end to the costs and harmfulness of the present legal approach."[42]

While writing *Marihuana Reconsidered*, Grinspoon was also dealing with an ongoing family crisis. His young son Danny had been diagnosed with leukemia and was reacting poorly to a medical regimen that was causing him severe nausea and vomiting. It was Danny's mother, Betsy, who decided to seek cannabis to try to ease her son's pain. She headed to the nearby Wellesley High School to buy some pot from a friend of Danny's. She didn't even tell her husband, the cannabis advocate, who did not smoke cannabis and would have rejected the idea because it was illegal. But after smoking a single joint, the young boy's vomiting ceased, his appetite returned, and he asked his mother to take him to a local sub shop.

Another son, Peter, now a Harvard medical professor and primary care physician who became a leading cannabis advocate in his own right, remembers his father as a stern man who took his academic status very seriously and never wavered in his convictions. That meant he could research marijuana but would not smoke it. That changed after his book was published, and he would be joined by Sagan and Allen Ginsberg in the Grinspoon home where marijuana reform was a nonstop topic of conversation. The young Grinspoon boys were smoking pot recreationally with regularity at the time, but they were sick of hearing about it from their parents, Peter Grinspoon recalls. Like other middle and high schoolers from time immemorial, they tuned their parents out. But Peter Grinspoon has an early memory of his father's resolve and how he dodged his critics. During a family visit to a popular ice cream parlor, Lester Grinspoon was set upon by a colleague for his cannabis views that were considered so radical in the day. Grinspoon got into a heated confrontation, telling his colleague that it was more dangerous to his health to drink a glass of whole milk than smoke a joint. The colleague became enraged, but Grinspoon stood his ground.[43]

Lester Grinspoon was the intellectual foundation in the push for legalization, and it cost him a full professorship at Harvard. He was one of the first to point to the disproportionate attack on racialized persons in the application of cannabis laws, and he knew that the government and the medical profession were peddling "bullshit" when it came to cannabis, Peter Grinspoon says.

Danny died, his suffering greatly eased until his death with regular cannabis use, and Grinspoon dedicated *Marihuana Reconsidered* to his lost son: "Children are the greatest high of all," he wrote in the preface titled "To Danny." With his best-selling and well-reviewed book (the *New York Times* called it the "the best dope on pot so far"[44]), Grinspoon had just lobbed a grenade into the Nixon bunker, resulting in some unexpected collateral damage in the War on Drugs.

The book gained national notoriety for its author who made the talk show circuit promoting what were then rather shocking views, but it not only cost Grinspoon support from the Harvard hierarchy, it also earned him the rage of the man in the Oval Office. "I want a goddamn strong statement on marijuana," Nixon ranted the morning the *New York Times* review of Grinspoon's book was included in his press clippings. "I mean, one on marijuana that just tears the ass out of them." According to another of his famous taped conversations, Nixon fumed about the "way left" Grinspoon: "Every one of the bastards that are out for legalizing marijuana is Jewish," he growled. "What the Christ is the matter with the Jews? . . . I suppose it's because most of them are psychiatrists."[45]

While Nixon was politicizing cannabis use for his own partisan purposes, Canada was tentatively staking out a more progressive position with the publication of a study that echoed much of Grinspoon's findings but carried more weight at home or, more accurately put, was supposed to carry more weight at home. The Le Dain Commission was named for its chair, Judge Gerald Le Dain. Le Dain, who was dean of Osgoode Hall Law School, had the highest profile in a well-credentialed lineup of commissioners. He had completed three years of study on the nonmedical use of drugs with a 1972 report, which called for the repeal of the law prohibiting the possession and production of cannabis, a recommendation that shocked parts of the nation and split the Cabinet of Prime Minister Pierre Trudeau. A couple of the commissioners had met with John Lennon. They also heard testimony from Led Zeppelin, the Grateful Dead, and Allen Ginsberg, and logged more than 80,000 kilometers holding hearings in 27 cities and at 23 universities.

Like Grinspoon, the Le Dain commissioners found no evidence that cannabis use was a gateway to harder drugs, concluded that there was no evidence that it led to criminal behavior, and reported that the country's excessively harsh cannabis laws were far out of proportion to the alleged crime. Given the tone of the times, Le Dain had delivered one of the most exhaustive and progressive studies of the criminalization of cannabis in the world. Certainly, coming from a leading democracy headed by an unorthodox prime minister also known the world over (whose wife was to gain further Canadian notoriety for partying with the Rolling Stones a few years later), expectations for a breakthrough ran high. Surely, Canada was about to take its place in the galaxy of progressive nations and legalize adult-use cannabis. In fact, the commission's work was well regarded and highly praised. It sparked national debate and was ignored by Pierre Trudeau and his Liberal government.

Even today, the Le Dain Commission report is praised for its ability to look beyond the immediate horizon. Yet, south of the border, Nixon was determined to yank North America deeper into the cannabis criminalization mess. He had one more kick at his report on cannabis aimed to undermine those promoting cannabis. For this, he turned to Raymond P. Shafer, a conservative Republican governor who had to leave his post under term limit legislation. Nixon knew him well, and he knew Shafer was a solid "law-and-order" Republican. Nixon also knew Shafer harbored hopes of a Supreme Court post. All he had to do first was deliver the "ass-tearing" study on the dangers of cannabis use and convince everyone of its threat to the very foundations of American culture. The president met with Shafer before he embarked on his study, told him he wanted him to stay within the lines drawn by a hard-line Congress, and warned him not to come back with something that would embarrass him.

Shafer took four years, delivered four thousand pages at a cost of about $24 million in today's dollars. It was the most comprehensive study of cannabis use in US history. And it drove Nixon nuts. Shafer compiled his report in 1972, a time when, according to the survey done by his own commission, 21 million, or 15 percent, of all Americans over the age of eighteen had tried cannabis, and approximately 6.9 million adults were regularly using it. "There is no systematic empirical evidence, at least that drawn from the American experience, to support the thesis that the use of marihuana either inevitably or generally causes, leads to, or precipitates criminal, violent, aggressive or delinquent behavior of a sexual or nonsexual nature," the commission concluded. "From the perspective of marihuana's relationship to anti-social behavior of a criminal or violent nature, the drug cannot be said to constitute a significant threat to the public safety. If its use, therefore, is to be discouraged, it must be discouraged on grounds other than its role in the commission of criminal or violent or delinquent acts."[46]

The skyrocketing number of marihuana arrests, Shafer wrote, showed that police were extremely serious about enforcing the law and responding to public (and political) pressure to crackdown on cannabis users. "Yet, in their experience with the marihuana user they have been placed in the unenviable position of having to enforce a law either disregarded or discredited by large segments of the population they serve." The commission recommended that possession no longer be a criminal offense and "casual distribution of small amounts" of marihuana similarly be decriminalized. "The Commission feels that the criminalization of possession of marihuana for personal use is socially self-defeating as a means of achieving this objective. Considering the range of social concerns in contemporary America, marihuana does not, in our considered judgment, rank very high. We would de-emphasize marihuana as a problem."[47]

An angry Nixon disavowed and buried the report. Back-to-back blue-ribbon reports in North America had recommended decriminalization. Had either Nixon or Trudeau taken the bold political step of deferring to science and research in loosening cannabis laws, the course of history on this continent would have been drastically changed. But neither could see a political advantage to such a move. It would have been seen as capitulation to the "radical left," would have denied police such an easy and effective—and racist—way to "clean up" the streets, and would have further outraged angry middle-class and right-leaning voters.

Still, in foreshadowing the road to legalization, a dozen US states moved on their own to decriminalize cannabis possession in the 1970s. Yet we have to lament that legalization was still decades away. Historians continue to calculate today how many racialized youth have been charged, convicted, and incarcerated, and how many lives have been ruined, since a former

Republican governor of Pennsylvania, hand-picked by Nixon, tried to tell America the truth about cannabis. Needless to say, Shafer never made it to the Supreme Court. It would be four decades after Shafer until the passage of the first legal adult-use cannabis laws in the United States in Washington and Colorado in 2012. It would take twenty-nine years from the Le Dain Commission to legalize medical use cannabis in Canada in 2001 and another seventeen years to legalize adult-use cannabis in Canada. But change was afoot. Through a 1996 ballot initiative, California became the first state to allow the consumption of medical marijuana. Alaska, Nevada, Oregon, Washington, and (for a short time) Arizona followed in 1998 (Arizona passed a ballot initiative, which was shortly overturned by state lawmakers).

Based on numbers provided in successive American Civil Liberties Union studies that we referred to in chapter 1, it is likely that, in the years between the Shafer report and the Colorado and Washington initiatives, there might have been 30 million (and counting) more cannabis arrests in the United States, targeting Black people and other racial minorities, often youth, stopping dreams in their tracks and turning neighborhoods into battlegrounds by ever more militarized police. Before we move on to that prelegalization era of decriminalization and the legalization of medical marijuana, we need to do justice to the unlikeliest of pioneers. This largely anonymous young man walked into the San Francisco police headquarters in what is now generally acknowledged as the moment the legalizing campaign began.

Every revolution has an iconic figure who flashes onto the scene in symbolic defiance and is just as quickly gone, back to the shadows but never forgotten. Who was the Chinese man who stood before the tanks in Beijing before the 1989 Tiananmen massacre? Who was the naked woman who sat mutely in the middle of the Portland street to challenge Trump's storm troopers in 2020? What happened to the young man planting carnations in the gun barrels of approaching police at the 1967 antiwar protest at the Pentagon? We are not equating the cannabis revolution with campaigns of political struggle that cost thousands of lives, but that doesn't mean it is a movement without its own essential revolutionaries. Meet Lowell Eggemeier.

Little is known of Eggemeier because Eggemeier wanted little known of him. But no history of prohibition can be told without including his story because he lit the match, tossed it, and then stepped back as others fueled the fire. Author Emily Dufton set the scene for Eggemeier's simple but profound act of defiance in San Francisco on that August 1964 day. The San Francisco Giants were set for a Sunday doubleheader against the Milwaukee Braves at Candlestick Park, and the city was anticipating the San Francisco appearance of the Beatles during their first North American tour. As Dufton wrote, "occupied by the arrival of the Fab Four, the police were taken by surprise when 28-year-old Lowell Eggemeier walked into the city's Hall of Justice, lit up a joint, and politely asked to be arrested for smoking pot. . . . 'I am starting a campaign to legalize marijuana smoking,' he told the stunned cops who watched him take a drag. 'I wish to be arrested.'"[48] So unfolded the nation's first "Puff In."

The police accommodated Eggemeier, who ultimately spent almost a year in jail. But he also drew the attention of an attorney named James R. White III, whose interest was piqued not because of cannabis activism but, rather, because of his libertarian bent. He argued futilely that Eggemeier was denied his constitutional rights when arrested for smoking cannabis. The two men may have been on opposite sides of the political spectrum, but they converged on the question of personal liberty. White went even further, establishing the first Legalize Marijuana (LeMar) advocacy group, the first branch of a movement that eventually went nationwide. His court arguments, and the unearthing of ancient documents from the US government extolling the benefits of cannabis, were embraced by the Haight-Ashbury hippie movement. He published *Marijuana Puff In*, his writ of *habeas corpus* in support of Eggemeier (listed as a coauthor), and the LeMar chapters, led by the activism of the poet Ginsberg, were established in Berkeley, Boston, New York, Chicago, Detroit, and Toronto.

Eggemeier would not have fit the profile of the typical hippie of the 1960s, and after his release from jail, he retreated from the public eye, living as quietly as he had been before his Puff In. But he had started a movement that could not be stopped—one that persevered despite continuous setbacks and one that has eventually forced the cultural revolution we are now witnessing. The road to that revolution began when Oregon decriminalized cannabis possession in 1973, making possession of up to an ounce punishable by a fine of one hundred dollars. Other states followed, and, five years later, New Mexico would become the first state to enshrine the therapeutic value of cannabis in legislation. It would take another eighteen years before California voted to legalize medical use cannabis in a 1996 voter-initiated proposition.

In Colorado, medical use cannabis had been legal for twelve years when Amendment 64, which would legalize adult-use cannabis, was placed on the state ballot for a vote on November 6, 2012, the day Americans returned Barack Obama to the White House. The amendment passed with 55 percent support. On the same day, voters in Washington State passed Initiative 502 with 56 percent support, legalizing adult-use cannabis. History had been made, but an extended period of regulatory debate ensued in both states. The Colorado governor of the day, John Hickenlooper, foreshadowed a year of legislative debate with this sharp analysis on election night: "Don't break out the Cheetos or the Goldfish too quickly."[49] The first retail cannabis outlet in Colorado opened on New Year's Day in 2014. Washington consumers had to wait until July of that year. It would take five more years for Illinois to become the first state to legalize cannabis for retail sale through state legislation rather than a voter initiative (Vermont acted a year earlier but did not include provisions for retail sales).

Canada became the first G7 nation to legalize adult-use cannabis in 2018, but the roots of that legislation are found in a YouTube video of the leader of Canada's third party speaking in Kelowna, British Columbia, five years earlier: "I'm actually not in favor of decriminalizing cannabis. I'm in favor of legalizing it," Liberal leader Justin Trudeau said in off-the-cuff remarks that initially received no media coverage. "Tax it, regulate. It's one of the only ways to keep it out of the hands of our kids because the current war on drugs, the current model is not working." One of the reasons the pledge received scant attention was because Trudeau had just won his party's leadership and was believed to have little chance of vaulting from third-party leader to prime minister in an election to come in 2015. It was one of a series of promises ranging from electoral reform to Indigenous reconciliation that was widely viewed as the easy musings of a leader who would not have to implement any of these promises. More than one of those promises was cynically discarded after his electoral victory, but a more fully sketched promise on cannabis was kept and never faced any serious opposition in Canada. The first retail cannabis outlets opened in October 2018.

However, this revolution remains in its infancy. The next step will be payback for the Black, Brown, and Indigenous victims of this war. It will mean the expungement of criminal records that have crushed dreams, it will provide room at the top of the legal cannabis chain for those who have paid the ultimate price, and it will include the legislated transfer of government funds from legal cannabis sales back into ravaged neighborhoods. None of these next steps were central to legalization debates in Colorado, Washington, Canada, or other jurisdictions that legalized early on. But more recent legalization efforts have begun to include record expungement and social equity provisions in providing licenses in the shiny new world of cannabis legitimacy. We have seen legalized adult-use cannabis long enough to reach some conclusions. Colorado, which we study more closely in the next chapter, is a prime example. In the years since legalization there, cannabis use among youth has remained largely static, but all cannabis arrests have come down by two-thirds.[50] One thing that has not changed is the racial disparity in cannabis arrests, with Black people in Colorado still being arrested at nearly double the rate of whites four years after legalization.

Harry Anslinger lived long enough to see the prohibition tide begin to turn in the late 1960s. But Anslinger was not for turning. In his retirement, he cited "permissive parents, college administrators, pusillanimous judiciary officials, do-gooder bleeding hearts and new-breed sociologists with their fluid notions of morality" as the root causes of the "marijuana menace" among America's youth. He warned of a coming "assault on the foundation of Western civilization" from drug addicts and dealers, adding in a 1968 interview with author Carol Parks in the Penn State magazine *Town and Gown*: "The only persons who frighten me are the hippies."[51] Anslinger died in 1975. Late in life, he turned to the morphine he had loathed to control his pain from a variety of ailments.[52]

3 THE PIONEERS

As the 1970s dawned, Richard Nixon had declared his War on Drugs, with Black Americans who smoked cannabis its specific target. The tumult of the previous decade had not receded, and America was embroiled in both racial and cultural conflict. Many thousands of miles from the epicenter of this war's Command Center, the candidate for sheriff in Pitkin County, Colorado, decided to get a haircut. And not just-a-little-off-the-top trim. No, candidate Hunter S. Thompson had his head shaved so that he might easily refer to his strait-laced Republican opponent, Carrol D. Whitmire, the by-the-book horse-riding incumbent who insisted that his deputies wear cowboy hats, as his "long-haired opponent."

As Nixon compiled his list of enemies, America was witnessing the beginning of the era of "Freak Power," the unlikely birth of "gonzo" journalism, and the dawning of the class war between the hippies and the moneyed and what used to be called the counterculture versus the establishment. The county seat of Aspen, now a ski destination in one of America's richest enclaves, was the perfect setting for that battle, and Thompson, a recent arrival to nearby Woody Creek, was the perfect man to take on the fight. It was widely viewed at the time that Thompson, who had already written a best-selling inside look at the Hell's Angels and would go on to write *Fear and Loathing in Las Vegas* and *Fear and Loathing on the Campaign Trail* (on Nixon's reelection campaign), was waging this campaign for a laugh, and it may well have begun that way. Thompson had pushed a local lawyer into the mayoral race in Aspen, impressed by the way he had used his office to defend the Aspen "freaks" who were being harassed by the local police. He had promised him that, if he became mayor, Thompson would run to be his sheriff. His mayoral candidate, twenty-nine-year-old Joe Edwards, lost by a mere six votes—close enough for Thompson to convince himself that a race for sheriff was still in the cards.

The campaign of a self-described "freak," who spent his days sipping whiskey and tripping on psychedelics and ran his campaign from the J-Bar in the local Hotel Jerome, drew national attention, particularly when Thompson wrote about it in an article titled "The Battle of Aspen: Freak Power in the Rockies" and had it published in a magazine that was gaining national attention. *Rolling Stone* was only three years old at the time, and Thompson's writing would eventually make it world renowned. In time, this gag morphed into a serious endeavor, featuring an election platform that included drug dealers being placed in stocks on the courthouse lawn (because no drug worth taking should be sold for money), roads being torn up and replaced with lawns, and Aspen being officially renamed Fat City to discourage wealthy speculators.

Ahead of his time, Thompson would institute a variation on what is now known as defunding the police force, barring himself and his deputies from carrying firearms. Because of fears over climate change (although it was not called that at the time), Thompson would have banned cars in favor of bicycles downtown, and he pledged to replace sidewalks with grass.[1] Central to his campaign, however, was the legalization of all recreational drugs—cannabis, first and foremost. "Marijuana laws are one of the reasons there . . . is a lack of respect that cops complain about all over the country," Thompson told those he courted, a target-voting bloc he described as "freaks, heads, funhogs and weird night people of every description." Thompson had already identified the breakdown in criminal justice caused by cannabis laws: "When you have a whole generation that grows up as felons and they know the law is ridiculous and they're told all this gibberish about it—it drives you crazy and your brain goes soft and your feet fall off—even the police know it's a silly law. . . . It's time that we either bridge that chasm with some kind of realistic law enforcement or else I don't think it's going to be real in this country. It's going to be revolution."[2]

Thompson may have been legendary for his love of liquor, drugs, and guns, but his analysis from more than a half-century ago sounds downright visionary today. Cannabis laws, he said, were passed in an era of ignorance and mass hysteria and have made felons out of an entire generation: "[Young people] consider cops to be narrow-minded racists who send out informants to spy on them and set them up for arrests, which can result in fantastic jail sentences."[3] He damn near won. Republicans and Democrats had to join forces to coalesce around a single candidate to suppress Freak Power, and although historical accounts of the margin of defeat quote a variety of numbers, one account had him defeated by a count of 204–173.[4] He never became sheriff, but he never left Aspen and died there, taking his own life in 2005.

He left a legacy as not just a writer who popularized a brand of journalism never before imagined but also as a reformer. Whitmire was ultimately forced to resign a few years later; Aspen became more judicious in land development, and its police were ahead of the curve in using conflict de-escalation methods; and Thompson's "freaks" were no longer harassed. And the year he took his .45 caliber pistol and ended his life at the age of sixty-seven—leaving behind a goodbye note titled "Football Season Is Over"—Denver became the first US city to legalize adult-use cannabis, a precursor to a larger, statewide victory in 2012. The spirit of Thompson may have been watching with amusement during that raucous Denver campaign. But there was no nod to his early efforts, even if the kid behind the legalization effort, who would not even be born until twelve years after Thompson's quixotic bid for office, was drawing on a solid Colorado tradition of in-your-face campaigning.

Mason Tvert knew a thing or two about audacious public events that would have made Thompson proud. And, just like Thompson, if you were on Tvert's side, you loved him. If you weren't, you might (as Thompson would say) loathe him. But before we tell you about Tvert, we will fill in the blanks between Thompson's wild campaign and the first great Colorado campaign of the twenty-first century. We have told you how Raymond P. Shafer, Nixon's handpicked commissioner to head his 1972 National Commission on Marijuana Use, suffered the humiliation of having all his recommendations rejected by the antidrug president. He also had his career aspirations stifled by presenting findings that were antithetical to Nixon's goal of scaring American kids straight or giving his administration the cover needed to escalate his War on Drugs. Instead, Shafer recommended that possession and "casual distribution of small amounts" of cannabis be decriminalized. Trafficking of larger amounts would remain illegal, but Shafer and his commissioners were really borrowing from the policies that ended Prohibition when the bootlegger was prosecuted, not the drinker.

Washington's Republican administration ignored Shafer. Nixon rejected decriminalization because he said it would make cannabis half-legal and half-illegal and criminal justice could not operate that way. It would remain illegal, he said—full stop.[5] In fact, Nixon had signaled his response even while the commission was still doing its work. His vice president, Spiro Agnew, went further, saying that the report frightened him.[6] Harry Anslinger one-upped even the vice president. He branded the commission's finding "terrifying," predicting its adoption would lead to "about a million lunatics filling up the mental hospitals and a couple hundred thousand more deaths on the highways—just plain slaughter on the highways."[7] Yet there was movement. Many states had already reduced penalties for cannabis possession from felonies to misdemeanors. Then the city of Ann Arbor, Michigan, home of the University of Michigan, passed an ordinance by a vote of five to four, which made the possession or sale of cannabis punishable with a $5 fine.

Then came the big move. In November 1972, the California Marihuana Initiative garnered enough signatures to put Proposition 19 on the ballot in America's largest state. That ballot initiative would decriminalize any form of recreational cannabis, from cultivation to possession, if it was for personal use. Expectations were high, but it failed miserably, losing by about a two-to-one margin, though it did pass in San Francisco and received 49 percent support in Marin County. The much-anticipated breakthrough was not at hand. Indeed, petition drives to put similar propositions on the ballot failed in Arizona, Florida, Oregon, Michigan, and Washington State for lack of signatures.[8] But other states that took heed of the Shafer report merely took a breath for the fear and loathing of the 1972 presidential election, then studied the issue anew. The dam broke in 1973 when Oregon became the first state to decriminalize cannabis possession, making it the same as a traffic offense. The penalty for possession of up to an ounce of cannabis in the state was set at one hundred dollars.

That set off a small wave of 1970s decriminalization. A couple of years later, Alaska (through a court ruling), Maine, Colorado, California, and Ohio followed suit. The following year, Minnesota joined the club; then, in 1977, Mississippi, North Carolina, and New York arrived at the party. When Nebraska partially decriminalized in 1978, providing a fine of three hundred dollars by citation for a first offense of possession (subsequent possession charges were criminalized as misdemeanors), it appeared that the dominoes would keep falling. Quite the contrary, it turned out. Instead, no other state would decriminalize until 2001. In 1997, the pioneering law in Oregon was overturned, a full generation later.

In fact, many of the decriminalization laws were torn down in the subsequent decades because legislators had not reckoned with the boom in cannabis-marketing paraphernalia that seemed aimed at kids. A parents-driven counterrevolution had been launched, and it reached its peak during the Ronald Reagan years and Nancy Reagan's Just Say No campaign. The decriminalization momentum had not just been slowed—it had been reversed. The sense of inevitability, the certainty that decriminalization would turn to legalization just as night turns to day, disappeared, which is perhaps a cautionary historical tale for those today who see the recent legalization victories in states as the inevitable opening act to legalization across the land. The decriminalization see-saw was emblematic of the two steps forward, one step back journey to legalization that has played out for half a century.

Colorado had joined the decriminalization movement, and, as early as 1973, a state Republican named Michael Strang, a rancher in Carbondale, introduced a bill that would have made possession and the use of cannabis legal for anyone older than eighteen. He used the revenue argument, proposing licenses for growers, wholesalers, and retailers with a six dollar per ounce tax on any cannabis sold, about 40 percent for the going rate of an ounce in 1973. His bill went nowhere (although Strang moved on to the US Congress), but, two years later, the Colorado legislature followed suit. It voted to decriminalize possession, transportation, and private use of cannabis up to an ounce, imposing only a maximum fine of one hundred dollars.

Another step on the road to acceptance of cannabis was gaining hold with decriminalization stalled across the United States. The legality—indeed, the need—for legal access to medical cannabis was beginning to take center stage. In 1996, California voters approved Proposition 215, allowing the use and cultivation of medical marijuana, and Colorado attempted to follow in the next election cycle in 1998. Amendment 19 got on the ballot, but the secretary of state of the day refused to count the votes, claiming it did not have enough signatures to be on that ballot. Undaunted, proponents tried again, and, in 2000, Coloradans approved Amendment 20, which made it the only state to enshrine access to legal medical cannabis in its constitution.

There is no clear consensus as to why Colorado so often stood at the forefront of cannabis reform and why its largest city made cannabis history. The state, along with Washington, would follow into the history books. It may have a libertarian bent, and the mountains may attract a younger, more progressive demographic, but, for many of these years, it was also staunchly Republican. Hunter S. Thompson may have had his Freak Power moment in the mountains, but none of this was playing out in the cities. In fact, Colorado is home to two of the most deeply entrenched bedrock conservative institutions in America—the fundamentalist Christian Focus on the Family in Colorado Springs and, just to the north, the United States Air Force Academy. This was not a state with a laissez-faire attitude toward cannabis, like much of California, Oregon, or its fellow legalization pioneer, Washington State. If Colorado were legalizing cannabis, it would have to be done differently there. So maybe it is no surprise that the road to legalization of adult-use cannabis in the state came about mainly because there was so much drinking going on in Colorado.

* * *

Mason Tvert nearly died.[9] He was about a month from graduating high school in 2000 when he awoke in the emergency room of a hospital in Mesa, Arizona. Tvert had been to a country music festival and nearly drank himself to death. He was taken by ambulance to the hospital and, when he awoke, he noticed it was ten o'clock. The attending nurse told him his parents had been called, and he dialed his mother's number with some trepidation to try to explain this predicament. His mom answered cheerily from the golf course. Tvert thought it was 10 p.m., but it was 10 a.m. He had been passed out for hours. His parents had not been notified, despite the nurse's assurances. So he checked himself out of the hospital and took a cab back to the music festival. "Now, I'm an eighteen-year-old who just consumed enough of a drug to almost kill me to the point that I was taken by an ambulance to an emergency room overnight, and there's no one interested, like no law enforcement wanting to ask where did I procure enough of this substance to kill me?" he recalls. "No interest. That's just how it is. Who cares?"

At the time, he remembered thinking how lucky he was that he did not get in trouble. Today, he looks back on it and wonders how he could have not gotten in trouble. And he wonders about the insanity of a system in which he could almost kill himself with booze and everyone collectively shrugged. He wondered some more during his first year as an undergraduate at the University of Richmond. He marveled at how campus drinking was sanctioned by the school. Parties at his fraternity house were registered with the school, you were eligible for free carbon dioxide for your kegs if you used a certain brand of beer, and a police officer was even stationed outside your door to ensure you were drinking properly.

Tvert admits he was drinking a lot, but he also liked cannabis, and one day he retrieved his mail to find a notice that he had been subpoenaed by a grand jury to answer some questions about cannabis use. He responded by thanking authorities for their kind attention, but he had to decline their invitation because he was headed back to Arizona for the summer and the hearing was in July. They graciously responded in kind, telling him that that was not how it works, buddy. He was going to have to attend or he would be cited for contempt and face jail time. Tvert was forced to answer questions about where he smoked cannabis. How much did he pay for it? What was the quality like? Where he did he buy his cannabis? He told them they were doing such an exceptional job, it was hard to find on campus. He was never specifically accused of anything, but the hypocrisy hit him upside the head: "When I drank to the point where I almost died, no one ever thought to ask me how I got that way or expressed any interest in punishing anyone who gave it to me. . . . But sitting around in my dorm room, with no medical issues, I was the subject of a multijurisdictional task force—campus police, state police, everyone wanting to know where I got marijuana. No one ever asked me where I got the alcohol."

When local officer Buddy Norton finished his questioning of Tvert, a cannabis activist had been born. As a postscript, the fraternity house at the University of Richmond—where eight kegs a night were allowed by the university, where he could drink until he passed out, the home of sanctioned drinking—was kicked off campus a couple years after Tvert graduated. Cannabis was found on the premises. Tvert was the product of upper middle-class parents who schooled him in the fine art of debate at the family dinner table before he headed off to college, seeking a potential career in politics or journalism. By his own admission, he was privileged and maybe just a little shiftless. Communications seemed to run in the family's blood. His father Steven owns an advertising agency, and his sister Jordan is in public relations. He was no political firebrand at school, but it looked like some future in politics beckoned after his parents got him summer work at Phoenix city council, including a short stint as an intern press secretary. A stint as an aide to a state senator in Virginia followed.

Upon graduation, he turned down a job in Phoenix city management and instead followed Phish and the Grateful Dead on tour. Mostly financed by his parents, some funding came from his earnings from summer work and sales from T-shirts he hawked in the parking lot at concerts, including a Dead shirt that featured a cannabis leaf and the title of one of their songs, "Let It Grow." But all tours must come to an end, so Tvert applied for a job at the Washington-based Marijuana Policy Project (MPP) as a legislative analyst. He did not get the position, but, at the age of twenty-two, his mentor at the MPP, the late Steve Fox, assigned him a project in Arizona. His new role included harassing a congressman who was opposed to the legalization of medical marijuana. And that tapped into a special talent that even Tvert may not have been aware he had.

It turns out that he was damn good at harassment. If you needed confirmation, ask mayors, governors, district attorneys, or other law enforcement officials in Colorado. Tvert says he has been branded a "brownshirt," a local newspaper called him "a fascist," and another official said he had "diarrhea of the mouth." Even the White House called him "snarky and juvenile."[10] This was music to Tvert's ears, who is a man who has admitted he was energized by being insulted by a district attorney, a man who got a buzz from the instant gratification of seeing his name in the news every day, and a man who enjoyed tearing down elite politicians with the most outrageous of gambits. "It's not so much I get off on pissing off people in power," Tvert says. "I get off on pissing off people who are assholes who are wrong." That made him a tough target for his opponents.

In the meantime, Fox, working for MPP, was poring over polling data and came up with an analysis that many credit with the key to Proposition 64, which legalized recreational cannabis in Colorado. He found that if a respondent believed cannabis was safer than alcohol, they could be counted as a strong supporter of legalization. Using a compendium of data from different polls, he pegged that number at about 25 percent and believed that if he could convince another 26 percent that alcohol was more dangerous than cannabis, legalization could be at hand. Colorado was going to be the laboratory to test that theory.[11]

He tapped Tvert to head up an experimental project that Fox had called "High and Dry," in which Tvert could speak to university students about cannabis being safer than alcohol. Tvert relocated to Boulder and threw himself into the task with his typical unbridled enthusiasm, launching into sermons at college campuses like a born-again evangelist. Selling university students on the merits of cannabis was, perhaps, not the toughest challenge of Tvert's life, but he was having success, and flush with his campus proselytizing prowess, Fox and Tvert then plotted their next act. They created the simplest cannabis legalization initiative possible for the city of Denver, one that matched the tenor of the times, shorn of any extraneous measures that would acknowledge racism in policing, disproportionate arrests of young Black men and women, the expungement of cannabis records, or the use of cannabis tax revenue to rebuild ravaged communities. Tvert set out to show voters that cannabis was safer than alcohol, and he very early on developed traction for that concept because of tragedy.

Samantha Spady, known to her friends as Sam, was a Colorado State University sophomore from small town Beatrice, Nebraska. She was a young woman who was somewhat reserved as a first-year student but had found her footing in her second year, her bright smile drawing friends from around campus. She was a business major with a future that knew no limits. She had been her class president and homecoming queen in her final year of high school. She had volunteered with the Special Olympics, the local food bank, and a mobile blood donor clinic. Clichés be damned—she was the All-American Girl.

Saturday, September 4, 2004, was football day on the Fort Collins campus with the rivalry showdown between Colorado State and the University of Colorado dominating local attention. Football day was also drinking day for many students, Spady included. She bounced from house to house that day, downing beers and vanilla vodka chasers, as well as just hanging out and not even drinking at other houses, students recalled. Later that evening, tequila was introduced into the mix, and Spady had likely been drinking for about eleven hours when friends, including her roommate, asked if she wanted to go with them to her home. She declined and said she would sleep it off at Sigma Pi house, where she remained in the company of many friends. She retreated to a spare room, and that is where she died. Her body was discovered the next evening by a student who was giving his mother a tour of the fraternity house. The coroner found her blood alcohol level was five times the legal limit in Colorado.

Her death received national attention—the homecoming queen found dead on campus was the inevitable story—but it shocked the state and forced a reckoning on alcohol abuse in Colorado. That sense of crisis was only heightened shortly thereafter when an eighteen-year-old first-year student, Gordie Bailey, died of alcohol poisoning during a fraternity pledge at the University of Colorado. Tvert was drawn back to his time in the emergency ward in Arizona, and he saw the familiar conditioning of people saying it was okay to drink, but not to smoke cannabis in a state that had medical marijuana legislation. There was an opening, but there was no well-funded legalization activism at play in Colorado.

Tvert had never been to Colorado except for school backpacking expeditions, and now here he was trying to fuel a debate about how penalties for cannabis use were harsher than for university drinking even though campus binging was killing young people. "We chose Colorado because of the drinking deaths," he recalls. Tvert and Fox came up with a new name for his movement, ditching High and Dry for SAFER—Safer Alternative for Enjoyable Recreation. Until the Colorado campaign, every failed bid to legalize adult-use cannabis had emphasized a similar array of arguments. It had to be kept away from kids; it had to be removed from the purview of organized crime or the cartels; it would provide tax revenue; or cannabis was bad, but prohibition was worse. It was 2005, so the overriding argument of fifteen years later was a nonstarter, Tvert says. "Going to Congress to say 'this is going to benefit people of color—well, you're not going to win," he said in 2015.

SAFER sought the requisite signatures for a 2005 Denver ballot initiative, which was pure simplicity. It merely stated that possession of up to an ounce of cannabis would be legal for anyone twenty-one years of age or older. SAFER needed 4,000 signatures to get on the ballot. It collected 10,000 for its ballot measure, Proposition 100. Still, no one was under any illusion that victory was at hand. SAFER would go on to spend a grand total of $32,000 on its entire campaign. But Tvert would prove to be a master of what could only be called media manipulation. SAFER put up its first billboard in downtown Denver across from Mile High Football Stadium, depicting a woman with a battered face with a creepy guy lurking in the background with the message "Reduce Community Violence, vote Proposition 100." While Tvert said his billboard was merely alluding to studies showing that alcohol was fueling domestic abuse, he received an explosion of media interest, including criticism from those working with abused women who did not want alcohol to be highlighted, giving abusers the chance to use booze as an "out."

When an abused woman contacted him to tell him when she and her husband smoked cannabis life was calm, but when he was drunk, he was abusive, he convinced her to attend a press conference where he created another billboard that was merely a computer-created PDF but which received extensive use on local television. It was a cost-free image on Tvert's laptop, but it was leading local newscasts and getting a splash in the daily newspapers. Tvert was enduring a barrage of criticism, but one of his talents was battening down and absorbing the hits, as long as he was getting attention. He easily gained enough attention to bring Denver Mayor John Hickenlooper out of his bunker with his public opposition to the initiative.

Hickenlooper was also a transplant, having moved to Colorado from his native Pennsylvania; his political career has taken him from Denver mayor to Colorado governor to even a short-lived and unsuccessful bid for the Democratic presidential nomination in 2019. He is now Colorado's junior senator, unseating a Republican incumbent in 2020. It was as a laid-off geologist in 1988 that Hickenlooper and some buddies pooled their money and opened the Wynkoop Brewing Company, Colorado's first brew pub in a state that, at one point in the 1990s, had more craft breweries than any other state in the country. Having a beer magnate as a foil in his campaign was a gift.

Tvert called the mayor a drug dealer on television and unfurled a huge banner in front of city hall that read: "What's the difference between Mayor Hickenlooper and a drug dealer? The mayor sells a much more dangerous drug." The next day, Tvert found himself a fake body bag, complete with a toe tag, and scattered empty cans of Hickenlooper's beers around at a downtown site. He labeled it The Harms of Alcohol beside a sign that identified The Harms of Marijuana—a package of Oreos and Doritos. Another Tvert sign read: "Sell a Couple Ounces of Marijuana, do 55 years, Sell Thousands of Gallons of Beer, Become Mayor." Simple? Sure. Outrageous? You bet. But Tvert and his supporters enjoyed the wave, and then they were at a Grateful Dead bar on election night, celebrating victory. Denver had become the first major city in the United States to legalize cannabis for personal use. Tvert was twenty-three years old.

But one victory did not necessarily translate into a larger victory. When Tvert and SAFER tried to replicate the campaign state-wide a year later, they failed, even when escalating the same tactics. Three weeks before the 2006 vote, authorities announced the largest pot bust in Colorado history and turned it into a huge media event at the Denver justice building. Tvert tried to hijack proceedings by doing his own media event in the parking lot outside of the justice building, bringing in beer from Hickenlooper's brew pub plus cans of Coors, highlighting one of Colorado's favorite sons, Pete Coors, the wealthy Republican donor and founder of the Colorado beer company. He put up "Wanted Posters" with pictures of Hickenlooper and Coors, who were wanted because they were dealing a more dangerous drug than cannabis. He challenged Hickenlooper to a "Drug Duel" at high noon, vowing to show up at the city hall stairs with a bunch of Hickenlooper's craft beer and Coors best-selling suds and an ounce of cannabis to determine, once and for all, who would vomit first, who would pass out first, and who was dealing the more dangerous drug.

When President George W. Bush and Vice President Dick Cheney made Colorado campaign appearances, Tvert ran ads about the president ("Tried to fight his father while drunk") and Cheney ("Shot his friend in the face while drinking") as reasons to vote for his proposition. He put a billboard made to look like a beer ad with a woman in a bikini with the message: "Marijuana, no hangover, no violence, no carbs." But with the campaign floundering, he stepped over the line. The first time was when his supporters shouted down the attorney general at an event, leading Governor Bill Owens to label him and his supporters "brown shirts," in remarks reported in the October 28, 2006 *Rocky Mountain News*, with the local paper dubbing Tvert's gang "fascists." The second time was when, at the same event, he faced charges of exploitation when he held aloft a banner with a photo of the two dead university students and the message: "Your drinking policies killed them."

When the votes were counted, Tvert and his gang of volunteers suffered a resounding defeat, but they still pulled a moral victory out of the ballot box mess. They knew they would lose, but they aimed for 40 percent support. They got 41 percent (and 55 percent in Denver). "I felt we lost, but we are winning," Tvert recalled. But if there was to be another successful bid, tactics would have to change, and time was needed to reboot. Tvert took a break from the Colorado wars and worked on cannabis campaigns that were more national in scope. But there was always going to be another run at legalization. By 2011, Tvert, teamed up with Fox and Denver lawyer Brian Vicente, was now looking at a general change in attitude, years of experience with the Denver experiment in legalization, and 2011 polling data showing they could win in 2012.

There was a similar campaign underway in Washington State, but there seemed to be little fear of legalization there. The Washington initiative had the backing of the governor and mainstream business. The biggest threat to victory appeared to be infighting among pro-legalization forces and medical marijuana patients who worried about gaps in their supply chain. It was sold as a tax revenue measure, and, years thereafter, Washington's legal cannabis business remained overwhelmingly white. With each state campaign undertaken along its own unique contours, Tvert and his associates were still dealing with fear in Colorado where an electorate was clearly still not fully comfortable with the concept of legalization.

This time, Tvert had more than a team of enthusiastic volunteers. He had cash. In 2006, the legalization campaign spent about $100,000, but, in 2012, according to nonpartisan tracking of campaign donations, his team had $1.7 million in donations from individuals alone, much of it from out of state. Scott Bannister, a California entrepreneur, kicked in a quarter million and a San Diego peace activist donated $30,000. According to VotersEdge. org, Tvert's Campaign to Regulate Marijuana Like Alcohol, ended up with $3.7 million, including $1.2 million from Tvert's Washington-based Marijuana Policy Project.

This time, a toned-down Tvert oversaw a much less edgy campaign. The billboards told the story. This time, instead of a model in a bikini, a billboard featured a more sedate photo of a woman, fully clothed, with the caption: "For many reasons, I prefer marijuana to alcohol. Does that make me a bad person?" The billboard was right above a liquor store. No need to shock, as before. This campaign already had voters' attention. This was a woman leaving the office, not showing off her figure. Another billboard featured a father backing the cannabis initiative, saying: "Please card my son." When the right-wing evangelist Pat Robertson unexpectedly backed the cannabis proposition, they slapped his face up on a billboard.

Momentum was building. The first ballot signature drive was tossed out on irregularities, so the undaunted organizers went back and got close to two hundred thousand signatures, even though only eighty thousand were required. They were making a statement. They had learned from previous losing campaigns in California and Nevada where support had been above 50 percent, and then, in the last couple of weeks, opponents had blanketed the airwaves and tried to scare the hell out of everyone. They had the money and the experience to head off the late slump. They kept people believing that cannabis was safer than alcohol. On election night, more people voted for marijuana legalization (55 percent) in Colorado than voted to reelect Obama (53 percent). Washington also passed a legalization measure, but Obama outpolled the ballot initiative there.

The Colorado vote received international attention. Tvert was hailed as a hero. He was on every morning American news show following a sleepless night. He did media all over the world, and he was flown to Los Angeles to appear on Bill Maher's *Real Time* where the host begged him to come to California and do the same there. Tvert told him he would if Maher would give him a million bucks. Two years earlier, California appeared poised to make history on legalization with Proposition 19 and that campaign did include a spirited intervention from civil rights organizations who backed the measure as a means to end the disproportionate cannabis charges against Black and Latino Californians. It was derailed, however, in large measure because of the decision by Governor Arnold Schwarzenegger, a Proposition 19 opponent, to sign into a law a measure that made cannabis possession a civil infraction, undermining much of the impact of the referendum measure.

And what of Hickenlooper, the man who was mocked, badgered, baited, and reluctantly dragged into the world of cannabis regulation at two levels during his political career? Hickenlooper's battle with Tvert and other pro-cannabis activists dogged him all the way to his Democratic presidential nomination bid. He had been dubbed Mayor Chickenlooper, a drug dealer and a hypocrite by his pro-cannabis opponents, and the campaigns worked. The *Denver Post* echoed Tvert's charges of Hickenlooper hypocrisy in an op-ed, in which editorial director Curtis Hubbard asked why, if Hickenlooper opposed cannabis legalization because of its negative impact on children, the brew master wasn't leading the parade for reinstatement of Prohibition?[12] Hickenlooper, a guy who says he smoked a lot of pot when he was younger, was very deliberate in setting out regulations for legal adult-use cannabis in his state, but he always believed in retrospect that he got it right. And while he was consistently worried about the effect of cannabis on young kids, his views eventually evolved.

Tvert and Hickenlooper, years after their battles, seemed to finally converge when it came to the effects of the War on Drugs on racialized youth in Colorado and across the continent. Hickenlooper acknowledged in a 2019 interview with Colorado's *Westword* that the old system sent millions of youths from low-income backgrounds to prison. But he also wanted to ensure that the cannabis experiment in his state did not lead to a surge in people driving while high or to a spike in young Coloradans using dangerously high-THC cannabis.[13] As a would-be presidential nominee, he advocated federal decriminalization in every state that had legalized, but he did not believe the federal government needed to go into individual states and tell them how best to regulate cannabis.

And still the cannabis versus alcohol dynamic created by Tvert haunted him. He had already sold his stake in Wynkoop when Colorado voted to legalize, but the "beer magnate" label stuck. "I've never been somebody who leads the fight that alcohol is safer or better than marijuana," he told reporter Thomas Mitchell in 2019. "I've been immersed in this issue for a number of years, and I recognize that there were, to my knowledge, no medical fatalities caused by cannabis in the country last year, when there was something close to 40,000 fatalities last year as a consequence of alcohol. I'm not defending one or the other, but our country decided many generations ago that beer was a legal way for people to relax, enjoy their meals or watch a ball game. We legalized alcohol in 1933, before I was alive."[14] But, he said, he grew up in an era when movies equated cannabis with heroin, and, until he was fifteen years old, he didn't know there was a difference between cannabis and heroin. As we know only too well, these are tough perceptions to shake. Yet the man, who as governor told voters in his state they were "reckless" to approve Amendment 64 and counseled the victorious side to keep their Cheetos sealed for the time being, climbed onto the stage at a Democratic debate and took credit for blazing the path to cannabis legislation in his state.

Despite the historic nature of the Colorado victory, today it seems almost a relic of another era. No one was talking about Black youth being disproportionately targeted by police for cannabis busts or the inherent racism in policing when it comes to cannabis. No one was talking about expunging records and redressing past wrongs. Tvert was intent on making things irreverent and simple. However, in Washington State, the campaign was centered around the failed War on Drugs and the unnecessary policing costs and incarceration of young Black people. The Washington ACLU crafted the successful Initiative 502 (I-502), led by primary drafter and campaign director Alison Holcomb. I-502 legalized cannabis in Washington, shaped with the injustice of the War on Drugs as a way of luring the undecided, centrist voters in the state. For her efforts, Holcomb was dubbed Washington's "Pot Momma."[15] Nevertheless, the state has lagged on social equity and diversity in its industry.[16]

At the same time, legalization efforts in both states benefited from years of advocacy by organizations such as the National Organization for the Reform of Marijuana Laws (NORML), whose work has spanned more than half a century, and the Drug Policy Alliance, as well as various studies from the ACLU. Tvert acknowledges that the times have changed, and he believes that today's focus on systemic racism in policing and racial injustice was made possible because Colorado led the way on legalization: "Those arguments are now at the forefront because of what we did. . . . Not entirely, I mean that in the context of cannabis policy. It was after marijuana became legal and support for legalization grew that it became more of a conversation because people wanted to get more into the nitty-gritty details about this." First, he says, you need a message to gain political traction, and his message worked: "If Colorado didn't happen, then we wouldn't be in the same place we are now and this discussion wouldn't be happening." Speaking in the 2020s, Tvert can look back and fully appreciate the fact that some would think his ballot initiative was incomplete because it did not include a social equity provision or retroactive expungement: "I understand why someone impacted by that would feel that way," he says. "But I know the faster way to accomplish their goals is through this incremental approach."

First, he argues, you need people to widely accept cannabis; then you can make the case for racial justice or preach to those attracted by the tax revenue generated by legal adult-use cannabis. Then there are the logistical concerns. In Colorado, only the governor can grant clemency, so record expungement would not be viable on a ballot initiative and raise objections about the separation of powers in the state. It could have also run afoul of a "single issue" rule on ballot initiatives in the state and the political fear that raising other issues could distract from the simple, easily understood, easily marketed question put to voters. Successful legalized cannabis initiatives in other states that followed the path blazed by Colorado and Washington, notably Alaska and Nevada, also resisted pressure to deal with things like home delivery or smoking in public settings in order to streamline their campaigns. In Alaska, which passed a ballot initiative in 2014 in a campaign largely driven and funded by the MPP, residents are allowed to use, possess, and transport up to an ounce of cannabis. Nevada voted to legalize in 2016, despite a $3.35 million donation to the No side by casino billionaire and native Nevadan Sheldon Adelson. It allowed legal possession of an ounce for anyone over the age of twenty-one, but similarly stayed away from regulation (other than a taxation provision) or social justice language.

But the pace of change in North America is quickening. Now, legalization efforts focus on social equity programs and giving back to those so badly hurt by prohibition and racist policing. "When I first announced my campaign for Governor, legalizing adult-use marijuana was one of my top priorities," said New Jersey's Democratic Governor Phil Murphy, explaining his support for legalization in his state in advance of the 2020 vote: "It was as clear then as it is now—marijuana prohibition causes serious, lasting damage to our state, especially to the 35,000 mostly young, Black and Hispanic residents who are arrested for possession of marijuana every year. . . . In fact, Black residents are 3.5 times more likely to be arrested for marijuana possession than white residents. Legalization would right those wrongs while also spurring massive economic development opportunities, job creation, and new tax revenue."[17] As he explained, young people of color in his state found it harder to get a job, find a place to live, and even to get a credit card because of cannabis arrests.

In November 2020, 67 percent of New Jersey voters approved a constitutional amendment legalizing the sale and consumption of cannabis for residents over the age of twenty-one, but legislative wrangling meant it took until February 2021 for New Jersey to officially become the fifteenth state to legalize adult-use cannabis. During those three months of political wrangling, an estimated 6,000 more New Jerseyans were arrested for cannabis offenses.

There is one postscript to the highly entertaining and ultimately historic cannabis battles in Colorado between the brash, young, self-described shit disturber and the brew-pub-owning political leader. The racial injustice argument in the state would have been a tough sell, but don't be fooled: Black Coloradans, like Black people in every other state in the union, were disproportionately targeted by police for low-level cannabis arrests. Nevertheless, the numbers are worth examining. According to the ACLU study, *A Tale of Two Countries: Racially Targeted Arrests in the Era of Marijuana Reform*, Colorado had the smallest racial disparity in cannabis arrests in the country in 2018, even though Black people were still 1.5 times more likely to be arrested for cannabis possession than white people in the state.[18] In its study of arrest rates up to 2010 (before Colorado legalization), *The War on Marijuana in Black and White*, the ACLU found that the ratio was 1.87, again, the smallest racial disparity except for Alaska and Hawaii, suggesting that, historically, Colorado has not had the same magnitude of the problem of targeting Black people found in many other states.[19]

In 2021, Colorado medical and recreational cannabis sales hit a record high of $2.22 billion. Since legalization at the beginning of 2014, total sales have hit $12 billion.[20] State tax revenue from sales has grown from $67.6 million in the first year of legalization to more than $423 million in 2021.[21] By mid-2020, the state had issued more than 40,000 individual licenses and almost 1,700 business licenses, creating an estimated 20,000 jobs.[22] While cannabis arrests are down, crime generally has risen in Colorado in recent years, sparking debate as to whether there is a correlation between legalized cannabis and crime. There is no data to indicate that there is such a correlation, and law enforcement authorities have cast doubt on such a theory.

Cannabis use among youth has not changed since legalization. According to the state's biennial Healthy Kids Colorado study, in 2019, 20.6 percent of high-school age Coloradans said they had used cannabis in the past thirty days, up slightly from the 2017 rate, but lower than prelegalization days. Some 22 percent of high school students reported using cannabis in the previous thirty days during the 2011 government survey. For middle school students, the thirty-day usage percentage was 5.2 in 2019, down from 6.3 in 2011.[23] These numbers are studied worldwide, befitting the pioneer status of the state of Colorado. They are positive numbers that offer a solid foundation for legalization efforts everywhere.

In March 2021, Governor Jared Polis journeyed to the Simply Pure dispensary in Denver, owned by cannabis advocate Wanda James, the first Black woman to own a cannabis dispensary in the United States. There, he signed legislation creating a social equity fund to help Black and Brown Coloradans hurt by cannabis prohibition follow in James's footsteps. It would be tempting to say Hunter S. Thompson would have been proud. But the good Doctor of Gonzo might have found the way in which the legalization effort unfolded fifty years after his Freak Power campaign a bit too tidy and shiny. We can only lament the fact that we never got to see Thompson take on John Hickenlooper.

4 MISSED OPPORTUNITY IN THE NORTH

AKWASI

Rural Ontario was a long way from my inner-city British childhood, but for a young teen with boundless energy and a love of the outdoors, the Peterborough area was the perfect landing spot. My mother had taken a teaching position in the central Ontario town of Keene on the north shore of Rice Lake, and, for me, this meant bouncing along on the endless trails on my dirt bike in the summer and learning to play hockey on frozen ponds in the winter.

I had a loyal group of friends, and they made the transition from the often bleak neighborhoods of the English city of Bristol to my new home feel seamless. In fact, they were already looking out for me and my future. One day, one sidled over to me and solicitously offered me some career advice. I should sell drugs, he counseled me earnestly. Of course, I should. I was a Black kid, and among the sheltered lily-white denizens of the Rice Lake area, being Black meant selling drugs. It was the logical step in my career path, it seemed, and it was not a view exclusive to that group of guys.

I laugh when I remember this event, but it was a bit of a jolt and a dose of street learning, and, even then, I was aware of some early teen racial profiling. But the fact was that I had grown up around drugs in England, and there were fields teeming with cannabis in the Peterborough area, and it was probably a bit of a wonder, looking back, that I did not land on the wrong side of the illegal drug trade. Maybe it was Mac—my neighbor the cop, who regaled me with stories of chasing bad guys—who kept me on the right side of the drug divide. Because of him, I spent my evenings fantasizing about the days when I, too, would don the badge and uniform and weed out those scoundrels in our midst. Or maybe it was what I saw as a younger boy that had me determined to avoid that perilous path to the dark side of the drug trade.

My British mother was a teacher, and my Ghanaian father a university professor and psychologist by trade. After my parents separated, I spent my early years in Bristol where, from the late 1980s to the early 2000s, heroin and crack cocaine reigned. I grew up in a neighborhood a healthy rock toss from an area known as St. Paul's, home to a large population of Caribbean immigrants and a district known for drug trafficking and gang rivalries. We were sandwiched between a poor white area and a relatively poor Black area. Public drug use and street trafficking were omnipresent on both sides of me—Lockleaze on one side and St. Paul's on the other.

I really knew no different, but I do remember my mom telling me that a house close to our friends was a drug house, with nothing in it but a toilet and a safe bolted to the floorboards. It was commonplace to see used needles in parks and people strung out on smack as we went about our business. I was too young to understand the full extent to which drugs influenced the environment around me—my parents did not partake, and my sister and I were too young for serious trouble—yet the drug trade enveloped me and many of my friends, and even their parents had disappeared down the rabbit hole of harder drug use and trafficking.

Had we stayed, it might have been different. A well-known member of a local gang would regularly ride by me and nod as I made my way to train at the nearby Empire Boxing Club, a gesture perhaps intended to let me know he knew who I was and where I lived. He appeared to be grooming me at the age of twelve. I was fortunate to leave the area when I did—not long afterward, police carrying semiautomatic weapons patrolled St. Paul's in an effort to avert gang warfare. The first time that Bristol had seen armed police in the streets, this was a world away from the cliché of the unarmed, benevolent bobby much of the world had been conditioned to think of when they imagined English cops.

The Jamaican Yardies and their gangs—the Hype Crew and the Mountain View Posse—had wrested control of the Bristol street drug trade from the Aggi Crew, who had been swept up in raids by local police. The Aggi Crew was British born; this was their turf and they had seen it claimed by newcomers as their leaders and members bided their time in British prisons. When the Aggi Crew's leaders returned from prison, they demanded the Yardies pay them taxes on the trade they now controlled. The Yardies, of course, would have none of that, and a street war loomed, involving desperate and ruthless combatants, many of whom were only a bit older than me.

The streets of St. Paul's were becoming a battlefield, and the Black and White Café on Grosvenor Road (since demolished) and the Jolly Roger Pub over on All Hallows Road had become the flash points. The tiny Black and White Café was one of the most notorious criminal hangouts in Britain, a well-known drug depot and the scene of a skirmish with police that sparked one of Britain's infamous race riots in the early 1980s. It was half-heartedly masquerading as a Jamaican diner, sitting amid derelict row housing. It became the scene of countless shootings and stabbings from warring gang members, and police raids on the café—it was raided more than any other premises in the country—had netted thousands of pounds of crack cocaine. The Black Swan, the Malcolm X Centre, Lebeqs, the Caribbean Club—everyone knew they too could erupt in violence in this battle of Bristol—an era that scarred the city in the southwest of England for years.

Drug use and trafficking and violence continued to plague the neighborhoods, and kids with big dreams that would transport them to a better place were being recruited into the drug trade by the time they hit fourteen or fifteen. That could have been me. I knew it then, and I know it much more clearly now. As recently as 2015, a police crackdown tried to clean up the streets. The police action sensibly attacked the supply side of the drug trade. The demand side did not slow down.

I had no idea the dirt bike trails of central Ontario beckoned, but we left Bristol and came to Canada because my mother applied for a teacher exchange under an international program in which you swap jobs and houses for a year. She asked for Australia or Canada, and we ended up in Canada.

We were initially supposed to stay for one year, which was extended to two. My mother saw a bright future for her kids in Canada and so decided that an exchange was not enough. Within a year of our return to Bristol, my mother sold our house and struck out for our new permanent home in Canada.

I soon discovered there was more than just the great outdoors around my new home. Peterborough was also an area where biker gangs and some of Toronto's most active criminal entrepreneurs had huge cannabis grow-ops; million-dollar busts in the area were common. A number of people I knew sold cannabis; some grew it for personal use on a smaller scale, so it was just part of my day-to-day existence growing up. But something inside me was stirring, and it was drawing me toward activism. Maybe it was inevitable that I would gravitate toward the field of justice, particularly the intersection of policing, racism, and cannabis laws. It led me to a path of advocacy and activism, both in the United States and in my new home, which was about to become the first G7 nation to legalize recreational, adult-use cannabis. My Canadian academic life coincided roughly with the legalization of medicinal cannabis in Canada, and one could see recreational legalization coming down the road. As a move to legalize in Canada bubbled beneath the surface, I dealt more deeply with issues of policing and race.

After receiving my master's degree in criminology, I dabbled in government work for the Solicitor-General in Ontario where I was a policy analyst, and I held files on grow-ops and cannabis-impaired driving. I knew I saw things differently than my peers. I quickly saw the potential for racial profiling when Mothers Against Drunk Driving (MADD) began an advertising campaign against drugged driving in Canada. An effective ad of theirs combating drunk driving, running in heavy rotation on television, piled one empty beer glass after another on the dashboard as a driver navigated the streets of Toronto with blurring vision and judgment before the inevitable screeching of brakes and crumpling of steel. MADD's logo was a red line through car keys in a martini glass, but when it merely replaced the martini glass with the cannabis leaf in its new campaign, I knew we did not have a proper method to test for drug impairment in driving, and I saw a recipe for Black drivers being pulled over. Everyone saw a new logo, but I saw racial profiling, and this was the subject of my first academic paper.

I later worked with a group at the Centre for Addiction and Mental Health (CAMH) in Toronto where we took self-reported cannabis use studies and correlated them with race to determine for the first time that there was very little daylight in cannabis use rates between white and Black teens. But, in working with Toronto journalist Jim Rankin, who had unearthed groundbreaking arrest statistics, we were able to document for the first time the huge gap in cannabis possession arrests between white and Black people in the city. By 2014, I had my sights firmly fixed on a postdoctoral position in California, but it was not in the cards. Instead, I was recruited for a criminal justice position at Indiana University in Bloomington, a city I knew nothing about. My sum total of knowledge of Indiana University revolved around its infamous basketball coach, Bobby Knight.

I was in a liberal college town, a blue dot in a red state. Because it had the liberal college vibe, my race was never an issue, even though my frequent trips to the airport involved a drive through Martinsville, known as the birthplace of the second generation of the Ku Klux Klan. I arrived in America at the time of protests over the police shooting of Michael Brown in Missouri, which were happening concurrently with the first rush of cannabis legalization in the United States. I also became close to a guy at Indiana University from California who had spent a lot of time in his late teens and early twenties in and out of jail for cannabis offenses. He was paying close attention to the legalization question, and he introduced me to the work being done to leverage legalization to right past wrongs. I wanted to plug into the extensive network in the United States that was doing the same type of work I was doing on race and criminal justice. There is a rich history of research and activism there, and it only grew with the upheaval around the deaths of Brown and Eric Garner, the Black man who police killed with a chokehold on a Staten Island street for allegedly selling illegal cigarettes. He was left prone, unconscious, on the sidewalk for seven minutes with police offering no aid, a chilling precursor to George Floyd.

The first summer I was there, I was placed into a scientific fellowship at the Ohio State University as part of a Racial Democracy Crime and Justice Network, a national network of scholars funded by the US government. A colleague I met through the network was doing work on Ferguson, Missouri, where Brown had been shot, and she brought me into her studies. My level of expertise and passion for this field of research was growing quickly. I had planned to be in the United States for three to five years, but a job at the University of Toronto came up, and I simply could not turn down such an academic opportunity, rare as they are. I was returning to a country preparing to legalize adult-use cannabis. I came home shortly after Justin Trudeau was elected, pledging to make good on a 2014 promise that came so out of the blue that it stunned his principal secretary who was at the other end of the country at a Nova Scotia dinner while Trudeau was beginning the quest to legalize cannabis in British Columbia.

This was a time for a self-described progressive government to break new ground in social justice and use legalization to begin to correct past wrongs. It began that way, or at least it was couched in those terms. But it ended much differently. Canada's legalization of cannabis has been a success on many levels. A Deloitte study estimated the legal industry had generated 11 billion Canadian dollars in its first three years, added CDN $43.5 billion to Canada's gross domestic product, and created 98,000 jobs. But it also said the industry needed greater diversity.[1] I believe that, at its heart, Canadian legalization was a squandered opportunity. A potential arc toward social justice became instead a functional, anodyne piece of legislation that missed a chance to expunge records rooted in past racism, provide a new social equity framework, and give back to communities who had been disproportionately harmed by a War on Drugs in which Canada had been an enthusiastic participant.

It meant that the moment when adult-use cannabis was legalized in Canada and, a year later, when a companion bill offering an inadequate pardon process became law, Canada had fallen behind US states that had tied legalization to efforts to make good on promises to reverse racial injustice during the War on Drugs. The Trudeau initiative may have caught many off guard and may have been initially dismissed by many as the musings of a rookie, third-party leader with little prospect of immediate electoral success. But it should not have been seen as something so stunning. It was also not particularly brave. Like the United States, public support for legalized cannabis had been on an upward trajectory in Canada for years. The only votes that Trudeau was likely to lose with this initiative were votes that were never headed his way anyway. Trudeau's move was merely the next logical step after many tentative decriminalization or legalization moves in Canada.

As we have noted, the years of Prohibition were rooted in racism—predominantly, anti-Asian racism in Canada—but an early progressive commission report led by Justice Gerald Le Dain did not study potential cannabis legalization through any racism prism. The commission was established by Prime Minister Pierre Trudeau mainly because of an explosion of cannabis use and drug experimentation among Canada's youth in 1969. In its 1972 final report, the Le Dain Commission recommended the legalization of simple cannabis possession and cultivation for personal use. It recommended that people addicted to drugs be afforded greater opportunity for treatment rather than be dealt with by the heavy hand of the justice system.

Le Dain had two allies to create the majority opinion of the five-member commission, but one of the remaining two felt it did not go far enough. Marie-Andreé Bertrand, a Quebec feminist (and perhaps, not coincidentally, a Berkeley grad) recommended the government take over distribution as it had for alcohol, a view that was, in some provinces, forty-six years ahead of its time. But the country was not ready for Le Dain. His report came under heavy criticism in media of all partisan stripes as well as from the health authorities of the day, including the Canadian Medical Association. Le Dain sparked an incipient split in Trudeau's Cabinet with Health Minister John Munro seeming to accept the recommendations and Justice Minister John Turner aggressively pushing back. Given the danger that the report would be too hot for his government to handle, Trudeau simply ignored it and quietly kicked it to the curb. In a determination that would become a recurring trend, it was decided that there were no votes in moving forward with any of Le Dain's recommendations.

Medicinal marijuana was legalized in Canada in 2001, and, a year later—thirty years after Le Dain—a Senate committee headed by Progressive Conservative Pierre Claude Nolin recommended legalized cannabis be made available at retail outlets to anyone over the age of sixteen. His committee, in its 2002 report, cited scientific evidence that cannabis was no more dangerous than alcohol and was not a gateway drug. The bipartisan committee also called for a blanket amnesty for all existing cannabis possession convictions. Nolin's committee concluded that criminalization of cannabis was not only ineffective and costly but also led to harmful consequences, particularly for racialized and marginalized Canadians who were far more likely to be arrested for cannabis offenses and be flung into the maw of an unforgiving justice system.

As the unelected Senate committee was reporting, the justice minister of the day, Liberal Martin Cauchon, was already musing about the decriminalization of cannabis, and, in fact, successive Liberal governments led by Jean Chrétien and Paul Martin introduced legislation to decriminalize small amounts of cannabis possession. But in neither case was it a government priority, especially with the minority Martin government, and both initiatives died when their governments were dissolved. When Conservative Stephen Harper took power in 2006, the meager momentum built by the Liberals ground to a halt. Six years later, the federal Liberals were still stumbling in the opposition wilderness when, at their 2012 policy convention under the interim leadership of Bob Rae, delegates voted by an overwhelming 77 percent to call on future Liberal governments to legalize, regulate, and tax cannabis production, distribution, and use. It also called for an amnesty for Canadians with past possession convictions.

Justin Trudeau was listening. A year later, he was chosen party leader in a landslide, and, a few months later, he and his wife Sophie Grégoire embarked on a trip through western Canada. At a town hall-style picnic in Kelowna, British Columbia, Trudeau, then the third-party leader, announced he was going to legalize cannabis when elected—never mind that he wasn't seen, at least in the eyes of the country's punditocracy, as a likely prime minister in the short term. "He did it completely on his own," his former principal secretary Gerald Butts recalled.[2] "There was no grand political strategy to it. That was him making up his mind." He had discussed it with his friend Butts in the past, but, that night, Butts was visiting with a Canadian senator in his native Nova Scotia when he heard the news: "I turned to my friend and I was like, 'I don't know why he is doing this now.'" Trudeau had told Butts the story about his late brother Michel being busted for cannabis possession after smashing up his car on a trip home to Ontario from the West Coast. Police had found a couple of joints in the wreckage. The family used its name and the connections that only a former prime minister could boast to make Michel's problems disappear. It was a story Trudeau would repeat publicly. Had his brother been an Indigenous kid, he would have been in jail, Trudeau said. He was right.

It sounded like he was building the foundation for a legalized cannabis regime rooted in social justice, and a progressive Canadian government under Trudeau would undo much of the damage to Black and Indigenous Canadians from the War on Drugs. For Trudeau, the timing was right for legalization, with Barack Obama in the White House. Obama did not legalize, but he instituted a hands-off approach to states that sought to legalize. Canadian governments had for decades feared a substantive US pushback if they legalized. Trudeau did not anticipate any pushback from Obama. But the idealistic "sunny ways" of the Trudeau government elected in 2015 gave way to a more cautious, cynical, and pragmatic government gearing up for reelection by the time his cannabis promise became law. And those early social justice pronouncements ran into the formidable wall of Public Safety Minister Ralph Goodale, Justice Minister Jody Wilson-Raybould, and Health Minister Jane Philpott, the trio in charge of the legislation—a trio given uncommon freedom from a prime minister who sought views on the issue from his full Cabinet but did not dictate to his trusted three. He uncharacteristically let them drive the bus.

It was an odd trio with vastly different political experience and priorities, with the former top cop in Toronto, Bill Blair, thrown into the mix as the law-and-order guy selling the legislation to the provinces and Canadians at large. Blair's proscribed message was that Canada needed to legalize to protect our kids' health through regulation and to eliminate the illegal market and its organized crime profiteers. Though Blair's overriding preoccupation at the time was winning a ticket into Cabinet (which he eventually got), his role as the sherpa for the legislation drew the ire of Black Canadians who knew only too well his role in overseeing a police force that was under investigation for racial profiling and discrimination by the Ontario Human Rights Commission.

Goodale had been a fixture in Parliament forever, it seemed, first elected when Justin Trudeau was two years old. He had served in senior Cabinet portfolios under both Trudeaus, Jean Chrétien, and Paul Martin. He is an affable and approachable man with a steel will behind closed Cabinet doors. Goodale had long been a conservative counterbalance—or impediment, depending on your point of view—in the Liberal Cabinet, particularly on matters of gun control, which was always opposed by voters in rural areas of his home province of Saskatchewan. He was defeated in the 2019 election and is now Canada's ambassador to the United Kingdom.

Wilson-Raybould, from the West Coast, the country's first Indigenous justice minister, and Philpott, an Ontario physician, the health minister, were political rookies, never before elected to office before being elevated to Cabinet. They were seen as principled idealists, lured by Trudeau's promise of doing politics differently. Wilson-Raybould would end up resigning from Cabinet after a protracted government scandal in which she said she was improperly pressured to defer prosecution of fraud and corruption charges against Quebec engineering giant SNC-Lavalin. She sat for one term as an independent member of Parliament before bowing out in 2021 (although she remained a high-profile thorn in Trudeau's side). Philpott, now the director of the school of medicine at Ontario's Queen's University, followed Wilson-Raybould out the door. The scandal also led to Butts's resignation and severely damaged Trudeau's government, but, as legalized cannabis loomed, Goodale, Philpott, and Wilson-Raybould were an impenetrable threesome when it came to using cannabis legalization as a springboard to greater social and cultural reforms.

After his election in 2015, Trudeau quickly proved to be a prime minister prone to overpromising and underdelivering, a man drawn to the symbolic, often at the expense of the substantive. He was first met by a bureaucracy full of ideas on how to water down his cannabis promise, but he stood firm, and the bureaucracy quickly fell in line. The next step was to go to an old government hand, Anne McLellan, who had handled key portfolios for the Liberals under Chrétien and Martin and was the rarest of creatures, a Liberal from conservative Alberta.[3] She had won elections with such microscopic margins that she was ironically known as "Landslide Annie." Goodale called her and asked if she would head a committee that would provide a regulatory framework for legalizing adult-use cannabis. "We were old friends from the

Chrétien and Martin governments over twelve years," McLellan recalled. "That was a smart move because I'm not sure I would have done it. I was always on the enforcement side. I was minister of justice, I was minister of health, I was minister of public safety. I was always enforcing and defending the rules. When Ralph called, I said 'Are you crazy? I've always been on the enforcement side and I'm not sure I'm the best person for it.' . . . He said, 'Annie, yes you are, these are the three ministries that you held in government. You understand these departments and pressure points.'"

McLellan, her co-chair Mark Ware, a McGill University doctor with a specialty in cannabis research (and now the chief medical officer at cannabis company Canopy Growth), and her team were given a fairly lengthy leash—and only five months to do their work. Her team met with the three key ministers twice during that time, and with Trudeau once, to provide updates. Her mandate was to look at how legalization would work, not whether legalization was a good idea. The decision had been made, and, despite that leash as a nod to the respect she had earned over the years, McLellan was not to color outside the lines. She did not probe the questions of record expungement or social equity, something McLellan argues was beyond her mandate. When her task force traveled to Colorado and Washington State to study legalization there, she heard discussions regarding record expungements, but it was not a driving issue at that point in either state. "It came up in our roundtables," she said. "We listened intently to people who argued for expungement, but we always made clear at the beginning of those discussions that we would not be making recommendations in relation to it." She also heard arguments from Canadian attorneys general in the country that record keeping, much of it not digitized, would make such an initiative extremely difficult.

She also had no Indigenous representation on her task force, and she came under fire from Indigenous leaders over a lack of consultation. This lack of representation, in retrospect, was a mistake, Philpott believes. McLellan agrees that an Indigenous voice at the table would have been "useful":

> We had Indigenous roundtables and discussed their concerns. Indigenous communities, not surprisingly, . . . you would hear from Elders about the

devastation of certain drug use in their community. . . . Then you heard from responsible, forward-looking chiefs who saw economic opportunities that came with legalized cannabis if it was done right. It is not for non-Indigenous people to tell Indigenous communities whether they see sustainable economic opportunity growing and manufacturing cannabis. That is up to the community to decide.

And so the Canadian government did not offer any incentives for Indigenous people looking to profit from the legal industry. Nor did it reach out to Indigenous people who were carrying records for cannabis possession.

If some states look more progressive than Canada, it was precisely because they were states, McLellan maintains. "We were creating a national legalization. So it's pretty darn progressive." But certainly not nearly progressive enough for the mounting voices seeking true social justice. They saw a window opening for social justice reform, and I worked with many of them. Our fight for amnesty in Canada began some seven months before the first adult-use cannabis was sold in the country. With the support of the Open Democracy Project, the Campaign for Cannabis Amnesty was launched during the Global Marijuana March at Queen's Park, the seat of the Ontario government. I had proposed the need for cannabis amnesty to Annamaria Enenajor, a civil rights and constitutional lawyer who shared my passion for the need to fully erase past criminal records. I told Annamaria we had to fight to get those records erased, but she said the law does not work that way. You cannot change things retroactively, she told me, but I told her she was thinking too much like a lawyer. I told her we had pardons for a reason.

I left it that. Shortly thereafter I got a text from her: "We need to charter challenge the shit out of this." A few months later, she said: "I'm going to form this organization and I want you to be part of this." And that's how Cannabis Amnesty was formed. She grabbed the idea and just ran with it, enlisting the help of her law partner, Stephanie DiGiuseppe, and a group of talented and dedicated volunteers in the process. I had previously been invited to take part in the government's consultation on legalization and had quietly reached out to some elected and appointed officials and told them they had to be aware of the social justice aspect of legalization. Initially, I got a bit of a hostile response from some of them who were not supportive of this perspective.

Gradually, but effectively, I was becoming known and began getting invitations to speak to senators or their staff and to people close to the prime minister, where I could advocate for expungement. I was being invited to conferences where I spoke of expungement and advocated for redistribution of tax revenue. I submitted written comments to the cannabis task force. As a campaign, we had a goal to pressure government by gathering at least ten thousand signatures on a petition demanding full amnesty, then reaching out to media to deliver our message. We found a lot of support for the amnesty piece as we were gaining signatures. We pushed our campaign at the 4/20 march at Queen's Park, and we partnered with a cannabis company, and they drove a "Pardon Truck" from Vancouver to Toronto raising awareness. It was like a UPS delivery truck covered in Doja marking, and when it reached Toronto we parked it on Queen Street near the old Much Music studios and stopped people on the street to get them to sign our petition and come into the Pardon Truck to check out the swag. We went to cannabis conferences; we grabbed every media opportunity; and we worked tirelessly for the cause. We got the ten thousand signatures we needed easily. It did not take more than a few months.

Signatures and swag were one thing. Petitions were fine. But, more importantly, we had allies inside the tent. Those allies all had something in common. They had been involved with cannabis reform, the criminal justice system, or the prison system in Canada for years. Or they were Black. Or they saw a parade of Black and Indigenous youths before them on cannabis charges as lawyers and judges. Nathaniel Erskine-Smith, a Liberal member of Parliament who represents a riding in the east end of Toronto, has carved out a well-earned reputation as someone who thinks and votes independently from the often-stifling caucus conformity that marks Canadian politics.[4] He consumed cannabis like so many other young Canadians, and he acknowledged the security of being white and middle class; and, ultimately, being a lawyer meant he never feared the law the way he knows others have. He came to realize that the country was criminalizing people for no good reason and hurting the very people it should have been trying to help:

> When I was an undergrad, I got to reading more about drug policy and it struck me how many people from across the political spectrum had all come to the conclusion that the War on Drugs had been a failure. . . . There was a letter to [United Nations Secretary-General] Kofi Annan from hundreds of signatories saying the War on Drugs had failed and was causing more problems than the drug use itself. You grow up learning drugs are problematic and you stay away from drugs and the War on Drugs is held up as a positive law enforcement intervention. And then the evidence is so clearly the other way.

While studying at Queen's University in Kingston, Ontario, Erskine-Smith brought a former cop from neighboring New York state to speak to the class. He told the class that the War on Drugs had been a failure and he had regretted spending all his adult life enforcing those laws: "I found that very powerful and decided that day we had to reform our drug laws. It marked one of the first times in my life I went: 'This is what I have been taught, but here is all the evidence and the experts are saying and there is a huge disconnect between these two things.'"

Murray Rankin, now a cabinet minister in the New Democratic Party in British Columbia but a former member of Parliament for Victoria, once tried to establish a branch of NORML at the campus at the University of Victoria.[5] Years before, in 1973–1974, a time of "social foment," he headed up the Student Legal Advice Services at Rochdale College where he was a law student at the University of Toronto law school. Rankin lived around the corner from Rochdale at a co-op building and volunteered with the Student Legal Aid Society, and he often met clients at the famous college.

Rochdale inhabits an almost mythical place in the history of Canadian cannabis laws, an experimental school that was a hub for drug dealing just west of Toronto's downtown core, where large quantities of cannabis were sold while the city's finest circled the blocks around the school. It was a time of freedom and paranoia, of giving the finger to the establishment, but watching your back. The college opened in the idyllic summer of free love in 1968 as one of the largest co-op residences in North America and the largest of some three hundred tuition-free universities on the continent. It closed in 1975 shortly after Rankin railed against existing marijuana laws in a legal handbook that he was preparing for Rochdale residents. (He was lightly reprimanded by university administration for inserting editorial comments about the existing law in a legal handbook.) "It was the 1970s! What is the cliché about if you remember, you're lying?" Rankin recalled, with obvious nostalgia.

More than four decades later, Rankin introduced a private member's bill in the House of Commons that would have expunged low-level cannabis convictions. His goal was an artificial intelligence program modeled after the San Francisco experience Clear My Record program, the subject of a separate chapter. Private member's bills rarely, if ever, become law, but a buoyant Rankin thought his plan so logical, so just, so easy that it must be a winner—when you were saddled with a record, you were last in line to rent an apartment. You were last in the employment line. You were denied the opportunity to coach your kid's soccer team. He set out to explain this to his fellow members of Parliament. "If that record were expunged, as my bill would do, they could honestly answer that they do not have a criminal record. It would be deemed in law that they do not have such a record. Imagine how many thousands of impoverished Canadians we could assist by doing the right thing," Rankin told the House of Commons in December 2018. He reminded his colleagues of the disproportionate price paid by Black and Indigenous Canadians during the War on Drugs. He called it a historic injustice: "Jaywalking is not an offense under the charter. However, if nine out of ten people we go after for jaywalking are Black or Indigenous, then it is a charter violation. After years of injustice, why would the government settle for a process that will not fully relieve the burden of a criminal record? The only way to right the wrong and finally give the half million Canadians a fair chance is expungement, to erase the records for simple possession."

Erskine-Smith and Rankin had other allies. Kim Pate, an Ontario senator appointed by Trudeau, has spent almost four decades advocating on behalf of the racialized and marginalized people who have been warehoused in Canadian penitentiaries. In 2019, she introduced a bill that went further, providing for the expiration of criminal records beyond cannabis possession. "The expiry of criminal records reflects the principle that when we, as a society, decide to hold someone accountable for their wrongdoing, we can only inflict so much hardship before we ourselves are perpetrating an injustice," she said in March 2019, during second reading of her Senate bill: "It also reflects the empirical data demonstrating that after a period of crime-free years, those with a previous conviction are effectively no more likely than the rest of the population to be convicted of another offense. A record expiry scheme is not a scheme for forgiveness. It simply reflects the principle that punishment should at some point come to an end."[6] Those who have paid their debt to society and are seeking to move on with gainful employment or settle into a better place to live should not have their records hanging above them like some sword of Damocles, Pate told her colleagues.

Trudeau had spoken of the overrepresentation of usually young Black and Indigenous Canadians in the country's prison because of cannabis convictions, but that injustice ran much deeper than cannabis convictions. In his December 2021 report, the country's correctional investigator, Ivan Zinger, disclosed that nearly 50 percent of all female prisoners in federal institutions were Indigenous and that 32 percent (and growing) of all prisoners were Indigenous, despite comprising 5 percent of the population.[7] In his annual report, released earlier that year, he said that, while Black people comprised 3.5 percent of the Canadian population, they comprised 9 percent of the prison population. In that report, he pegged the Indigenous population in Canadian prisons at 28 percent.[8]

Meanwhile, Celina Caesar-Chavannes, a Black member of Parliament from a riding east of Toronto, had been appointed as Trudeau's parliamentary secretary, but she was chafing as her voice was muted, her influence waned, and she was denied any access to the prime minister. For Caesar-Chavannes, her appointment increasingly appeared symbolic, part of Trudeau's embrace of political choreography and stagecraft. She ultimately announced her resignation from Trudeau's caucus during the Wilson-Raybould-Philpott tumult, citing the government's decision not to expunge cannabis records as one of the many reasons for her departure. In urging her former government to get serious about systemic racism in Canada, she was clear about the first thing it could do: "Let's start with the expungement of criminal records for those folks, predominantly Black and Indigenous, who have been charged with marijuana possession. . . . The government has introduced pardons; however, the over-surveillance of Black and Indigenous communities, which is a violation of our human rights, has led to disproportionate over-representation of these groups in the prison system. It is time to right that wrong."[9]

Melvyn Green has a long history of advocating for cannabis reform and the wrongly convicted, beginning with his days as a researcher for the Le Dain Commission, then during his quarter century of private law practice, and, since 2005, in his position as an Ontario Court judge.[10] He has sat on the bench and watched as kids, most often Black or Indigenous, were brought before him after being busted on the street and treated in a "mechanical, sausage-processing kind of way. The sentencing was also based on priors. If he got thirty days last time, then it is six months now and the next time is penitentiary time and they ought to know that, accompanied by the old finger wag. . . . I tried to level the playing field." Green says he believes the government should have introduced an amnesty program for those convicted of possession right off the hop. But he was also advocating for an equity initiative in which those racialized groups who had disproportionately borne the weight of the War on Drugs be "given a leg up, or loans, or education or commercial support or licenses on a basis that recognizes both the harm they have suffered and the otherwise unequal opportunity for them to enter those markets."

And Green would have gone further. He would have moved to what he calls reparations. It is a concept most often associated with slavery in the United States, but it is pertinent in Canada as well, even if it is rarely discussed. We will discuss a reparations program begun in Illinois in a later chapter. "There are communities that have suffered because to a large degree they were Black or of some other racialized origin and their economic opportunities were clearly uneven," Green says. "Yet the manifestos of entrepreneurism, in sharing in the Canadian dream, were as entrenched for them and bought for them as for anyone else. But the opportunities were limited." The white population has insulation based on their color, as Green explains, and they use that insulation, or protection, when they seek drugs from those who have only a limited opportunity to engage in any other form of entrepreneurial endeavors: "Because that's the way the system is built. That may sound like a glib, reductionist analysis, but there is truth in it. That's why there is that guy sitting on the [inner-city Toronto] corner of Wellesley and Parliament."

These voices were largely ignored. Erskine-Smith told his own government that it was missing an opportunity to correct an injustice when that opportunity "stares it in the face": "We went with the pardon process, but the evidence is clear today it failed to do the job we wanted it to do. It's frustrating to see American jurisdictions doing the very thing many of us had asked for when the answer back from the government is it's 'too hard.'" Rankin, in fact, had suggested that if the government thought this was so damn difficult, teams of summer students could be hired to ferret about cannabis records that were still only on paper. Those of us pushing for expungement did get quick pushback, but part of that was simply that records were not as accessible as they were in San Francisco or Illinois, which were fully digitized jurisdictions where you could let an algorithm loose on them.

In Canada, there are convictions under the Controlled Drugs and Substances Act, but they do not specify cannabis, and there are no codes specifically for cannabis, so you would have to go through the records literally one by one.[11] This is a federal act and federal governments create the laws, but the provinces administer the laws. These convictions are kept in provincial jurisdictions. It was going to be very resource intensive to go through all these records and identify the cannabis convictions and downgrade or clear them; but it was very labor intensive to create these records in the first place. People had to be arrested, they had to be charged, they had to be convicted. We poured massive resources into the criminalization that harms these people and harms our society, and I think it is reasonable that we pour resources into clearing those records for them. Canada had proved it was possible to expunge criminal records. Trudeau had ordered just that in 2017 in offering a formal apology to lesbian, gay, bisexual, transgender, queer, and Two-Spirited (LGBTQ2) Canadians whose lives were ruined by charges and criminal convictions simply because of their sexual orientation. Today, politicians from Trudeau on down march in Gay Pride parades and celebrate those once persecuted for their sexuality. But smoking a joint is also legal, accepted, and often celebrated. Do times change for one injustice, but not another?

Erskine-Smith was the only Liberal to vote for Rankin's bill: "I remember standing up and thinking 'Shit, am I the only one?'" Among the handful of Conservatives who backed Rankin, however, was Erin O'Toole, who led the party for a short time before being ousted. Why would the government gradually go from social justice rhetoric to its mantra of protecting children and busting the illegal market? Why would it not go further? Surely the nation's first Indigenous justice minister would be aware of the injustice done to Indigenous youth for years during this War on Drugs. Wouldn't she be advocating for putting cannabis revenues toward improving the life of Indigenous kids in urban settings or pushing for guaranteed access to positions of power in the legal market for Indigenous entrepreneurs? Philpott, as health minister, worked assiduously to provide clean drinking water to Indigenous communities, but she did not push to right the criminal injustice perpetrated on Indigenous people convicted of cannabis possession.

Blair, who was Trudeau's point man in shepherding cannabis legislation to fruition, had been the police chief in Toronto and had once appeared to find his way to repudiate the practice of "carding," police checks in predominantly Black neighborhoods in his city that targeted racialized youth. If anyone knew the damage done to Black people in Toronto by cannabis busts, it would be Blair. Yet, when Rankin approached him, Blair argued that the Trudeau Liberals could expunge records of those charged for homosexual offenses because those convictions represented a historic injustice. When Rankin argued that cannabis possession convictions also represented a historic injustice, Blair was unmoved. Wilson-Raybould did not seem engaged as the legalization saga unspooled, preferring to rely on advice she was getting from her department. (Blair and Wilson-Raybould declined to be interviewed for this book.)

Both Erskine-Smith and Rankin called Goodale the immovable object. "Goodale was a real problem for me. He had no open mind, he was Mr. Law and Order," Rankin said. Goodale, when pushed on expungement of records before the original legalization bill had passed, had a talking point that he would not diverge from, a variation of: "We will not presume the will of Parliament. Until the law changes, the law remains the law and should be enforced. Currently people convicted of a minor possession offense can apply for a record suspension five years after their sentence expires."

Philpott, a doctor and health minister, understandably came to cannabis legalization from a public health perspective, but she had long been in the legalization camp, going so far as to speak out in favor of the decriminalization of harder drugs. She came to believe criminalizing drug possession was the wrong approach during her days working as a physician during the HIV epidemic. To be sure, there were Cabinet voices pushing for the expungement route, primarily those from Quebec. Melanie Joly, then the heritage minister, later the foreign affairs minister, was one. David Lametti, then a parliamentary secretary but, today—notably—the country's justice minister, was another. But simply put, there was a lack of political will, as Philpott concedes today. Expungement always "popped its head up," as the government was formulating legalization policy, Philpott says: "But I think for the sake of getting the job done there was a deliberate effort to say that was out of scope for the process. . . . There were questions about it, there was advocacy around it, and everybody had an opinion, but we knew we had to get legalization across the line first, then get a commitment to deal with the issue of expungement secondarily." She continued, "It would be interesting to know, if the same piece of legislation was working its way through the House right now [2021] in the context of raised social consciousness on racism, [whether] it would have weighed more strongly on the discussion." Her government's courage waned over time, she explained:

> We also knew that there were voters out there who opposed expungement because it might be a slippery slope that would lead to exoneration for serious criminals or opposed it because those convicted knew they were breaking the law at the time, or thought expungement was wrong because it was essentially retroactively changing laws. We knew it because we were hearing it, but we also knew this was a tiny minority. The government also knew these voices were faint. . . . The aspirations of the Trudeau campaign of 2015 versus the Trudeau government of 2018–19 as you get closer to an election . . . there is less desire to push on harder policies.

But were there votes to be lost by pushing harder? Was there political capital to be spent? "I don't have a good explanation on that one . . . if you are saying there wasn't enough political will to do it or not do it, so the government chose the easiest route," Philpott says, "I would agree with that."

Legal adult-use cannabis became law in Canada on June 21, 2018, and the first legal cannabis became available on October 17, 2018. On that date, the government announced it would table legislation allowing those with simple cannabis convictions to apply for a pardon, with the $631 application fee waived, provided the applicant's sentence had been completed. That law, Bill C-93, passed exactly one year after cannabis became legal, and the law came into force on August 1, 2019, shortly before Parliament was dissolved and the Liberals sought reelection. Canadians, in fact, have gone to the polls twice since recreational cannabis use was legalized, and no political party has tried to make legalization an issue.

During committee hearings on cannabis pardons, the Liberals heard repeated calls for a more progressive approach to dealing with those whose lives had been upended by a criminal record for something that was now legal. My voice, along with Enenajor's and the rest of the team at Cannabis Amnesty, was among those voices. Another voice was Samantha McAleese, a Carleton University doctoral candidate and research specialist on the collateral consequences of punishment. She studied the legislation and the committee testimony and concluded: "Overall, the government ignored the endorsements for a free and automatic expungement process in favor of a standard bureaucratic process that has already been the subject of comprehensive critique. Despite seeming to meaningfully engage and reflect on evidence presented by experts during the parliamentary committee hearings on Bill C-93, Goodale and others within the government settled for the status quo as a result of time constraints and a lack of innovation."[12]

Ralph Goodale is adamant that the question of expungement was seriously considered by him and his Cabinet colleagues who were also tasked with rolling back changes to the pardon system by the former Stephen Harper government.[13] That Conservative government had restricted eligibility and raised fees, making the entire process more onerous. The historic expungement granted to the LGBTQ2 community came about because Goodale and his government believed the section of the Criminal Code under which those convictions were brought was inherently a violation of human rights and had to be eliminated—as if they had never existed. Simple possession of cannabis was similar to the LGBTQ2 convictions in that the original offense had been abolished.[14] "But they were also different because the cannabis offenses had not been unconstitutional," Goodale says:

> The law itself was not inherently a violation of human rights—the problem was in its manner of enforcement which had become highly discriminatory, affecting certain minorities most harshly. . . . Consideration was given to a blanket expungement. This approach was not adopted with respect to cannabis convictions for several reasons. As a matter of principle, it would likely have blurred or diminished the critical point in the LGBTQ2 cases which involved an inherent violation of human rights in and by the very law itself. The distinction was considered important.

There were other reasons, according to Goodale. There was no ready access to a "complete and coherent" portfolio of simple possession records, which are stored by provincial and municipal authorities at multiple locations, often in paper form. He also argued that many of the charges refer to only violations dealing with controlled substances, and possession charges are often intermingled with more serious charges. As he explained, "Finding and combing through all records everywhere to identify those specific convictions that could be proactively or generically dealt with would take years of highly labor-intensive work, delaying the value and practical effect of any proposed blanket declaration for everyone."

Another legal view was provided by a judge. Green agreed that if the charges involved different drugs, the process could be messy, but not impossible. If someone pleaded guilty to simple possession, he said, all the rest is tantamount to background noise: "If that was what they were convicted of, that was what the Crown felt, or a judge felt, was the appropriate offense. . . . It would be perverse to read anything more than that into it. If someone was convicted of manslaughter, are you going to presume twenty years later that it must have been murder?" This is what Canadians got—a five-step process leading to a suspension that still costs the applicant money and makes it almost impossible for those living in rural or northern locales to apply.

For starters, the applicant is told their paperwork must include original documents with original signatures and original office seals or stamps from the court. Duplicates of forms will be tossed back at you. You must get your fingerprints taken and wait to receive your criminal record. If you have more than one, you need proof of each one from the court that heard your case and/or the police service that arrested you. You need to ensure you have proof of conviction that includes the date and court where you were sentenced, the offense that led to your conviction, your sentence, and the arresting police force. Still with us? Now you must obtain local police record checks for the city or town where you live currently and everywhere you have lived for the past five years. You must contact the police force where you live and where you may have lived for those five years. You better have the dated signature of your local police, along with its official seal or stamp.

So far so good. Now, if your criminal record or local police record check does not clearly show that you were convicted only of simple possession of cannabis and that your sentence was only a fine or a victim surcharge, you must obtain your court information and include proof of payment if there was a restitution order. You must contact the court that heard your case—or each case, if you were sentenced in more than one court. Make sure each court fills in the proper sections, includes all your convictions from that court, signs and dates the forms, and includes official seals or stamps. Moving along, you must now fill the Parole Board of Canada questionnaire (both sides, don't forget), include a photocopy of your identification, and fire it off in an envelope to Ottawa. If you served in the military, another step may await you. It can be no wonder that the take-up on the government program has been abysmal.

There are an estimated 500,000 Canadians with cannabis possession convictions, according to the CAMH, but the government disputes this, saying there is no reliable figure and only 10,000 might be eligible.[15] Regardless, according to government statistics, as of October 2021, two years after the program was introduced, only 484 "pot pardons" had been granted.[16] This means that only a small fraction of Canadians who might be able to seek a pardon have successfully applied. Meanwhile, a national survey done by Cannabis Amnesty and Responsible Cannabis Use found nearly 80 percent of respondents did not even know the government was offering pardons, and more than 90 percent had no idea of the eligibility requirements. Some 70 percent of respondents supported expungement of criminal records for possession.[17]

Given such a poor response to its program, Public Safety Canada, then headed by Blair, provided a list of talking points for government members of Parliament and distributed them on its website to try to justify the response. Here are some proposed excuses if Liberals were questioned about the low cannabis application approval rates:

- While the numbers may be lower than anticipated, this may be due to the fact that people with other criminal convictions, apart from simple possession, whether drug-related or not, are ineligible for the expedited process. Also, individuals may have already sought a pardon before the program was brought in.
- Due to the COVID-19 pandemic, PBC's [Parole Board of Canada] capacity to process record suspension applications, including those for cannabis record suspensions, was reduced, which resulted in delays in their processing.
- Recently, the PBC has returned to regular operations for the record suspension program. Less than 3 percent of record suspension applications that are pending processing are cannabis-related. The number of cannabis record suspension applications has declined since the beginning of the pandemic.

And what about those mounting questions about expungement versus suspension:

- Expungement is intended for extraordinary circumstances where the criminalization of an activity was historically unjust, such as where a law violated the Charter. This is not the case for convictions for simple possession of cannabis. Record suspensions are the appropriate recourse for these convictions.[18]

Goodale, like Philpott and McLellan, agreed that times may have changed, and, as he put it, "the shaping of various federal initiatives could still benefit from a specific assessment of impacts and distortions caused by outmoded drugs laws and, especially, discriminatory enforcement practices. Legislators should always be open to consider further information and new facts." The most charitable view of the Liberal legislation is that it was a product of its time, but, if that is the case, then I have to presume that views on diversity and equality in the legal market and the treatment of those who paid the price for misguided laws have moved at warp speed. Canada just recently passed the third anniversary of legalization. More likely, the Trudeau government could not see, or chose not to see, over the horizon, despite the urgings from me and other activists.

There was some movement from the Trudeau government on issues that were key for us, but they have not been specifically linked to cannabis legalization. Belatedly, the government introduced legislation that would end mandatory minimum penalties for drug offenses, but it stopped short of eliminating them. While the Trudeau Liberals said the legislation was an acknowledgment of the overrepresentation of Black and Indigenous people in the justice system, the bill would have still given police and prosecutors the option of laying charges. We know too well that police do not exercise their discretion evenly among social groups and that racialized and Indigenous people are the least likely to benefit from positive police discretion. The bill died when the Canadian House of Commons was dissolved for a late summer 2021 election, but it was quickly reintroduced in the new Parliament with Justice Minister David Lametti saying that mandatory minimums disproportionately locked up Black, Indigenous, and marginalized Canadians. The legislation would remove mandatory minimums on all drug convictions under the Controlled Drugs and Substances Act.

On another front, the Trudeau government, in partnership with eight financial institutions, established a $350 million loan program for Black entrepreneurs. But there was no specific incentive to give racialized Canadians a leg up in the legal cannabis market, although, as we will see later, successful Black entrepreneurs are seeking to change this situation. Butts said he always felt cannabis legalization was one of those things that, once it was done, people would look back and think it was insane that it was ever illegal, and, in retrospect, it would seem most of the country feels exactly that way. But he lost a lot of internal battles on the legalization file. As he explained, "I thought we were blowing a big opportunity to make Canada a global center for an emerging industry that was going to grow exponentially over the next five to ten years. The way we restricted the commercial aspect was short-sighted, and I also thought the expungement issue should have been dealt with as a no-brainer and the fact that we didn't do it weakened it from the social justice aspect." Today, Butts says it pains him to see the legislation being outstripped by more progressive jurisdictions in the United States. When he looks back, he sees two files during his time in the prime minister's office on which Trudeau's Liberals were overly cautious: "The two areas where we left money on the table were gun control and drug policy."

So, we watched in frustration as a cumbersome record suspension program paled in comparison to the use of artificial intelligence in San Francisco, Los Angeles, and Illinois. We watched as jurisdictions like New Jersey introduced a constitutional amendment to ensure cannabis tax revenues are steered to communities harmed by the War on Drugs. In later chapters, we will explain programs like the one in Evanston, Illinois, which channels cannabis revenue back into damaged communities as part of an ambitious reparations project. We watched as the federal Marijuana Opportunity Reinvestment and Expungement Act passed the House of Representatives promising exactly what its title says.[19] US federal legalization may not be on the immediate horizon, but it is clear that, when that hurdle is finally cleared, it will include provisions for minority involvement in the industry and will use revenues to pay back to damaged communities.

We will highlight the good—and the bad—of social equity programs in the United States while pointing out that, according to a study of seven hundred Canadian cannabis industry leaders I coauthored, 84 percent of them are white, only 2 percent are Indigenous, 1 percent is Black, and 1 percent is Latinx. Some 73 percent of those leaders are white men, and only 2 percent are non-white women. If one were to strip out the involvement of the Assembly of Nova Scotia Mi'kmaq Chiefs and its 51 percent stake in the licensed producer AtlantiCann, Indigenous leadership drops to 0.6 percent.[20] Indigenous numbers revealed a similar story. By the start of 2022, there were forty Indigenous-affiliated federal cannabis license holders (out of approximately 750 federal licenses) and sixty-nine new license applications (cultivation, processing, sale for medical purposes) in various stages of the federal licensing process that have self-identified as Indigenous, according to Health Canada.[21] Critics have taken issue with the government term "Indigenous-affiliated," meaning that the numbers may be reported higher than those that are exclusively Indigenous operations.

I have been working for criminal justice reform for almost twenty years, and I am constantly faced with resistance. Some of the wins I have had were due to another war, the war of attrition. Some of these politicians and bureaucrats will no longer be in their positions while I, as someone just starting my academic career, will still be around. By the end of my career, I can be confident that some of these things will happen in Canada. In the meantime, we will be pushing the government to study the racial impact of this legislation three years in, in addition to its mandate to study the effects of legalization on youth and Indigenous Canadians. The government put a lot of effort into criminalizing people and creating these records. They created laws, empowered and encouraged police to enforce the laws, spent money pushing them through the court system, and ultimately spent a lot of money punishing people and incarcerating people.

It took a lot of time and money to criminalize people for behavior relating to cannabis. Knowing what we know about how a criminal record negatively impacts an individual's ability to function in society, it seems only logical that the government would spend as much time and money—perhaps more—to identify these people who have been criminalized and clear the records for them. This move would benefit not only the person whose record is cleared but also a society that would no longer have to spend money on social assistance and housing for people who, cleared of their records, could contribute to society. The Canadian system is light years away from the free and automatic keystroke click to expungement that is needed in this country and, indeed, the continent. We will continue to push Canadian legislators until they adopt policies that are in play in US jurisdictions—the models of best practices that are with us today.

5 THE COST OF CONVICTION

By the spring of 2012, Evelyn LaChapelle was working on getting her life together.[1] She had ended a toxic marriage, left her job, and headed back to Oakland with her young daughter to live with her mother. Any dubious decisions or detours seemed to be behind her. She always had lofty goals, and she just needed to take a bit of a breath to ready herself for her next chapter after earning her insurance license. On this humid August night, she needed to take more than a figurative breath. It was the kind of night where the walls were closing in a little in her mother's condo as they sometimes did. It was 10:30 p.m., and she and a friend headed out to his Nissan 350Z to smoke a joint. They sat there smoking, with no lights on, no music playing. Sitting in a car while being Black.

A neighbor spied them and called police about a "suspicious" vehicle in the quiet gated community, home to mainly older residents living in about forty units stretched along a road no longer than five hundred feet. A Nissan 350Z looked out of place in that neighborhood and maybe somebody thought things were a little too quiet. Then there was a knock on the window. LaChapelle rolled it down to greet a sheriff's deputy, a seemingly innocent encounter that would change her life forever. It would be years before LaChapelle could again be the mother and independent woman she was before she walked outside that late night in Oakland. She is still adapting to being a mother, a sister, a daughter, and a friend. In some ways, she is still not there; she is still working on the happy ending. LaChapelle was a smart kid from Hayward, California, who took a rather conventional path to adulthood and, in fact, had advantages that were not available to many young Black women. Yet she ended up in a jail cell on suicide watch, shrieking uncontrollably and gasping for air.

Corvain Cooper was a hustler from east Los Angeles.[2] It was the family trade. He was the son of a hustler, driving a Benz by the age of nineteen. He loved the flash and the sleek cars. Cooper was a guy with street smarts who loved the hustle; a guy with a stubborn streak that often served him poorly, but a guy with a deep well of empathy for others. That empathetic side drew LaChapelle to him. However, all his traits put Cooper on a path that took him to one of America's most notorious prisons, where he would watch one night as a fellow prisoner had his neck slashed.

Michael Thompson remembers sleeping on the floor as a boy in a house shared by five families on St. John Street in Flint, Michigan, a bustling thoroughfare populated by families from the south as part of the great Black migration.[3] It featured rail tracks at one end and a slaughterhouse at the other before it was razed in the early 1970s to make room for an interstate highway. He, too, was lured by the fresh clothes and hot cars that he could only find by working the street, the only way he thought he could get out of St. John. It took him to the entertainment industry, hanging with the likes of Aretha Franklin. Yet, after being set up by a friend who lived in that same street culture, he lost twenty-five years of his life to the struggle and despair of prison life in Muskegon, Michigan.

Although seemingly unconnected—two young people from the West Coast and a middle-aged guy in the Midwest—this trio had one thing in common. They were all convicted of nonviolent crimes involving the sale of cannabis. Beyond that, these three languished in prison while a new, largely white, entrepreneurial class flocked to the legal cannabis gold rush of the 2000s. Those young speculators made money. These three who were Black and had done the same thing, sat in prison watching news reports featuring Beverly Hills blondes pitching their new cannabis outlets. Importantly, all three are now free, but it took the tireless work of champions for their cause, the steadfast faith of their families, unlikely interventions from the likes of Kim Kardashian and Donald Trump, and ongoing advocacy on their behalf from organizations like the Last Prisoner Project (LPP). Yet reintegration can be difficult. They live with restrictions that shrink their world, and they must rebuild skill sets and reset relationships. Still, they have that chance.

According to best estimates from LPP, there are at least 40,000 Americans—60 percent of them Black or Latinx—doing time for nonviolent cannabis offenses, even though adult-use cannabis is now legal in nineteen states and the District of Columbia.[4] None of these three—LaChapelle, Cooper, or Thompson—deny they made mistakes, and none of them blame anyone but themselves. But neither can any of them understand the severity of their penalties, while others profited. When the sheriff's deputies pulled up beside LaChapelle's car that night, there was no cause for concern. Cannabis had been decriminalized in California in 2010, and even the most hardline, by-the-book cop could not give her anything more than a ticket. Besides, there was no weed in the car. They had smoked it. "Hi, I'm going in the house, no big deal," LaChapelle told the officer, who, in turn, told her that someone had reported a "suspicious" car. Nothing suspicious here, LaChapelle assured him. "My mom lives here."

The officer asked for identification, but LaChapelle had none. She had thrown on a pair of sweats and didn't grab her wallet since she was within a stone's throw of her house. She had been out of the house for no more than fifteen minutes and just wanted to go back in and call it a night. This had become a major irritation for a woman who had simply walked outside to smoke a joint and thought this police data check was a waste of everyone's time. Just two weeks earlier, LaChapelle had been pulled over by an officer because her vehicle registration had expired, and the officer ran her name and nothing came up. But this time, a sheriff's deputy in her mother's community, using a different police database, found a warrant for LaChapelle's arrest. The officer would not—or could not—tell her what the warrant was for, but he did tell her she was going to jail, and the warrant involved the Immigration and Customs Department. With only that sliver of information, LaChapelle stood there, now joined by her mother, the silence pierced by her exasperated arguments that she was not an immigrant, had been born just down the road, and lived in a condo that she could see from the street. As she sat in the squad car, she suddenly heard a squawk from the radio, and her heart dropped from her chest.

"North Carolina," she heard. North Carolina. North Carolina meant another time and another space and a time with Corvain Cooper, a time she thought was firmly in the rearview mirror: "I was sitting there thinking this was all a huge mistake and I'll be out of here in an hour, but I heard 'North Carolina,' and I thought, 'oh, this is something that I actually did.'" She knew what this was about. It all began when LaChapelle and Cooper met in a grocery store parking lot. LaChapelle's beauty was not lost on Cooper, who was driving a Porsche and was used to women flocking to him because of his swagger, his clothes, and his luxury wheels. "Woah, I've got to have her," Cooper recalls saying to himself. LaChapelle wasn't impressed by any of the glitz or the smooth talking that was Corvain Cooper, but they got together a couple of times. Before a third date, and before anything went to what LaChapelle likes to call "the next level," she learned that she was pregnant. She and her daughter's father lived a volatile life. There was cheating, there were loud fights, and the news of the pregnancy traumatized LaChapelle.

But Cooper was there for her. "He became my best friend during a pretty rough pregnancy," she recalled. He became the "pregnancy friend," the guy who was there for lunch every day, who sent flowers, who bought dinners, took her to doctor's appointments and pregnancy massages, walked in the woods with her, and provided the shoulder when LaChapelle needed support. "Every woman needs one," she said. "Not every guy would do that. He is extremely loyal. He wants to take care of people. I don't know how he chooses, but from start to finish, he takes care of you. Even from prison, he was trying to look after me." There could be no doubt that Cooper was attracted, but, rather than a conquest, Cooper came to be comfortable with the fact that, in that moment, LaChapelle needed a friend more than any-thing else. "The cars and the clothes—she was never impressed by that and I really liked that about her," Cooper said. "She was pregnant and she told me her problems and I told her my problems and we liked each other. But we were not taking it there."

A customer at the Citibank where LaChapelle worked was also taken by her beauty and fancied himself an artist. He wanted to pay her to sit while he painted her portrait. But he wanted to do it at 9:00 p.m. in his apartment. Cooper and LaChapelle both still laugh at this one. She was worried and did not want to go alone: "I mean, nine o'clock at night at his place, I don't know about this, that ain't right, you know what I'm saying?" So he did the honorable thing. He went with her and sat there and kept an eye on the guy painting his friend. Their bond was tight.

LaChapelle knew Cooper was selling cannabis, but that elicited nothing more than a shrug. She came from a culture where she and all her friends smoked weed and bought it on the street. It had always been that way, and she had been buying it herself since she was nineteen. Besides, Cooper was earning money elsewhere as well. He was in the process of buying a house in downtown Los Angeles and opening a clothing store. "He certainly didn't carry himself as a drug dealer; we weren't in drug dealing situations," she said. "I wasn't in the 'hood with him." But they were linked, nonetheless, even though LaChapelle and Cooper took two radically different journeys to that fateful day when their paths crossed in that Los Angeles parking lot.

She was born and raised in Hayward, a small community southeast of Oakland. It was more industrial than urban, and her upbringing meant mixing with Filipino immigrants, other Black kids, and a smattering of white kids. Her parents separated when she was three or four, and her father married someone else. They shared their time with young Evelyn, and she forged a strong relationship with her stepmother, spending weekends with her and her father and weekdays with her mother. Her mom was a bartender, and her dad worked at Cisco Systems, a Silicon Valley maker of networking hardware and software. She did not come from a tough part of town, and she was not exposed to crime on a daily basis, but she had a bit of a rebellious streak in her that manifested itself in her first year of high school where some Ds and Fs—and a couple of fights—had her on the verge of flunking. So she was shipped off to Catholic School in Oakland to straighten her out.

After high school, she headed to Los Angeles. She had a trust fund established by her grandfather that paid for her rent, car, bills, and tuition at Santa Monica Junior College, then West Los Angeles Junior College, and finally Loyola Marymount. She was studying business administration with an eye to opening a strip club, but Loyola Marymount was a Catholic school, and it was having none of that. She appealed her plan all the way to the dean, but he gave it a firm thumbs down. Instead, she joined a team with some white guys who wanted to install energy-efficient lighting, and she half-heartedly saw it through so she could get her grades and graduate.

During this time, Cooper was following in his dad's footsteps. "He always kept me fly and kept me up to date, but I just didn't have a father in the house," Cooper recalls. "He always made sure I was taken care of financially. He was a hustler, so I always looked up to a hustler. He sold drugs, he was with the top guys. He was fly with the cars, I mean I was wearing gators in high school." His uncle, too, was a player, and was friends with a star Los Angeles Dodger of the era, Eric Davis, so young Cooper saw the money from both sides—on the street and courtside at a Lakers game or a visit to the Dodgers dugout. His dad hustled for twenty years, never even getting a parking ticket, before he was caught in an indictment when Corvain was seventeen. Both of his parents did jail time—but just once. They paid their price and changed their lives.

His mother, Barbara Tillis, was a graduate of Cal State, a woman with a promising future who was absorbed into the crack epidemic in the 1980s. Their divorce drove each of them to the streets and the streets drove her down. "As a little boy of six or seven, I would pray that she would get off drugs and she did," he said. He maintained that faith and the power of prayer his entire life. His mother wanted him to be an actor. He went to Hollywood High School, a school steeped in diversity that opened his eyes to different cultures. But there was no Hollywood ending, and his time there came to an abrupt end. For the young hustler, it ended with seven months in a juvenile correctional facility. Cooper was the "locker keeper," and maybe he wasn't the right man for this task. His job was to watch the lockers while classes were in session. He was given the codes to all the lockers. He had no idea there were kids at Hollywood High coming to school with thousands of dollars in their backpacks.

One day, as he explains it, out of boredom and just being nosy, he started opening lockers and realized what was in there. He spent about forty-five days skimming a little cash here and a little cash there, maybe scooping three hundred dollars from a wad of one thousand dollars. It would have lasted longer, but he brought a buddy into the scam after the friend wondered why Cooper looked so fresh and was wearing new clothes all the time. The friend got caught and ratted him out—"So I really never did get caught"—and there was Cooper doing a handcuffed perp walk through the halls of Hollywood High, now known as the "Locker Bandit."

He did graduate, just as he promised his grandmother he would, and went to El Camino College. But he wanted to be a firefighter. Cooper was a scrawny kid, and no matter how many protein shakes he drank, how many weights he lifted, he could never put on the requisite weight, and the dream died. He started passing bad checks, and after a couple of years dabbling in forgery, he was busted and got jail time. When he got out, he decided that selling cannabis—just like his dad—was the way to go. He learned the ins and outs of packing and shipping it to the other side of the world (well, initially to Atlanta, ultimately North Carolina, places foreign to him), and when he saw he could double his money in a day, he was sold. Business was good, very good.

In January 2009, right after LaChapelle found out she was pregnant, Cooper very nonchalantly mentioned to her that he had money coming in from North Carolina and was using Western Union to transfer the funds. "I'm paying this money to Western Union, I could be giving it to you," she recalls him saying. (Western Union was also too easy to trace.) "Do you mind if I drop this in your account?" Years later, the two differ over how much money LaChapelle made for her help, but it was not much, and she did not really need the cash anyway. She was still living on a trust fund, and she really did not give the question a second thought. Neither did she try to hide what she was doing. She even brought a friend in to help out and ended up sharing a jail cell with her as a result. "If he had said it was for heroin, I would have said 'No way.' But pot? I never had a second thought. I grew up in a very pot-enthusiastic atmosphere and couldn't see what the problem would be." Cooper explains it this way: "Western Union was bringing too much of a trail and we were already using other peoples' bank accounts. I thought, she already works at a bank and we're kicking it every day and she knew banking."

As a leader of the operation (even though North Carolina was not his plug initially), Cooper never touched the weed and did not have any of the money in his own bank account. LaChapelle was paid $200 for each deposit to her saving account and $200 for each deposit to her checking account. There were a lot of deposits. But, as Cooper saw it, she wouldn't even be committing a crime: "I mean, if you are depositing $9,000 in an account and then you take out that $9,000 from the same account, what crime are you committing? . . . She was a trust fund kid, she already had money. That was another reason it was good to work with her, because if you had to be away for a few days you didn't have to worry about her running off with the money, because the money didn't move her. We trusted each other. There have been people who have run off with the money."

The arrangement lasted about ten months, but the business was getting a little too much scrutiny for Cooper's comfort. His partner was getting a little too reckless, and he was starting to incur significant losses. Initially, business had been so lucrative, he wanted to mail pot until his "hands broke." Now it was becoming troublesome. "You move to boxes and crates, that's what brings the heat." The feds grabbed more than three hundred pounds, but they kept sending it:

> We took a loss and kept on ticking, but if you can do that, the feds take greater notice of that and you're drawing attention to yourself, even as you keep losing money. So the feds thought there has to be some big money somewhere. If you send forty pounds in a box and you lose it, you can withstand it, but when you start losing $200,000 on a shipment at a time, they're noticing and they're following people. . . . We were taking loss after loss after loss and I was ready to throw my hands up, take the little money I had and move on to the next thing. And that's what I did. I thought, "Man, I made it out."

In 2009, he was finished with the "drug thing." He had to lay down a foundation for his kids, and he opened a clothing store in 2010. Enough was enough for LaChapelle as well. She was having her baby, and her partner was not a fan of Cooper: "I just wanted to end this period of drama in my life." Cooper had proudly "backed up," as he termed it. He had been out of this thing for four years, but the statute of limitations on conspiracy was five years, which is why the police showed up in his driveway on a January day in 2013 as he returned home with his dry cleaning, about to take his oldest daughter to drill practice.

LaChapelle had never been to jail before she was shipped to a holding cell in Oakland, then moved out to Santa Rita prison in Alameda County, one of America's largest prisons, where she sat for four days until she was released on bond. That first night in a holding cell, she was afraid, but not desperately so. This thing was going to get cleared up real fast, wasn't it? The first morning at Santa Rita, there was a knock on the cell door, and she was moved again. Her mother's God sister, who worked for the sheriff's department, was worried about her safety and had her moved to protective custody, known in prison shorthand as PC: "I was completely on my own. I'm dressed differently than the other women, I was PCed. They wanted me to be away from others who could harm me, because I was now in a prison housing violent offenders."

LaChapelle was in solitary for twenty-three hours per day for four days. She was allowed an hour of freedom every morning at 7:00 a.m. and talked on the phone the entire time, seeking solace or help. It would take a day or two before one of the prison guards told her she should take a shower during that hour: "I refused to do anything other than talk on the phone. I was in a daze." When she was released on bond, she went to North Carolina to hire a lawyer, but the public defender said she should just sign a plea deal, do three years, and she'd be out before she hit thirty. LaChapelle thought that solution was ridiculous. There was no way she had done anything that merited three years behind bars. She felt she had really played no role in this conspiracy, despite the charge, so she hired a lawyer in North Carolina, went there for discovery, and gathered the information she needed.

There was an affidavit from the kingpin of this operation saying LaChapelle did not have a clue about what was going on in this lucrative cannabis operation. That was her fuel. She was not signing any plea deal. She was going to trial where she would be exonerated. On the first day of her trial, LaChapelle strode into court supremely confident. She did not even have any butterflies because she thought this awful charade was about to end, and she would go home to her little girl, Venise. But she and her lawyer were immediately blindsided by a second, much more incriminating discovery, and suddenly the wheels of North Carolina justice turned with dazzling speed.

The trial started on Tuesday, and the jury came back with a conviction on Friday. Deliberations by the all-white jury lasted about an hour. LaChapelle sat in the county jail in North Carolina, a maximum-security institution that housed violent criminals and drug addicts, for two years, facing a potential twenty-four years in prison. The first night, when the jail cell closed behind her, she could only think of her daughter. She couldn't breathe, she was borderline uncontrollable. She was with her codefendant who had been convicted with her. Her cellmate sat there with her head down, silent: "I was hysterical, screaming, thinking of my daughter, and thinking this should just be it for me." They ushered her into another cell, told her to strip down, and gave her a prison suit with a green padded vest, known as the turtle vest. She was placed on suicide watch.

The nights in the maximum-security county jail stripped the dignity and hope from LaChapelle. She was facing a maximum penalty of twenty-four years, and this preyed on her nightly: "That's when it started sinking in. You're a criminal. If they can give you twenty-four years in prison, you fucked up. I would think of the twenty-four years every night. It was the twenty-four years that broke me." There is little wonder such a prospect could break her because she had to live with such a potentially soul-destroying future for two years until she was finally formally sentenced to eighty-seven months. For those first two years, she did not see Venise at all. She was in North Carolina, and her family was in California. When her mother would fly in for a visit, it would be behind glass for thirty minutes. Then she would turn around and fly home. She was not going to make her little girl see her mother behind glass.

LaChapelle did not see Venise again until July 2015. Venise had just turned four ten days before LaChapelle was imprisoned in North Carolina on October 18, 2013. Now her little girl was about to turn six, and, as the meeting approached, LaChapelle felt a mix of anticipation and dread: "I didn't think she was going to know me, but she did. She said 'Mommy.' She ran and jumped into my arms after not seeing me for two years. It was definitely bittersweet, but it was the happiest I had been in two years. . . . We hugged and we played games and got snacks out of the vending machine." They spent about three hours together, but LaChapelle kept her emotions in check. She could not be seen to be an emotional wreck around her little girl. At such a young age, Venise was also learning to mask her emotions. There was no outburst when she hugged her mom, and when they said their goodbyes, Venise got back in the car with her great grandmother, who had brought her to see her mom.

As soon as the car hit the freeway, the little girl had a meltdown so traumatic that her great grandmother had to pull the car over on the shoulder of the interstate. LaChapelle beat herself up for years, believing that she was a bad person, a criminal, who deserved her fate. She was worthless. She had screwed everything up. She had lost her daughter. Twenty-four years. There was no daylight ahead. But the self-flagellation ended, and there were two catalysts for a change in her outlook. "I had been in there for two years and I was feeling guilty and I was a criminal and I had ruined everyone's life," she told an LPP audience:

And then I see the Channel 7 News at 11 and the cannabis industry is booming and I see the founders of the Beverly Hills Cannabis Club, two beautiful blonde blue-eyed white women, come on the screen, and the reporter asks how business is doing and she says, "business is booming." . . . And I'm sitting in prison watching business boom for the Beverly Hills Cannabis Club and that's when my prison sentence shifted to this righteous anger and—even though I hate the word "victim"—[the realization] I was a victim of unjust laws. How do you on one hand legalize and on the other hand criminalize? It set me on this path. That one thirty-second news report.

Another turning point was when she shared her story for the first time in an interview with long-time cannabis activist and author Steve DeAngelo. "That's when it kicked in. I started realizing this was just an unjust system and I didn't deserve what I got. . . . When I started fighting this case, it's like I've got this major ego thing and this pride that kicked in, and I was all 'I'm a trust fund kid, I got my degree, I've got my job, there is no way I'm going to let them win.' So my ego takes me into this and I am defeated." She had never considered the fact that she was a Black person being tried in North Carolina in front of an all-white jury and what that could mean for her fate. She had never been to North Carolina, and, in her mind, she had committed no crime there. After all, everything she had been involved in was happening with Cooper in Los Angeles.

Evelyn LaChapelle is a smart woman. But she had not seen the true picture of being Black in a state so foreign to her, where the justice system was stacked against her. But one thing had changed: "I no longer feel like a criminal." LaChapelle served sixty-three months of her eighty-seven-month sentence. She received a 15 percent reduction in her sentence for good behavior and another twelve-month credit for completing her residential drug program while incarcerated. She was released from prison on February 1, 2019, but her ordeal was not over.

Cooper had stepped away from business in 2009, but he was busted again in 2011, did his time, paid his price, and promised his daughters he would be with them forever now. He did not run. When the police pulled into his driveway in 2013, it was that promise to his daughters that he thought of first: "I wanted to start my clothing line. I thought my past was behind me. I hadn't seen any of those people, including Evelyn, since 2009." So when they came to his door that day on January 28, 2013, they mentioned North Carolina: "I pull up to the house, and the feds jump out talking about Charlotte, North Carolina. I'm like 'Shit, I've never even been to Charlotte, North Carolina.'" But he, LaChapelle, and her friend Natalia Wade had been named by one of Cooper's associates, among fifty-five people swept up in a federal effort dubbed "Operation Goldilocks."

Cooper's stubborn streak meant he vowed he was not going to be locked away on the word of someone else. "So, we all agreed. We had to go to trial. They had no hard evidence, no one had ever seen me commit any crime." A defiant Cooper refused a plea deal that might have got him fifteen to twenty years. He was proud, and he was a fighter, but he also thought such a deal was absurd: "To me, that was life. I was going to miss my kids' graduations. I would never see them grow up. I would miss everything. I wanted to maintain my rights. They wanted to take everything away, but I wanted to protect my rights. I was going to fight this to the end." But Cooper was a three-time offender in a world of three-strikes laws, and he was being threatened with a life sentence. He refused to believe he could ever get life for something that was legal in his home state; for a crime in a state in which he had never set foot; for a nonviolent crime. No one was hurt, he had caused no pain.

But, he wouldn't be human if the walls weren't closing in and the doubts were clouding his thoughts. "I can tell you, when you're facing life, you're going to have some trouble sleeping." And then the gavel came down from US District Judge Robert J. Conrad Jr. in a Charlotte courtroom, on June 18, 2014. Cooper had been sentenced to life behind bars without parole: "You feel empty inside. You think you're going to die in prison. This is how this movie is going to end? And it's going to end for something like this?" While he was serving his time, he, like LaChapelle, had to sit there and watch reports of the Green Rush sweeping the nation, while his life slipped away behind bars for doing what others were now celebrating: "I saw it regularly on the television, but once I saw it on the stock market and I saw it juice up from $5 to $40 for Canopy Growth Corp. and Tilray and . . . We're not even talking millions anymore, we're talking billions":

> My kids had to go through this while I was being buried alive under a bunk. It was a hard pill to swallow, a very hard pill to swallow because I'm reading Barron's and I'm keeping up with all this stuff because I was very big on stocks and that's when it really hit. The stocks are what changed it for me. I saw it in movies, I saw it on commercials and everyone was talking "weed, weed, weed," and everyone was making jokes about it. But when I saw it on the stock market that changed my entire outlook on things.

Cooper started his sentence at Atwater, a maximum-security prison southeast of San Francisco, where family could visit him. But he was gaining too much attention there. He was too popular, and his story was too big. Authorities believed Cooper wielded just a little too much influence: "They thought I was the shot-caller or a leader, the guy that people wanted to go to when there was a problem [in] the yard." That kind of popularity confers power. You have fans in there, and it almost always guarantees a trip out. It is known as diesel therapy. If you get too much attention as an inmate somewhere, the federal prison system will fly you somewhere else, so they can send you to Oklahoma, then to Kentucky, or fly you up north, for two to five days at a time, without any of your property. And that is how Cooper ended up at Pollock, one of the nation's most notorious maximum-security institutions. He had never been to Louisiana in his life. He was far from family, a nonviolent offender in a darkly violent atmosphere.

He never saw his daughters, Clyr and Scotlyn, while he was in Louisiana. They flew out to see him for his birthday, but the day before his birthday, there was a stabbing, and Pollock went into lockdown. They had flown all the way from California and could not see him. In fact, Cooper went four years without seeing his girls. But he did see assaults and stabbings. He watched one night as one prisoner was dragged from his cell with his neck wide open. There were stabbings over the most mundane things, such as a broken radio, a disrespectful look, or someone cutting the line. Shortly after Cooper got out, he was in a Walmart buying a phone when he saw someone cutting the line. It gave him chills: "I was like, 'Man, where I just came from, that is disrespect and I saw a guy stabbed in the neck because he cut the line.' . . . Everything you do in there, everything is serious. I still get calls from guys, telling me about stabbings. They say there is a hex on that prison. It's got a bad omen. If you've been at Pollock Max, everybody has an experience that is the worst. To walk out of that pit without a scratch on me is a blessing."

Cooper had petitioned Barack Obama for clemency in 2016 as the president was leaving office. Obama, after all, had vowed federal prosecutors under his watch would not seek lengthy sentences for nonviolent drug offenses, yet the outgoing president denied his clemency appeal. Cooper's chances of walking out of Pollock took an uptick in 2017. California's Proposition 64, which legalized adult-use cannabis, also reduced both of his previous convictions from felonies to misdemeanors. He appealed his sentence, logically arguing that he was no longer a three-strike offender because he had been convicted of only one felony, but this effort, too, would only lead to despair. His appeal was dismissed, and the US Supreme Court refused to hear his case. But his mother never gave up on him. Neither did his girls. "They motivated me," Cooper said. "Them not giving up and still having hope their dad was coming home, that kept me going." Clyr told him there had been a fly in her room one time, and she thought her dad had sent the fly in there to look after her. Scotlyn was only three when her dad had been imprisoned, and she had already lost him when he did a year on a weed offense when she was two. "She just wanted to experience kicking it with her dad," Cooper said, "getting to know me and me being there for her prom. She really only had two years with her father."

His appeals had been exhausted, but his case kept drawing attention from the mainstream and cannabis media through LPP. Cooper's case was featured in Black Entertainment Television's documentary *Smoke: Marijuana + Black America*, which propelled his profile through the roof. His lawyer, Patrick Michael Megaro, launched a Change.org petition that ultimately garnered more than 150,000 signatures asking for clemency from an unlikely source—Donald Trump. On the morning of Joe Biden's inauguration, Cooper had again heard nothing from an outgoing president. Trump was fleeing the capital at noon, and at 11:38 a.m., Cooper decided he had to go about his usual routine. "I was still trying to have faith that I'm leaving when Trump leaves, but he was getting on that helicopter while I was heading into the shower," Cooper recalled of that January 2021 morning. "I was back in the cell for five or ten minutes and then, out of nowhere, I hear: 'You've got five minutes. Pack your shit up!' Donald had hit a 'last-second shot,'" as Cooper related it. A buzzer-beater that flipped his world: "Ivanka (Trump) called my mom to tell her they chose me because I had two daughters, and he had daughters and he wanted me to get back to my daughters."

In the chaos, Cooper missed the call from Trump because he was doing a media interview and let the phone ring. When he was finished, he saw a "missed call" notification from POTUS on his phone, then a text message from Trump: "Corvain, have a nice life." . . . I called my mom and I was crying. She said, 'What are you crying for? I talked to Ivanka and she said you were coming home.' I said, 'No, mom, these are tears of joy. This is some kind of once-in-a-lifetime stuff.'" The clemency papers signed by Trump hang in the hallway in his new home to this day: "I was set to die in a prison. Everything I do now has to be for a reason."

Michael Thompson was born in Oxford, Mississippi, delivered by a midwife in the family home because in 1951 in Mississippi, Black babies were not born in hospitals. Maybe it was a law, maybe not, but it was just understood that that was the way of being Black in the South. In the mid-1940s United States, very few Black mothers were able to give birth in hospitals during the Jim Crow era. The year Thompson was born, 88 percent of white births were in hospitals, and only 22.7 percent of non-white Mississippi births were in a hospital or clinic.[5] During this racially segregated period, the maternal mortality rate for Black mothers in Mississippi was nearly five times that for white mothers. Mississippi was the strongest holdout to desegregation of hospitals, and it would take until 1966 and Lyndon Johnson's threat to cut off Medicare funding for the state to begin to desegregate under the civil rights legislation that the president had passed two years earlier.[6] Thompson was born in a different era than LaChapelle or Cooper, but one could be forgiven for thinking very little had changed by the passage of years.

As a baby, Michael and the Thompson family, including five boys and one girl, migrated north to Flint as many southern Blacks did. Thompson and his family joined four other Mississippi families in one house on St. John Street in the Michigan city. "We didn't have enough beds," Thompson recalled, "so I slept on a mattress on the floor. The mice would become my friends, there were so many of them. They played with my ears at night. . . . It was a big house, but it was nothing to brag about. There were at least a dozen of us living in there. Still today, I can't stand the smell of roach spray. That house was always filled with roach spray, but those roaches just never died. They just kept coming." Thompson's father eventually landed a job at the Flint General Motors plant, and his mother was a beautician who took in clients in the family home. There was always food on the table, and hot dogs and baloney were staples for young Thompson: "I had a good upbringing. I had no excuses."

St. John was a strip, but it was also Thompson's playground, marked by those rail tracks and that smelly slaughterhouse; it was also a magnet for pimps, hookers, hustlers, and drug dealers. In Thompson's words: "I was raised right there in the belly of the ghetto." He grew to just shy of six feet—five feet, 11 3/4 inches, to be exact—but Thompson could dunk a basketball, and he was a terror on the court. His mother was a basketball player, his mentor and his biggest fan. She went to every game her son played, sometimes beating the team bus so she could be sitting there in the bleachers as the team arrived. He played hard for his mother and was offered a scholarship in the basketball program at fabled Michigan State.

But Thompson left high school and never touched another basketball. "I was just a stubborn kid," he said. "You know, it was like your mother made you play basketball and I was rebellious, so I never played another game." Instead, the streets sucked him in. He was fascinated by the street money, and he got lost out there. There was a guy named Bill Glover who, in 1974, was a starting guard for the Michigan State Spartans. He was a six-foot, two-inch wonder with the ball who averaged twelve points per game, and one day there he was on television in the big game that Thompson watched with his mother. "Isn't that Bill Glover playing for Michigan State?" she asked him. When Thompson allowed that it was, mom added: "Didn't you put up twenty-eight against him?" Mom's message was plain. Thompson's basketball future was playing out on the screen, but he squandered that future. Instead, his future was playing out on the streets.

By seventeen, the teen known on the street as "Meeko" was selling coke and weed. "Some slick cat who drove a pretty car left a great impression on me and he introduced me to cocaine," Thompson recalled. "I wanted to be him with the shiny car and the slick suit and the Gators. Everybody wanted some of them." He was busted, but that was not what turned him away from cocaine. He saw what it was doing to his friends who were freebasing, destroying themselves and their families. He was hooked, though he kept trying to get clean. Meeko could hustle, and he had some mighty big plans, but the damn coke kept getting in the way. It took daughter Rashawnda to finally get Thompson to think straight and get straight: "One day I picked her up and we looked in the bathroom mirror and she said, 'Daddy, why don't you wear pretty clothes anymore?' I was wearing bib overalls with sandals. . . . She said, 'What happened to your pretty clothes and pretty shoes? Why don't you put those back on?'" He had lost that sense of style and, more importantly, that personal pride that coursed through his veins, and, from that moment, Michael Thompson never touched another drug: "The love of my little girl was far more powerful than those so-called friends who were trying to lure me back in. She was offering me love. They were offering me an illusion. I knew who really cared about me and that was my daughter."

Finally clean, Thompson embarked on a path that led him to business and music. He was working at General Motors, but he was known for Meeko's, a business he had named for himself and proudly established on North Saginaw in Flint. It included a hand car wash, video game, and a four-car body shop. He was also helping to get kids off the street, and, for his work to reduce gang violence, he was given the keys to the city and was honored with a National Association for the Advancement of Colored People Youth Award for his work organizing a "Unity Day" event in 1984. But Thompson really hit his stride as a music promoter. This kid who once slept on the floor on St. John Street was now hanging with Aretha Franklin, Bobby Womack, Patti Labelle, The Impressions, The Temptations, and The Dramatics. "I had a thing about arenas," he remembered. "I would walk in, see them empty and just think of all those asses in the seats. I said to myself, 'Let's put some asses in those seats.' You could see an empty arena and know as a promoter you could put 20,000 asses in those seats. It was magical. It was like a high to me. I would have done it for free."

Initially, he did do it for free, but he had a talent. He knew a couple of guys doing this, and he tagged along to help them, for nothing. He linked up with a DJ known as Sweet Meat Cool, and he was loving things, learning the ropes of the promotion business, and he was good. So good, it only took a year before everyone he had been working for was now working for him. Aretha called Thompson her "bad ass," and he loves telling stories about the Queen of Soul. You can hear the delight in his voice as he regales you with tales of that time. He will tell you about how Aretha counted her own money before she went on stage, and how she only wanted to be paid in cash, even if it was $50,000. One time, Thompson recalls, an associate, mesmerized by Aretha's physical charms, counted out $52,000, and Aretha was about to take it, using the assistant's distraction to earn another $2,000, but he stepped in and told Aretha that wasn't "no $50,000." She feigned surprise, gave back the $2,000, and they both laughed about it. Michael fired the assistant: "Aretha didn't want no check. She wanted her own money, and she could count. Aretha gave me an opportunity of a lifetime. She opened up a lot of doors wide open for me, with corporate sponsors. She was good to me and I screwed it up, not Aretha. I screwed it up. I owe Aretha everything. Even when I went to prison, she told me the best promoters in the country have gone to prison."

It all sounded so good. Business was booming up just nicely at Meeko's, he had the award, the contacts in the community, and the entrée into the world of musical celebrity. But he had opened Meeko's with money he was making by dealing weed. He wasn't doing drugs, but he was still hustling on the side. He wanted to use the drug money as a steppingstone into the world of legitimate business; he certainly had no intention of being a lifelong drug dealer: "[Yet] if I had a third leg, I'd be kicking my ass every night. I didn't need to sell marijuana." But he did, and it all came crashing down that night in 1994. Thompson had a good friend who was running a muffler company. At least, he thought he was a good friend. What Thompson did not know was that this guy and his wife had been caught in something by the local drug cops, and they had turned. He thought he was doing his friend a favor that night, selling him the pot which he delivered to the front of his friend's house, and when the money had been counted and the pot delivered and the police duly informed by the snitch, Thompson's world came crashing down on him.

As we outlined in chapter 1, there were the guns found in Thompson's home, but they were never used as part of the drug deal. His wife testified that she had the guns, and she said she needed them when Thompson had been in jail on a previous charge and she feared for her safety in the empty house. One of the guns was an antique in a case: "The guns were in a locked closet. Where were the guns connected to the crime? I didn't have any gun on me, there was never any gun used in the commission of a felony." In fact, Thompson had never been convicted of a gun crime. But he was prohibited from having guns—regardless of Michigan being an open carry state—because of a previous nonviolent drug felony conviction, and, though no guns were involved in the cannabis sale, he was deemed to have "constructive possession" because the guns were in a house that he was ruled to have control over.

But there was more. The same cops who seized Thompson's Porsche and his jewelry bought them back for a song at auction, then turned around and sold them at a huge profit. They sent Thompson a note with a smiley emoji to thank him for their good fortune. The charges against him were stacked under Michigan's habitual offender legislation. He hired a lawyer without doing his proper due diligence, falling for what he now characterizes as a "used car salesman spiel," from a guy who was lurking outside the courtroom with a business card. He found himself up against a judge who overruled a plea deal that he had struck with state prosecutors that would have given him four years in prison. Instead, Judge Judith Fullerton declared that he would face a trial with the gun infractions stacked on previous drug infractions, making him a habitual offender under Michigan law.

On the day of sentencing, Thompson sat in the prisoner's dock as Fullerton fixed her eyes on him and said: "No more than 60 years, no less than 42 years." What?

> I had to ask my lawyer. Man, what is she talking about, 42–60 months? And he was scribbling something on his page, he couldn't even write it, and he said, "Hold on a minute, man." And I said, "What did she say, man?" . . . He said, "Your honor, for clarification for the court, are you saying 42–60 months?" And she said, "No, I am talking about 42–60 years." . . . And I looked at him and I said, "What did she say?" I couldn't snap out of this. He said, "Wait a minute, I'll come talk to you in a minute, just hold on, don't worry we'll get this overturned on appeal." So I thought I'd be out of there in one year. I thought I'd be back on appeal. Unfortunately, it was 25 years later.

Thompson considers himself an honorable man, and he operates on principle, a strict adherence to beliefs that many might consider obstinacy. That is what drove him to refuse visitors for some twenty years. He saw how his family and friends were treated when they came to visit, how they had to remove their shoes, and how they were patted down like they were criminals. "They were shown complete disrespect," he says, so he would no longer force them to go through that. Then a preacher from Texas arrived claiming to be his savior, but Thompson didn't need his help: "I didn't need him and I didn't need his lies. That put an end to all that. I'm honorable and I don't like liars. I don't like phonies. I don't like people who gossip a lot, I like real people—and I love all hustlers, even the ones who pick up pop bottles. I like people who know how to survive, who can take nothing and turn it into something. As long as they don't hurt anyone, I love all hustlers. I respect a person who is creative, who knows how to create their own way."

So, he rejected the lies, and this was the moment Thompson decided he would spend his life in Muskegon with very little contact from the outside world. Except, of course, he never envisioned twenty-five years, a quarter century of waning hope and prison drudgery:

> I never thought I was going to die in prison, but it got pretty dark at times. . . . I never thought I'd spend a year in there for what I did, but when you get to like fifteen years and you're still in prison, then you're calling people and good friends and you tell them I think I'm going to be out pretty soon, things are going good in here and you think, damn, shit, what the hell is going on? Why am I still in here in this prison and you get to twenty years and then you say to yourself when am I ever getting out?

His mother died while he was behind bars. And when it was time to bury the woman who doted on young Michael, who used to beat his basketball team to the gym on game day, who sat in the bleachers and cheered on her son and dreamed of his future in the National Basketball Association, Thompson was further humiliated. He was forced to wear leg shackles and handcuffs to mourn the mother he loved so much, becoming a spectacle at her funeral. The man who had never been convicted of violence was treated like a threat to his family and friends at his mother's gravesite: "I didn't like all my friends and family seeing me handcuffed in public." His pride was deeply wounded:

> Me walking like that was a great embarrassment, seeing me handcuffed and shackled. It was a low point. A very low point. . . . The only thing that made it beautiful was the little kids there. They didn't care about no shackles. They hugged me by the legs with the damn shackles on. They didn't care. They just called my name, holding onto me, calling me, "Meeko, Meeko," I was thinking, where did they come from, how did they know me, they weren't even born when I went into prison? That made those shackles disappear because those kids didn't care about no damn shackles. They just wanted to hug a man.

Throughout his ordeal, friends say Thompson never wavered, never changed. He also was given only two low-level citations for misdemeanors over almost twenty-five years, never letting his frustrations get the better of him, becoming the quintessential model inmate. He watched the onset of cannabis legalization in Michigan on a television in prison in 2018, and he wondered why the hell he was still behind bars: "It was frustrating. Who was making the rules? Who is supposed to correct the rules? Who governs people like me who get in a trap like this, who do I talk to?" When it got dark in there, and it surely did, there were legions outside bringing the light, shining it on the injustice of Thompson's sentence, even though he was often oblivious to the efforts building across the United States.

Shaun King, a writer and activist, used his Twitter account with more than one million followers to highlight Thompson's case. "He brought the thunder," Thompson says. Journalist Tana Ganeva wrote about Thompson in *Rolling Stone*, telling her readers that Thompson knew he had made a mistake, but he had more than repaid his debt to society.[7] Deedee Kirkwood, a cannabis activist, began a letter-writing campaign on Thompson's behalf when all efforts to have him released seemed to have hit a wall, and she took Thompson's case to LPP. Kirkwood also raised $266,000 for Thompson in a GoFundMe campaign so he would have a house when he was released. Legal Michigan cannabis entrepreneurs began raising money for Thompson's campaign for freedom, citing the fundamental unfairness in that they were earning cannabis revenue, while Thompson was serving what was believed to be the longest sentence for a nonviolent offense in state history.

The LPP took up his case. When that happened, it got the attention of the woman Thompson called that "Kardashian girl," and, indeed, Kim Kardashian did write a letter in support of Thompson and drew attention to his plight as Thompson's lawyer, Kim Corral, filed the formal clemency application. Sarah Gersten, the executive director of LPP, said Thompson's case "was shocking to the conscience to hear about Michael being incarcerated for decades for something that others in the state of Michigan are now profiting [from]."[8] This collective effort set the political machinery in motion.

Michigan's Attorney General Dana Nessel appealed to Governor Gretchen Whitmer to free Thompson, calling his disproportionate sentence a relic from another era. In fact, Thompson's sentence was in line for those convicted of second-degree murder or rape. "Given that recreational and medicinal marijuana is now legal in Michigan, allowing Mr. Thompson to continue serving the very draconian sentence in this case is even more distasteful," Nessel wrote.[9] Whitmer did eventually grant Thompson clemency, and he walked out of prison at 4:00 a.m. to the cheers of supporters, standing in the late January chill, snow flurries swirling, looking more than just a bit amazed. "I'm just going to let you know—I'm happy," Thompson told those supporters.

He was free, but neither his story nor those of LaChapelle, Cooper, or the legions of others whose life was interrupted by cannabis incarceration end with the cheers and the hugs and the tears. The road to reintegration can be painful. The regret over the lost years never fades. Despite that, these three want to give back. Life on the outside has its rewards in relationships reborn, embraces, TikTok videos, and wonder at what the rest of us take for granted. But freedom is often a misnomer. Thompson, despite the clemency, must still spend four years on probation. He cannot travel, he cannot be around people who carry a gun, even if they are properly licensed. He cannot be around bars or alcohol and he definitely cannot be in the company of anyone carrying drugs. "I've got to be damn near like the police, I've got to pat people down," he says. "But I ain't going back to prison."

Then there are the wonders awaiting a man who spent nearly twenty-five years cut off from societal and technological changes. Thompson had no idea what an iPhone was. GPS almost made his head explode: "Everything was different. The cars. The feel of the car. You know, talking to it and it's telling you where to go, that was mind blowing, absolutely mind blowing. I had to just tell myself take it slow, man, take it slow, because you've got to know that was some mind-blowing technology, the creative minds out there, the technology like that." He has learned from the teachings of children. They may have often laughed at his struggles, but they were proving to be effective tutors to a man whose life was frozen in 1996: "You know, I thought I got to start in kindergarten again, they better put my ass back in kindergarten." He wanted to eat things that he hadn't tasted in years; orange ruffage, tomatoes, cucumbers, and fruit. A lot of people would want a drink, but Thompson doesn't drink. He didn't ache for a steak or hamburger but for fruit and vegetables: "And I love liver. I smothered it with onions and all that kind of stuff."

The most remarkable trait found in LaChapelle, Cooper, and Thompson is the apparent lack of resentment and anger. It truly startles an outsider who cannot imagine a victim of such a miscarriage of justice being so devoid of rage. The way Thompson looks at it now, he feels he has been truly blessed, and he thinks things happen for a reason. He holds no grudge against the "friend" who set him up. "I think that was God's plan," he said. Another blessing—friends and family never abandoned him. His daughter's faith never wavered. "There's nothing like holding your father's hand or giving a hug," Rashawnda Littles told a television reporter in Flint.

Cooper is rediscovering his children. The three could be seen on a TikTok video made by the kids in which Cooper plays their chauffeur and butler. He has a video of his girls greeting him when he got out of prison, and he sometimes just sits and watches it over again and again: "The first thing was seeing my kids. I hadn't seen my kids for three or four years. Seeing my mom. Seeing Evelyn. Just seeing everybody. Just hugging everybody."

LaChapelle has been out longer than the two men, but she has had more setbacks since she reentered this world. When she got out, she went back to her old job at the Marriott in Oakland, but she quickly landed a better role at the Omni in San Francisco. She was asked about her employment gap, but she had been trained in prison to deal with this, and her response was well rehearsed. She told them her life had taken a turn for the worse, and it did not allow her to work but she was now prepared to get back in the workforce. The general manager asked a follow-up question: What was the worst decision you made? LaChapelle was truthful and told him that she had been involved with someone who was selling cannabis and her inability to be truthful led to major consequences. He said we all learn from our mistakes. She got the job. She has been honest about her background at all times.

She had passed all the checks and felt she was on the path to redemption when, two months into the job, she got a call from Human Resources. A coworker had Googled her name and found her conviction and passed it on to management. She does not know who and she does not know why, but she was told to pack up her belongings and leave: "Reentry is a much bigger problem than most of us imagined. As a first-time nonviolent offender I still faced judgment and as a result I lost my job." LaChapelle had support from her family, a college degree, and a resumé, and it still took her two years to find housing for herself. She and Venise have been sharing a room at her sister's home. For those without that support, it is exponentially tougher. Despite all of the tax revenue rolling in from legal sales, a cannabis conviction means you cannot get government housing aid.

LaChapelle persevered, joining the advisory board of LPP. She was asked to speak at a fundraiser, so she got up and told her story. She was barely offstage when she was approached by two senior executives of Vertosa, a cannabis and hemp infusion technology company, who told her they needed her expertise in events coordination. She served as the community engagement manager for Vertosa until December 2020, and today, she hosts their IGTV series *Canna Be Honest*, is the Community Engagement Manager for LPP, and is the founder and chief executive officer of her own firm, 87, which provides consumption essentials and amplifies the voices of women imprisoned during the War on Drugs. "Healing is a marathon, not a sprint," she said. To unburden herself from the shame and the guilt that comes with a prison stint, LaChapelle learned to get up in front of a room and talk about her experience, honestly and from the heart.

As part of their reentry into society, all three have become advocates— for justice reform, for cannabis reform, for racial equity. "This industry and this nation will have to acknowledge the wrongs of the criminalization of cannabis," LaChapelle says: "We have to recognize that this plant which we have just deemed essential (during the pandemic) must have benefits. If you are legalizing it, you are recognizing that this plant has medicinal qualities for the community. In the same breath, when you leave people in prison, you are saying the plant is beneficial to the community but these people who sold the plant are not beneficial to the community." Cooper is trying to raise his voice for criminal and prison reform: "I have to tell people that there are people still alive in there. You see suicides, you see murders . . . it is not an easy ballgame in there. People are still in there for this plant that people are selling. You see these billboards on the interstate advertising cannabis shops, we should also put up billboards saying there are still people serving time in prison for this." Thompson is also trying to draw attention to the need for prison reform. The man who used to put those asses in arenas for concerts is now trying to get asses in the seats of community halls to hear him push for the end of the habitual offender law:

They've got all these studies on prison reform and they know what the problem is. Now, after these studies, there is supposed to be action. Instead, we get more studies. Where are these millions of dollars on studies going? Who is getting these millions of dollars? Who is responsible for no action being taken? . . . And these prisoners are a burden on taxpayers, but they don't vote so the politicians don't care so they don't listen to them. When are people just going to say enough is enough?

Cooper, who is facing ten years of parole, is the brand ambassador for 40 Tons, a social-impact cannabis brand that markets swag including an homage to his freedom. You can buy a T-shirt emblazoned with "executive clemency is better than a lottery," the phrase he uttered upon release, a phrase he has now trademarked. The brand was launched in Cooper's honor while he was in prison as a means of raising money for his campaign for freedom. A percentage of sales goes to helping cannabis prisoners fight for their freedom and work for restorative justice upon their release. "I want 40 Tons to be the biggest thing in cannabis," he said, and the hustler is reborn as he gives a quick tour of the swag for sale: "I want everyone involved in it to be those who got taken down." That is Cooper's social equity program.

And LaChapelle is marketing 87, her brand of luxury cannabis accessories and smoking devices, named for her prison sentence of eighty-seven months. She speaks on cannabis reform on behalf of LPP. None have forgotten those who have been left behind. As we push for social equity programs and advocate for record expungement, we also cannot forget those who paid for the War on Drugs in years lost. "This has put me on a better path with more purpose in what I have to do with my life," Cooper said. "I want to thank the plant. It took my life away, made me recreate myself and make myself a better man for my children."

6 ERASING THE PAST

By any measure, George Gascón's life has been lifted from the archives of the American Dream, that mythical ethos the privileged like to spin to their immigrant and racialized citizens. According to this story, anything is possible in the great land of opportunity, and hard work will translate into success. Any little boy or girl can grow up to be a doctor, lawyer, a Hollywood star, or a famous athlete—even president. It is nothing more than a fable. Well, almost always a fable. As a boy, Gascón was spirited out of Fidel Castro's Cuba on a freedom flight to Los Angeles. His father had lost his job for speaking out against the new Castro regime, his uncle was imprisoned because of union activities, and the family knew it must flee. California and the Gascón family did not immediately bond. His parents, haunted by the Castro oppression and threats, lived in fear of police and other figures of US authority. Gascón, who had arrived with nothing more than a change of clothes in a cardboard box, struggled with his English and dropped out of high school.

He joined the army, but, after a few years, he returned to Los Angeles and enlisted in the Los Angeles Police Department (LAPD), where he was a self-described "warrior," patrolling the toughest streets in Los Angeles as an uncompromising agent of by-the-book law and order. Gascón's biography takes many turns. He left the police force to sell cars, becoming a manager at a local Ford dealership, then returned to the force. However, he did not return as a hardliner this time but, rather, as an officer who witnessed firsthand the destructive outcome of overzealous policing at the apex of the tough-on-crime era. Oh, he also went to law school in the evening.

He is a man with a reputation for listening and learning, and his is not a born-again belief in justice reform. It is the evolution of a belief learned on the street. It has earned him enemies at every stop, it has often left him isolated and has severely tested his resolve. It has led his own employees heading to court to block his reform and a move by voters to remove him from office. But Gascón has stood firm. His ascension within the LAPD was as swift as it was startling, and he sprinted through the ranks all the way to deputy chief before leaving to helm the police force in Mesa, Arizona. There he clashed repeatedly with the infamous anti-immigrant crusader "Sheriff Joe" Arpaio, the headline-seeker who gained renown as the right-wing media darling of Maricopa County for his lawless raids on Latinxs in his community. While Arpaio chased headlines, Gascón chased progressive reform, focusing on repeat offenders to achieve reductions in crime levels. He did not buckle against the conservative headwinds of Mesa.

Three years later, Gascón was in San Francisco as the city's police chief, where he would remain for seventeen months until he became San Francisco district attorney, replacing Kamala Harris, who had become state attorney. Those who know him believe his upbringing made him the type of prosecutor who could understand how a bad, potentially life-changing decision can be made in a moment. There was no privilege laid at his feet. He led the life of those he would encounter as a district attorney. He relied on digital tools and deep data to measure the success of prosecutors in the county. When a Black man was acquitted of charges of assaulting police officers and alleged a white man would never have been charged in the first place, Gascón responded with an experimental project in which an artificial intelligence program masked the race and name of suspects and the location of the offense to guard against unconscious bias as charges were being laid. "Blind charging" to confront racism in the justice system had never been tried before.

In 2020, he rode his progressive reform agenda to a sweeping victory in his first US home, elected as Los Angeles district attorney. That race was keenly watched nationwide as a major test of the movement for police and justice reform. But that ambitious reform agenda quickly ran into serious post-election headwinds, trouble in the form of a court challenge claiming he had overstepped his power and an incipient recall effort by those who were convinced Gascón had tipped too far in the direction of criminals' rights. That recall effort fizzled, but his reforms—including banning the death penalty, ending the prosecution of juveniles as adults, severely limiting the use of sentencing enhancements (which can add years to prison terms for factors such as gang membership or the use of a firearm in an offense), and banning prosecutors from opposing the release of previously convicted defendants eligible for parole—earned him the enmity of police unions, venom from the families of victims, and the disdain of district attorneys in other jurisdictions who refused to work with him on joint prosecutions. Such is the history of any reform movement. Change cannot be plotted on a linear, upward graph.

Gascón's biography can leave you breathless. It is constantly marked by accomplishment and controversy, often in equal measure. As San Francisco district attorney, Gascón appeared to be the progressive who was needed in a city that would embrace criminal justice reform, and he battled the powerful police union, opposed their bid to acquire more tasers, reduced drug and theft felonies to misdemeanors, kept nonviolent offenders out of jail, and became a powerful voice against the racism inherent in the War on Drugs. But San Francisco's liberalism did not immunize it against the disturbing trend of police violence against people of color, and Gascón's golden resume was not without tarnish. He was accused of allowing petty crime, particularly a rash of car break-ins, to flourish because he was soft on crime.[1]

Opponents reached back to his days on the Los Angeles police disciplinary board to show he had exonerated an officer who had shot and killed a suspect carrying a serrated weapon. The officer had shot the man some twenty-two feet away (adhering to the widely spread, but now debunked, police theory that anyone within twenty-one feet with an edged weapon is a deadly threat). More seriously, as San Francisco district attorney, he declined to prosecute police officers who shot and killed a knife-wielding Mario Woods, blitzing him with more than twenty bullets, including six in the back. Gascón called the officers' reaction unnecessary and excessive and pledged reform, but he would not lay criminal charges.

The killing of twenty-six-year-old Woods in December 2015 was significant beyond the brutal police reaction. It led to widespread protests in San Francisco and was the catalyst for 49ers quarterback Colin Kaepernick's protest of kneeling during the national anthem before National Football League (NFL) games. Kaepernick was ostracized, vilified by white Donald Trump–backing NFL owners and the president. After two more fatal shootings by San Francisco police, the killing of a forty-five-year-old homeless Mexican immigrant named Luis Góngora Pat and a twenty-nine-year-old Black woman named Jessica Williams, San Francisco police chief Greg Suhr was forced to resign. None of the officers in any of the shootings were charged, and, as his opponents will remind you, Gascón declined to prosecute a single San Francisco cop for their involvement in a shooting over more than eight years as district attorney (even though he criticized his Los Angeles opponent for the same record).

San Francisco police officers killed twenty-four people during Gascón's time in office, yet Gascón survived, a teflon district attorney who stood tall while others around him were stumbling. In fact, in an era in which ballooning police budgets are being challenged by Defund the Police movements, there are demands to address the systemic racism in law enforcement agencies. The fundamental role of police in North America and abroad is being questioned by a historic movement, and the criminalization of the mentally ill has cost far too many lives. Gascón was becoming a progressive icon. But still, San Francisco was grappling with racial tension. It was also the home of some of the country's most innovative technological visionaries.

Jennifer Pahlka had gravitated to the West Coast like so many others on the cutting edge of technology in America. She was becoming a legend in the gaming industry as an organizer of huge tech conferences and a mentor to game developers in the private sector. She would go on to spend a year as Barack Obama's deputy chief technology officer. But when she arrived in Oakland, work in the government sector would have been the last thing on her mind. Pahlka, like most who believed in the transformative power of technology, also believed that governments could be technically inept. Innovation, if it permeated government at all, moved at a glacial pace, and bureaucratic red tape, requests for proposals, and timidity was poisonous to progress. Procuring software can take two years and lead you into a bureaucratic labyrinth. Tech visionaries could not become entangled in that mess.

One night at a 2009 family reunion, according to an article in the *New York Times*, Pahlka was lobbied by the husband of her best friend who wanted her to bring her technical expertise to government, where he worked at the local level in Tucson, Arizona.[2] Dismissive at first, Pahlka allowed the concept to play out in her head, and her friend's husband proved persistent. She finally came to the belief that the talent, passion, and skill that has made life easier and more efficient through technology could be used to allow citizens to reconnect with government. That year, she founded Code for America, which she described as a Peace Corps for Geeks. It was a melding of a commitment to social justice and high-tech wizardry. In essence, Pahlka had decided to buy back into government, and she was going to convince others to follow. It was a hard sell, but Code for America's early work for local government was not just innovative, it was playful. It likely needed that playfulness to reestablish a lost sense of community at the city level and to bring cynical citizens back to the government fold.

Code for America created an app in Boston in 2011 called Adopt-a-Hydrant, which urged citizens to dig hydrants out of snowbanks, saving the city time, money, and manpower. It was launched during a particularly snowy Boston winter, and an interactive map allowed residents to "adopt" a hydrant and volunteer to dig it out after a storm. If you did, you got to name it, but if you abandoned your adoptee to a snowbank, other volunteers could remind you. If you did not act, a competitor could "steal" your hydrant and name him (or her). This idea caught the attention of a city bureaucrat in Honolulu who brought a team of Code for America fellows to Hawaii to establish Adopt-a-Siren, which allowed residents to become a "parent" to a tsunami siren, ensuring that the batteries were functioning (or even that they were there, as some had been stolen), bringing the community together in the name of safety. Another program had Seattle residents clean clogged storm drains. Today, many such programs dot the urban landscape.

Pahlka and Code for America were reengaging Americans with governments that appeared hidebound and out of touch. "When you strip away all your feelings about politics and the line at the DMV and all those other things we're really mad about it, government is at its core . . . what we do together that we can't do alone," said Pahlka, quoting her fellow tech guru and husband, Tim O'Reilly, in a 2012 TED Talk.[3] You can hate politics, Pahlka said, but politics is not government. It was time to make bureaucracy sexy because that is where the work of government is done, which, to put it mildly, was an ambitious goal. Bureaucracy wasn't sexy, it was a partner wrapped in flannel snoring under the covers.

San Francisco, then, was witnessing revolutionary behavior on two tracks—from a progressive district attorney and a visionary technical mind. Gascón continued to build on his upward political mobility, and Pahlka continued to build Code for America. One thing was not changing, though. Americans were still being arrested at record rates, and its jails and prisons were filling up. Young Americans, particularly young Black Americans, continued to be arrested for cannabis possession at disproportionate rates. In San Francisco, a 2013 American Civil Liberties Union (ACLU) study found that Black people were four times more likely than white people to be arrested and charged for cannabis offenses in the city.[4] The United States may be a country often besotted with second chances and heroic comebacks, but it can also be rigidly unforgiving to those who have veered from the straight and narrow. The road back—the path to redemption—is seemingly available to everyone, but clearly not everyone, because those second chances are not equally distributed in our society: Black, Latinx, and Indigenous people saddled with the heavy burden of a cannabis conviction often find their path to redemption blocked.

With the proliferation of online criminal records, there is a term for this oppression—"digital punishment." In recent US history, depending on the severity of your conviction, a criminal record in some states could have barred you from becoming an accountant, a teacher, an architect, a hair stylist, a cosmetologist, a roofer, a chiropractor, a plumber, an interior designer, or a land surveyor. In many states, private or public employers or licensing agencies were even permitted to consider arrests that never led to conviction when making hiring decisions. You could be barred from adopting a child, obtaining a driver's license, or serving on a jury. You would not be eligible for a student loan, and you could not possess a firearm or serve in the military. You could also be banned from playing certain video games. Federal student aid could be suspended if the recipient of that aid was convicted of a drug offense. Aid could only be restored by passing two unannounced drug tests, or two unannounced drug tests administered by a drug rehab program, or having the conviction "reversed, set aside, or otherwise rendered invalid."[5] If you were not a US citizen, no American Dream for you. You could be deported.

And what about the cost of fighting a misdemeanor possession charge? Prepare to dump out your wallet. You could easily spend $10,000 because of a decision to light up in a park one night. If you are ordered into a rehabilitation or some other type of program as part of your sentence, you could be ordered to pay for that as well. The cost to the state is even steeper. If you extrapolate figures we have quoted from the 2020 ACLU study, you will find it costs taxpayers more than $70,000 for every cannabis felony conviction—from policing to sentencing. The benefits of arresting, convicting, and jailing someone for a cannabis offense are suspect at best, counterproductive at worst. You are not protecting society against anyone. A Human Rights Watch report cited in the *New York Times* found that 90 percent of New Yorkers jailed on cannabis charges without prior convictions did not reoffend. Only three in one hundred committed a violent offense after release.[6]

According to research by Bruce Western, the codirector of the Justice Lab at New York's Columbia University, if you are an American high school graduate whose working life was interrupted by incarceration, your lifetime earnings can be cut by up to 40 percent, a drop that comes accompanied by shorter job tenure, higher unemployment, and lower hourly wages.[7] In a 2010 study for the Pew Charitable Trusts, Western and his colleague Becky Pettit found that serving time reduced hourly wages for men by approximately 11 percent, annual employment by nine weeks, and annual earnings by 40 percent. By age forty-eight, the typical former inmate will have earned $179,000 less than if he had never been incarcerated, and, over a lifetime, Black males who have served time lose 9 percent of total earnings.[8] But the repercussions are felt by the entire family, and it is handed down to the next generation, meaning the children of the man or woman convicted and incarcerated for a cannabis offense start behind other children and face a greatly diminished labor mobility outlook.

Western and Pettit have also shown that prison time is a normal life event for Black men who have dropped out of high school, with fully 68 percent of those born since the mid-1970s carrying prison records around with them at the time. Traditional means of upward mobility for Black Americans—military service or a college degree—are not accessible for these people. "For the first generations growing up in the post–civil rights era, the prison now looms as a significant institutional influence on life chances," they write.[9] There are obvious social costs, as well. Largely because of the demands placed on women raising families while their partners are incarcerated, there is a significant uptick in divorce and separation, family poverty, and delayed development and behavioral problems in children, particularly boys:

> Clear majorities of the young men in poor communities are going to prison and returning home less employable and more detached from their families. . . . In this situation the institutions charged with public safety have become vitally implicated in the unemployment and the fragile family structure characteristic of high-crime communities. For poorly educated young men in highly incarcerated communities, a prison record now carries little stigma; incentives to commit to the labor market and family life have been seriously weakened.[10]

For far too many with criminal records, their place in society has been closed. The sentence is life. When it comes to cannabis, too many of these restrictions have remained even after legalization. Expungement of records and the racism of the War on Drugs was often treated as an afterthought by some of the first states to legalize. In most instances, expungement—or any provision dealing with a current record—was left off ballot initiatives so as not to muddy a question put to voters. In some cases, the question of dealing with existing records was the purview of the executive branch and could not be changed by referendum. In some cases, the reason was simple—there was loud opposition to expunging convictions.

The United Nations has adopted the International Covenant on Civil and Political Rights, which states that when a change of law benefits a person previously arrested or convicted, the new law should retroactively apply.[11] Yet, as recently as the end of 2019, in three states that have legalized cannabis—Maine, Michigan, and Nevada—there had been no serious consideration given to expungement. In many jurisdictions that legalized early, a cannabis conviction was still a hurdle to entering the legal cannabis industry. There are various methods to show compassion to those who have been wrongly convicted or have paid the price for a crime of possessing or selling a plant that is now legal. We are all familiar with the terms *clemency*, *pardon*, and *expungement*. They are three distinctly different acts, although the public can be forgiven for using these terms interchangeably because they are not well understood.

Clemency has been historically grounded in a philosophy of forgiveness, compassion, and redemption, an act of mercy and justice often cloaked in articles of religious faith. More recently in US history, clemency has been selectively gifted by politicians who may cite moral grounds for granting it, but it is generally available only to the powerful, the wealthy, or the well connected. Political support, particularly financial support, often clears the road to clemency. Because of its arbitrary nature, clemency often distorts justice instead of facilitating justice. Among the types of clemency available, the pardon is the most commonly used in North America. Pardons are an official act of leniency that are imparted on a case-by-case basis in recognition of the individual's good conduct and acceptance of responsibility after they have served a sentence or paid a price.

Sometimes pardons are preemptive, such as Gerald Ford's grossly unpopular pardon of Richard Nixon for any Watergate crimes after the disgraced president resigned. Others can be amnesties, blanket pardons such as Jimmy Carter's amnesty, announced during his second day in office, for hundreds of thousands of Vietnam War draft dodgers. Ten years later, President Ronald Reagan also granted a blanket amnesty for immigrants who illegally entered the United States before 1982. With this collective pardon, 2.7 million undocumented immigrants became legal permanent residents, and, of those, 1.1 million later became citizens. Donald Trump pardoned the aforementioned Joe Arpaio, Gascón's foil, who had been convicted of criminal contempt. He also pardoned a dozen Americans who were serving prison terms for nonviolent federal cannabis convictions, including his last-minute decision to pardon Corvain Cooper. More recently in Canada, the government of Prime Minister Justin Trudeau issued an amnesty and automatic expungement of the criminal records for all those who had been convicted of crimes because of their homosexuality during a particularly shameful period of Canadian history.

In most jurisdictions, people with criminal records are ineligible to receive a pardon until a set period has lapsed following the completion of their sentence. Those seeking a pardon must initiate the process themselves, triggering a probe that involves the justice system as well as the applicant's employers and associates. A combination of waiting periods, distrust of the legal system, and financial barriers have led to what is known as the "second chance gap," and if the onus remains with the person seeking judicial relief to begin the process, the number of successful petitioners is woefully small. A University of Michigan study found that those who had their records cleared in that state saw their income rise by more than 20 percent within a year. But because of a waiting period and the work and cost involved, barely 6 percent had that record cleared, leaving a huge second chance gap. A pardon is a formal expression of forgiveness but not a declaration of innocence. You may have been pardoned, but you are still guilty. The US Supreme Court has ruled that acceptance of a pardon implies the acceptance of guilt. A pardon can open avenues largely closed to convicted criminals, allowing one to vote or run for office. It may lessen the stigma associated with a criminal record, but it does not make you less of a convicted criminal. Your record can still be easily searched by would-be employers or landlords.

That brings us to the only air-tight, fail-safe mechanism to right the wrongs perpetrated on those who have been criminalized through cannabis use—automatic expungement. There is a moral imperative in expungement that is lacking in a pardon. Whereas in the case of a pardon, the government signals that it forgives an individual for their past wrongdoing by fully clearing a criminal record, expungement sends a message that the government was wrong to have criminalized that behavior in the first place. For it to be perfectly fair, this expungement must be free, fast, and initiated by the state. The onus must be on the government, not the person carrying the record. An expungement destroys or erases one's record, making it disappear as if it never happened. It allows one to answer "no" if asked if they were ever arrested or convicted of a crime.

Amnesty confers automatic expungement, but few of us will be on a presidential radar, so expungement must be initiated at a more local level. Any attempt to right the injustice of a cannabis conviction in an era of legalized adult-use cannabis has been fraught. It can be costly, complicated, triggering, and puts the onus on the applicant, not the state. Expungement should not require an in-person hearing, and the decision should not rest with a powerful oligarchy. It should not require opening new investigations or give new, onerous responsibilities to a bureaucrat. It should be streamlined under one jurisdiction.

Opposition to expunging or sealing conviction records ran into stiff Republican pushback in Colorado, which, along with Washington State, became the first North American jurisdiction to legalize adult-use cannabis in votes in 2012. Arguments against expungement generally fell into four categories: (1) it would create a pathway for expungement in years ahead for even more serious criminal charges; (2) those convicted of low-level cannabis crimes were breaking the law as it was at the time, and they were doing so knowingly and thus deserved the penalty; (3) blanket amnesties could emancipate those who were guilty of the more serious offense of trafficking in cannabis because many of those cases are pled down to simple possession in agreements before the court, so expungement should be dealt with on a case-by-case basis; and (4) cannabis possession was still illegal at the federal level and that government should take precedence.

But a survey of initiatives at the beginning of this decade showed progress was being made. In Oregon, anyone convicted of possession, delivery, or manufacture of cannabis can file a motion to set aside that conviction after a year, providing they have not been convicted of another offense and have completed all aspects of their sentence. In Washington State, anyone over the age of twenty-one convicted of a cannabis misdemeanor can apply to a court to have that conviction vacated and the court is compelled to do so. But, in both those cases, the onus remains with the applicant. Eleven states and Washington, DC, have passed measures to force courts to expunge, destroy, set aside, seal, or annul low-level cannabis convictions: Colorado, Connecticut, Delaware, Hawaii, Maryland, Massachusetts, Minnesota, Nevada, New Hampshire, Rhode Island, and Vermont.

Further, for the record, all those states place the onus on the person looking to have the record expunged, plunging them back into the world of bureaucracy and justice with all the financial costs and emotional trauma that entails. Take up on those programs is minuscule. North Dakota, Pennsylvania, and Washington State offer expedited pardons for those convicted of low-level cannabis offenses.[12] But, in a clear sign of more enlightened times, four states that legalized recreational cannabis use in 2021—New Jersey, New Mexico, New York, and Virginia—all included some form of automatic cannabis record relief. The first three states have extended expungement to distribution convictions. Virginia's program offers expungement only for misdemeanor convictions but allows the expungement of felonies, by petition, if a court approves.

The cannabis expungement moves came as part of a growing trend of justice relief across the United States. According to the nonprofit Collateral Consequences Resource Center, twenty-five states enacted fifty-one laws authorizing sealing or expungement of criminal records in the first six months of 2021. The US Congress has failed to act, leaving those with federal convictions without any remedy short of a presidential pardon. Waiting for a phone call from the president can be one long, fruitless wait. In parts of the country, pop-up expungement legal clinics have sprouted. In Oregon and Washington, DC, the expungement clinics have been paired with a quasi job fair where those with cannabis convictions learn to prepare resumes and participate in test job interviews in preparation for a return to the work force after their record has been cleared.

Since 2018, an annual National Expungement Week has offered legal relief clinics and workshops that dispense guidance and advice to some 77 million Americans with criminal records. So far, it has helped more than a thousand people begin the process to seal or clear their convictions while also providing help with health screening, voter registration, and job seeking. It is a grassroots operation run exclusively by people of color, with a particular focus on cannabis records. Code for America and Canopy Growth help sponsor the workshops. These events are crucial because, by and large, adult-use cannabis has been legalized with no restorative provisions for those still serving a lifetime of vanished opportunity because of a conviction for possession of something now proudly sold from pristine dispensaries.

These efforts were important, but something much more was needed. Today, that something much more—automatic expungement with the onus on the state—is available. California, Illinois, Colorado, and Vermont led the way, but millions were still weighed down with the cannabis conviction millstone. This level of progress was sparked by a more progressive outlook on justice, but it still needed a revolution. That revolution happened in San Francisco in 2018. It took the legalization of adult-use cannabis and a partnership between a district attorney who embraced change and a nonpartisan, nonprofit institute in the city that offered a unique blend of twenty-first-century technological savvy and a commitment to social justice. The joining of Gascón and Code for America was the most significant contribution to cannabis justice in the history of the War on Drugs.

It started in 2016 when California voters passed Proposition 64, legalizing recreational cannabis. It also mandated resentencing for those with felony convictions for the cultivation, sale, or transport of cannabis, reducing them to misdemeanors, making it easier to obtain public housing or employment. If you were burdened with a misdemeanor conviction for possession, it could be wiped out. While the proposition was hailed for reversing the injustices of past drug laws, it still left a cumbersome, labor intensive, time-consuming process. It did not require a public defender at the front end, but one was recommended. Otherwise, applicants would likely find the process, which required another deep dive into the justice system, too intimidating. The vast majority of people in that category felt they should not have been convicted in the first place. Why would they think the justice system would now be on their side? The courts had to review the process, and the petitioner had to attend a hearing. It cost petitioners, on average, $3,500 to navigate the process.

Under Proposition 64, a mere 3 percent of those eligible for expungement in Gascón's jurisdiction actually petitioned the court for relief. Those numbers are in line with other jurisdictions that have failed to streamline a system to expunge records. In Canada, for example, where the fee to apply for a pardon was waived, more than 80 percent of those eligible did not even know there was a program available to them two years after the 2018 legalization. The Parole Board of Canada reported a paltry 428 applicants—and 257 approvals—of the estimated 10,000 Canadians eligible for record suspension under the program.[13] Faced with such daunting figures in his jurisdiction, Gascón, in early 2018, became the first prosecutor in the nation to proactively expedite the process, placing the onus on his department.

The impetus came from his chief of staff at the time, Cristine Soto DeBerry.[14] It took the Guatemalan-born Soto DeBerry and the Cuban-born Gascón to form the team to free tens of thousands of Black and Latinx people from the bonds of past convictions. For almost nine years, she was at his side, pushing for criminal reform. Before the technical glitz of Code for America drew widespread attention, the policy-makers first had to make a move to make the partnership possible. "The big innovation here may not be the technology but the policy decision that we were not going to put the burden on the individual," Soto DeBerry recalled. "This had not ever been done before. The process had always been the individual petitions the district attorney and the court and says, 'I have this conviction I would like to have removed from my record.'" Soto DeBerry looked at the existing situation and went to Gascón with a logical proposition: "If we knew as a policy matter that we would grant every single one of those requests . . . why does somebody need to request it of us? Why don't we just affirmatively perform that duty for them?"

Gascón readily agreed, but that still entailed processing each case by hand, an arduous exercise that taxed resources and offered a long path to any finish line. It was taking between eight to fifteen minutes to process every single one of the thousands of eligible convictions, and they were dealing with a database dating back to 1975, about 9,700 cases. Once the list of eligible charges was compiled, they had to be cross-referenced, then the court petitioned for the relief, and they had to ensure the court was comfortable in having the district attorney's office do the petitioning. The courts could only process about 100 petitions per week, so it was creating a huge bottleneck, even with three or four paralegals working on the project, on top of their regular work. It would take up to nine months of heavy slogging by Gascón's office just to get the petitions to the backlogged court. But it had to be done. "I was frustrated that we spent forty years criminalizing people for something that we were now prepared to turn the corner on and make it a legal marketplace . . . and we had permanently damaged so many people's opportunities to be full economic citizens because of a conviction we had given them over this now-legal activity," Soto DeBerry said:

> It felt to me to be unconscionable to allow this marketplace to open up, to be largely dominated by the white community, and continue to shackle African American and Latino community members with these convictions that would prohibit them not just from the cannabis marketplace industry or other gainful employment—but student loans, housing opportunities, so many of the other consequences that come with those convictions. It's not just enough to flip the page and say everything is legal. You have to address and redress what the previous framework left in its wake.

Code for America saw opportunity and a chance to put its slogan, "We help government work for the people who need it most," to work. Alia Toran-Burrell, whose background included a stint at a public defender's office in the Bronx and time spent as a youth community organizer, was Code for America's codirector. She spent years observing up close the embedded racism in policing of young Black and Brown kids, and she was increasingly frustrated by the number of people with cannabis convictions being left behind in so many ways. Code for America saw a government in San Francisco saying it was going to tackle this issue, and it jumped.

The nonprofit was already in the record-clearing business, having established a program called Clear My Record in 2016 that connected people with convictions to attorneys who could help them. It simply made things a bit easier for those seeking help from the court. She reached out to Soto DeBerry, and the response was instantly positive. When the call came, Gascón's office had cleared about a thousand of the convictions on its plate. There was none of the usual government speak about "considering the plan" or "let us think about this" or "we'll get back to you." "They were excited to do it," Toran-Burrell recalled. Soto DeBerry took the call: "That's amazing,

I'm super interested," was her immediate response. A meeting between the two sides happened within days, and it was symbolic of the changed times. The historic meeting consisted of a diverse group of nine women.

The nonprofit Code for America's team assured Gascón's team it could help them more quickly sort through the list of eligible candidates for expungement, and it would do this work for nothing. A deal was struck quickly, and, on May 15, 2018, Gascón stood at a podium beside Pahlka to announce the partnership. He spoke of the damage done to Black and Brown people and their neighborhoods and how America's obsession with incarceration entirely perpetuated the nation's cycle of crime: "Housing and employment opportunities are two of the . . . major factors in keeping people from committing crimes. . . . So if we are able to reduce some of the areas that preclude people from getting housing and getting employment opportunities that will improve the public safety picture for all of us." And Gascón spoke of social equity: "Drug use in this country has not been limited to people of color. . . . But if you look at our courts, you look at our jails and you look at our prisons, overwhelmingly the people who have been arrested and prosecuted and incarcerated for drug use in this country, over and over again, have been people of color."

Gascón explained that his initiative had really nothing to do with drug policy. It was all about giving people a second chance. It was about treating them with respect and restoring their pride and dignity. Otherwise, Gascón believed, we end up with a huge segment of society that has lost hope and has no stake in that society, a dangerous road for any society to navigate. As the partnership began, Code for America was operating under the assumption that it would have to develop technology to read rap sheets in bulk. Gascón's office had been pulling rap sheets with cannabis convictions in his county and was reading every single sheet, one by one, to determine whether they were eligible for relief.

While it was developing its technology, the scales of justice were about to tip most decidedly in the direction of social justice. In late 2018, then Governor Jerry Brown signed California Assembly Bill 1793, which required the California Department of Justice to provide information on all Californians potentially eligible for sentence reduction or expungement to the California

State district attorney's office by July 1, 2019. Soto DeBerry testified twice before the state legislature about the San Francisco initiative that was gaining attention statewide and that helped swing political support for Bill 1793. The legislation meant that every district attorney would have to do what Gascón was already doing, but the onus was now on the state, not the petitioner. Instead of pulling rap sheets one by one, the state justice department would provide datasets in spreadsheets to every district attorney in the state.

Instead of working with rap sheets, Code for America developed technology to read a bulk dataset. Instead of that previous eight-to-fourteen minute, one-by-one perusal of each potentially eligible conviction, Code for America was developing an algorithm that could read ten thousand potentially eligible records per minute. The technology uses optical character recognition to read criminal records and then maps the data to determine if the person is eligible. The program then auto-fills the necessary paperwork to have the charge expunged, which is then sent off in bulk to the courts. "We saw this as a momentous thing that had never been done before and had the potential to help tens of thousands of people that way," Toran-Burrell recalled.

To have the record expunged, you would not have to do anything. No lawyer, no court, no interview, no trudging to a downtown office, no revisiting a justice system you felt had already victimized you. If you were ineligible for relief, the attorney's department would have to make a "good faith" effort to inform you of that. A website was established with a phone number you could call to determine whether you had been cleared, so the burden to the citizen was this: make yourself aware and make a phone call. Predictably, the phone line was rarely used, so justice was largely being dispensed without the knowledge of the recipients. Toran-Burrell knew the program had turned a corner with the latest legislative victory. She also knew she was going to be part of history: "Fundamentally this was a matter of social justice. . . . That is the base of everything we do. We do this so we can help people move past barriers that criminal convictions unjustly pose."

By the summer of that year, Code for America, working with the freedom it had under Bill 1793, had moved beyond the five California counties in which Clear My Record was operating on a pilot basis and developed a desktop application that could be used for cannabis record expungement in every county in the state. And, in 2020, Clear My Record moved outside California and was adopted by Chicago's Cook County in Illinois. Kim Foxx, the Cook County attorney, was elected as a criminal justice reformer and was a major driver of the cannabis legalization push in her state. She oversees the nation's second-largest team of prosecutors. Watching the success of Clear My Record in California, she reached out to Code for America to partner in her campaign to expunge low-level cannabis convictions. She is moving faster than the state, but the Illinois legislation is progressive.

Statewide, criminal records resulting from offenses that became legal under Illinois's new cannabis law (possession up to thirty grams or one ounce) would be automatically expunged, while a streamlined clemency process with assistance from legal aid groups was created to handle offenses involving higher quantities (from 30 to 500 grams or 17.5 ounces). The state estimated that almost 800,000 convictions were eligible for expungement under the new reforms. All records, dating back to the last century, are scheduled to be expunged by 2025.

One year after the law came into force, Illinois Governor J. B. Pritzker had issued 20,236 cannabis pardons, and the Illinois State Police had expunged 492,129 low-level (nonfelony) arrests from state records.[15] Illinois created three different categories of cannabis-related records eligible for expungement. The first two classifications were automatically expunged with no action required by the person with the record. The third classification of more serious offenses required a petition to the court to start the expungement process. Illinois has estimated some 572,000 minor cannabis offenses would be automatically expunged under the legislation, with another 119,000 eligible under the court process.

Pritzker went a step further, promising to invest revenues generated by legalized cannabis into harmed communities where historic wrongs must be made right. Those who were convicted for minor offenses and those who lived in disadvantaged communities that could be statistically proven to be police targets were given preferential treatment in obtaining licenses to market legal cannabis. The law provided for financial aid if needed and legislated a financial payback to those Illinois communities that were damaged by the often-violent enforcement of cannabis-related laws. We will examine the Illinois social equity legislation more closely in the following chapter.

Code for America caught a minor expungement wave in its infancy and was now driving it far beyond its California roots. But for it to continue to push the merger of technology and social justice, it had to produce results. The success of Clear My Record is indeed clear given the numbers. California district attorneys using the program, by the summer of 2020, had identified approximately 144,000 marijuana convictions to be reduced or dismissed from people's records, representing two-thirds of all eligible marijuana convictions in California. In total, as many as 220,000 convictions were eligible for clearance. Code for America estimated 113,000 people will have had marijuana convictions reduced, dismissed, or sealed, and another 42,000 people will have no felony convictions on their state records. Felony convictions are the toughest to overcome in background checks when seeking anything from licenses to jobs and state benefits.

The program in California expanded beyond its San Francisco roots, first to Contra Costa, then San Joaquin, Sacramento, and Los Angeles. In Los Angeles County, one of Code for America's five pilot projects, it teamed with District Attorney Jackie Lacey—the incumbent who Gascón displaced in 2020—to clear nearly 66,000 cannabis convictions. The social justice impact was also clear from the numbers. Of those who were given relief from past convictions in San Francisco under the initiative, 33 percent were Black, and 27 percent were Latinx.[16]

Since this groundbreaking move in California, signs have appeared of an incipient social justice awakening. In June 2019, Pennsylvania became the first state to start automatically sealing eligible criminal records so that they cannot affect people's chances for employment, education, and housing. As many as 30 million criminal cases could be sealed, but law enforcement agencies retain the records. Utah became the second state to approve "clean slate" legislation, automating criminal record clearing, and California, beginning with convictions in 2021, began automatically scrubbing other low-level convictions and denying the power of courts to publicize prior arrests that did not result in convictions.

While states are indeed moving, at the federal level of the United States, actions on record expungement and social equity have been virtually non-existent. The Marijuana Opportunity Reinvestment and Expungement Act was passed by US Congress in December 2020, but President Joe Biden continued to oppose full legalization and Vice President Kamala Harris, one of the sponsors of the Senate version of the bill, appeared to be moderating her position on legalization.[17]

The bill would finally remove cannabis from the Controlled Substances Act, ending its classification as a Schedule 1 drug with no medical benefit but with a high risk of abuse.[18] Federal penalties for cannabis would be expunged, and legalization would be left to states. It would impose a 5 percent sales tax on legal cannabis sales and redirect that money in the form of grants into treatment programs, communities devastated by the War on Drugs, and licenses for the legal cannabis business for racialized Americans. As expected, the act died in the Senate, but Democrats reintroduced it in the House of Representatives in May 2021.

Biden has embraced automatic expungement of low-level cannabis use and possession convictions and will push states to funnel cannabis revenues back into hard-hit minority neighborhoods. Both were recommendations of his party's criminal justice reform committee in the prelude to the 2020 presidential election: "Under my plan, if a state decides it wants to implement an automated system for the sealing and expunging of certain nonviolent criminal records, if a state chooses to do that, the federal government will help put together the process and allow them the money to be able to know how to organize to do that. That's what racial equity in our economy looks like." Biden agrees that smoking a joint as a youth should not deny you a "good paying job or a career or a loan or an ability to rent an apartment . . . states should recognize the costs to their economy when residents with non-violent criminal records can't fulfill their full talents and capacity."[19]

The Code for America program is still new, and as with anything new, many will look at it and think it expensive and complex; it will take time to reassure them that neither perception applies. The combination of saving government money, freeing up funds for other programs and simply doing the right thing should be an irresistible combination for governments worldwide. "The concept of automatically clearing records is gaining momentum and growing across the country. People are seeing it is the just thing to do, the right thing to do . . . so few people get the relief to which they are entitled for so many reasons," Toran-Burrell says. "We want to clear all eligible criminal convictions across the country using automatic record clearance. That is our North Star. People should not have to go through the petition process."

Soto DeBerry has said that the real breakthrough was an elected official deciding he was going to help people who deserved that help and then eliminating all the hoops and barriers that stood in the way of justice. It started small in San Francisco, but it has grown to help hundreds of thousands recapture their lives. She knows her legacy is important, but there is still work to do. Neither Soto DeBerry nor Toran-Burrell is prepared to rest until everyone adopts this form of criminal redress. We should all strive toward that goal—it is ambitious, but just.

7 PAYING IT BACK

Mon-Cheri Robinson was born on Chicago's South Side in the shadow of a city icon.[1] Everybody knows Fat Johnnie's Red Hots and the promise of a hot dog "Fit for a King," delivered from the same shack on Western Avenue for almost half a century. Fat Johnnie's is her touchstone when she describes her birthplace, but the irony is not lost on Robinson or those closest to her, who still live around 73rd and Artesian. The hot dogs may be fit for a king, but there is not much in the way of royalty wandering the streets of this neighborhood. It is a neighborhood where you can be pulled over by police for walking on the wrong street at the wrong time. Police harassment does not necessarily wait for darkness; daytime can also bring unwanted police attention. "They see you're in the neighborhood, they shake you down," Robinson said. "It comes with the territory. It's just understood that if you live in that neighborhood, you have done time before, or you are ganged, or you have been recruited by gangs. That's just the minimum that comes with living in that environment."

But this is not to suggest that police attention is always unwarranted. Chicago's gun problem has been well documented. House parties have been shot up. Your life can be threatened for wearing the wrong NFL team gear. Robinson has seen that happen. Cannabis use is endemic, just as it is in white suburbs. But here, arrest rates are high and income is low. Good jobs, upward mobility, and hope are in short supply. In other words, it is a classic example of a neighborhood in need of social equity, based on income or arrest rate, under an Illinois program that aims to bring some of the new profits from legalized cannabis back to those whose lives have been disrupted or derailed by the racist War on Drugs.

Illinois was not acting alone. There was some form of social equity legislation or record expungement legislation (or both) in more than twenty states by the summer of 2021, but Robinson's frustrating quest for cannabis justice is illustrative of the problems that so many of them have encountered.[2] They have been slowed or derailed by litigation, by lack of transparency, by political hesitancy, by bureaucratic inertia, and, to varying degrees, by a global pandemic. The result is a patchwork of efforts. On the progressive end, Connecticut identified 215 census tracts, home to almost 23 percent of the state population, eligible for state help accessing the legal market because of a historically disproportionate arrest rate or a present-day unemployment rate above 10 percent.[3] Almost two-thirds of all drug convictions in the state between 1982 and 2020 took place in those census tracts, even though it comprises only 22.8 percent of the state's population.

Advocates say unlimited licenses and small entry fees will foster social equity. Oregon has created such an environment, and New Jersey has approved regulations that only cap cultivation, not dispensary licenses, and require only 20 percent of the license fee for an applicant upfront with the balance to be paid on approval. The total license fees will not top $2,000. In a Chicago suburb, history was made. The first reparations payments were approved in Evanston, Illinois, using cannabis tax revenue to fund this groundbreaking initiative. Whether this was a one-off or the first ripple of a momentous wave across the country will be explored later in this chapter.

On the other end of the spectrum is Nevada, where applicants for retail licenses who can prove they have at least $250,000 in liquid assets score higher on permit applications, and licensing fees can be as high as $30,000. The state did not include any social equity provisions in its legalization legislation, and, by August 2020, there was only one Black-owned retail outlet, and only two Black-owned cultivation licenses were awarded out of 330 permits.[4] And then there is Oklahoma, where the lack of rules means that anyone, including those who would be classed as social equity applicants elsewhere, can open a medical dispensary. The term "medical" is so loosely defined in Oklahoma that the dispensary is essentially a recreational outlet. In the Oklahoma free market, dispensary licenses cost $2,500, local municipalities cannot ban them, and medical cards are available without qualifying conditions.

What are the results? There has been a Green Rush since medical cannabis was legalized in 2018, in a state in which one in ten Oklahomans have a card that allows them to buy medicinal cannabis at any of more than 2,300 dispensaries. The state had issued 12,000 marijuana licenses, including more than 8,600 grow licenses.[5] Is it social equity? Most assuredly not. But is it accessible? Absolutely. There is no other market like it in North America. Still, in the nineteen states (and Washington, DC) where adult-use cannabis has been legalized, only thirteen have social equity programs. In another eighteen states that have legalized medical cannabis, only two have social equity programs. According to a February 2022 study by the Minority Business Cannabis Association, of the fifteen state social equity programs, not a single one has led to an equitable cannabis industry when measured across the pillars of industry, justice, community, and access. Of the total thirty-eight states that have legalized medicinal or recreational cannabis, twenty-six have license caps, which inflate the price of licenses, a disincentive to equity-seeking groups, and fourteen of the eighteen legalized recreational states have disqualifications for would-be license holders for previous criminal convictions, regulations that run counter to the spirit and substance of social equity.[6]

Other studies have shown that more than 80 percent of all US dispensaries are owned by white people, with Black entrepreneurs accounting for a mere 4.3 percent of ownership.[7] The Initiative, an organization that promotes women in the cannabis industry, pegged that number even lower, at about 1.7 percent. The statistics may vary study by study, but they all point to the same fact: the cannabis industry in North America is overwhelmingly white, and those harmed by prohibition policing are overwhelmingly Black and Brown. The numbers in Canada are similar. Our 2020 study, done jointly by the University of Toronto and the Centre on Drug Policy Evaluation, showed 84 percent of cannabis industry leaders in that country were white, 6 percent South Asian, 3 percent East and Southeast Asian, 2 percent Indigenous, 2 percent Arab, and only 1 percent Black and 1 percent Latinx.[8]

What kind of potential windfall is the largely white industry chasing? The growth potential in legalized adult-use cannabis needs to be repeated again and again. New Frontier Data reported legal cannabis sales of nearly 6 billion dollars in the United States in the first quarter of 2021. It estimated 43 billion dollars in projected annual sales in 2025, 62 percent of that in recreational purchases with the remainder in medicinal sales. Deep-pocketed lobbyists in closed-door meetings with white politicians still ruled the day in too many jurisdictions, and the threat of big pharma and big tobacco and mergers and consolidation across US state lines controlling lucrative markets were real threats to social justice.

Social equity applicants were caught in an endless cycle. Those with the assets to secure a lease, buy much-needed infrastructure, or secure a favorable long-term loan had the advantage over those who were social equity applicants largely because they lacked those advantages. Without capital, good intentions were hollow. Those applicants were shunted to the sidelines by the very programs meant to provide incentives to get them into the legal cannabis business. There were few Black and Brown entrepreneurs who could boast the type of white network replete with friends or family members with the type of available cash needed to invest in a nascent cannabis initiative. Would-be investors shunned Black men and women who needed that cash to get started.

And what about the banks? Many individuals reported they would not even bother because they would be laughed out of the building, and the numbers show the scarcity of help from financial institutions. Over the course of 2020, the number of banks and credit unions loaning funds for cannabis-related enterprises declined. By December 31, 2020, only 684 financial institutions (515 banks and 169 credit unions) were banking cannabis-related business, down from a peak of 747 a year earlier.[9] Those who can partner with financial institutions must expect higher fees because of the risk involved. As long as cannabis remains illegal at the federal level, these disheartening numbers will likely remain rather static. Under the Secure and Fair Enforcement Act, which has repeatedly passed the House of Representatives but run aground in the US Senate, bank regulators would be prohibited from penalizing individual banks that dealt with businesses in the recreational or medicinal realm in legal states.[10] Proponents say the business will be safer because it no longer has to deal in cash only, more convenient because it could accept debit and credit cards, and, more crucially, more accessible for Black and Brown would-be social equity entrepreneurs. But, by the end of 2021, passage in the Senate looked unlikely.

People like Mon-Cheri Robinson must be convinced that when it comes to social equity, the system is not still rigged against them. Robinson's tale is rooted on Chicago's South Side, and, despite her upbringing in East Nashville, her heart remains on the South Side. As we shall see, those pushing for true social equity have been motivated by similar life experiences in neighborhoods deeply scarred by the War on Drugs—neighborhoods in Buffalo, Cleveland, Orange, New Jersey, small-town Virginia, Lakeland, Florida, or the Toronto suburb of Scarborough.

Illinois made recreational adult-use cannabis legal in June 2019, becoming the first state to legalize commercial sales in a legislative vote rather than in a separate referendum (Vermont had gone the same route a year earlier, but with no framework for retail sales). When recreational cannabis became official on New Year's Day in 2020, Governor J. B. Pritzker promised a world-class social equity rollout. The sales side of the legislation has been a booming success. In July 2021, Illinois logged almost $128 million in cannabis sales, double the figure from the pandemic months of summer 2020. July marked the fifth consecutive month that adult-use sales topped $100 million, and the state was poised to top $1 billion in sales in 2021, way up from 2020 when it sold $670 million of cannabis and reaped $205 million in tax revenue.[11]

There was another side to this tale of success, however. By mid-summer 2021, new legislation had to be crafted and passed to try to remedy a social equity program that had failed to deliver a single dispensary license. The program was beset by a litany of legal challenges. It faced challenges to its scoring system, pushback over its lack of transparency, and charges that it favored white entrepreneurs with plenty of cash, not those social equity applicants it was supposed to be helping. Intentions written into legislation may have been sincere, but the numbers in the results were a world away from the arrest and incarceration numbers for Black and Brown Americans caught up in the fervor of cannabis prosecution over the decades.

Robinson had lived this frustration since making the decision to plunge into the cannabis industry as she traveled to a college football game in Blacksburg, Virginia, in September 2019: "We saw who was considered social equity and we thought we could really make a play. . . . We could pool the best of our family and get together and finally break this vicious cycle that we were born into." She recruited four family members—husband Quintin Robinson, brother Marvin Butler, cousin Kendrick Slaughter, and aunt Tanya Dawson. All were from the South Side, and all but her and her husband still lived there. Her parents had started a restaurant in Nashville, so there was some entrepreneurship in her genes. She worked in higher education, and her husband worked in agriculture at Virginia Tech. Her brother and cousin are nurses. They all had what Robinson called the "soft skills" but knew they would need help in coming up with a first-class, quality application.

They vetted top consultants and settled on Next Big Crop, a Denver-based company that billed itself as "a full-service cannabis consulting firm . . . a dedicated group of passionate and seasoned cannabis experts with decades of collective expertise devoted to license procurement, facility design and construction, systems engineering, equipment and materials sourcing, management and compliance." Next Big Crop did not come cheap. It charged $80,000 for its work and requested another $80,000 if the application was a success. Robinson and her team searched other firms that had comparable rates, but they wanted 2 percent of the equity in the licensed enterprise, something she felt was predatory.

That was $16,000 each, a good chunk of change for most people, let alone a social equity applicant. On top of that was the $2,500 application fee, professional memberships they were urged to take out, legal fees, the cost of establishing a website, and other ancillary costs, bumping the final bill to close to $95,000. That meant emptying saving accounts, liquidating 401(k)s, scrimping, scraping, searching under sofa cushions, doing whatever it took. "It was a lot of money for sure," Robinson said. But she and her team had no doubt that it was worth rolling the dice because of what could be theirs down the line. They were sure they were the perfect social equity applicants—"the friggin' Unicorn," as Robinson put it. She felt if they could get in on the ground floor, they would not have to worry about being pushed out by larger competitors in a saturated market: "And we knew, at the end of the day, when we were dead and gone, this would outlast us. I looked at this like green cotton. People are still eating today from the wealth generated from cotton. This new cash crop was this generation's cotton. It would feed our families for generations."

They submitted their application, and they waited. There was no communication from the state, so Robinson set up Google alerts, searched executive orders, and enlisted the help of a local journalist to keep an eye out for press releases. She received a deficiency order, dealt with it, and submitted her application again, as per the rules. Then COVID hit. Results were due in May, but nothing happened. So, she waited some more. On Labor Day 2020, Robinson and her husband were driving on Chicago's Dan Ryan Expressway when she checked her email. The state had sent out the list of top scores that were heading to a lottery process. She was not on that list: "I was numb. I couldn't even breathe, reading the email. I just kept looking at the email, looking at it and looking at it, and I couldn't believe our names were not on that list. I couldn't control my emotions. I was hurt. I was confused."

Out of sheer frustration, she hit "reply" and demanded her scores, which she received, even though it was against regulations. "That's when I was pissed off," she said. "I could make my peace with God, believing this wasn't our time. But when I looked at those scores, that didn't have nothing to do with God. That was about the Man fucking up." If there was one thing Robinson knew for sure, she knew she was a qualified social equity applicant. But she did not even get her social equity points. The Illinois system was plagued by scoring irregularities and lawsuits from applicants who felt they were scored incorrectly. She was no activist; she simply saw a path to a better life for her and her family. But her experience changed her outlook. She became an outspoken advocate for cannabis justice, and she ultimately joined a lawsuit against the state. She wanted to know why the numbers of Black and Brown persons in prison serving terms for nonviolent cannabis offenses outstrip, by a huge margin, the number of Black and Brown dispensary owners across the United States. She wanted to know why a program aimed at helping the most vulnerable ends up hurting those who are most vulnerable: "Equity should not be for sale."

Kara Wright gets that. She understands Robinson's plight and is trying to do something to help her and other social equity applicants in Illinois.[12] Wright took a circuitous path to her present position. She thought she was destined to be a professional singer; she once had a recording contract, working with the likes of the late Whitney Houston and Pink, before she realized the music business was not for her. The music industry's loss turned into a huge gain for those who believe in equity and diversity. Wright returned to university and, while there, volunteered at a residential program for teenagers who were wards of the state of Illinois. It was while taking diversity training for that program that she realized that there was something about diversity and inclusion that she connected with, and her music career was suddenly in the rearview mirror.

She has worked in the diversity field for twenty years and is now the managing director of Chicago's Envisioning Equity Work, a consulting firm with domestic and global clients who are seeking to better understand and dismantle inequitable systems and equip businesses to transition to a diverse work force. She did not live a cannabis lifestyle, and, looking back, she thinks it is borderline crazy that she is deeply into this field now. But her experience with the initial licensing process for Illinois's medicinal dispensaries gave her a different perspective on a recreational licensing system that looked so chaotic to others. Like so many others whose stories are chronicled in this book, it was Wright's compassion that drew her to cannabis in the first place. Several years ago, Wright was caring for an ailing grandmother suffering from cancer. Her grandmother was taking opioids to ease her pain: "If I knew then what I know now, I would have absolutely given her cannabis instead," she said. "I would have tried to convince her to smoke weed. I would have at least provided topicals or do some interesting cooking or infusions or something."

It was her grandmother's suffering that took her to the Illinois medicinal pilot project. Illinois's program was all about compassionate care. And Wright also saw it as a social justice issue with a restorative justice component. She became an equity owner in the only minority-owned license, Illinois Grown Medicine, which was awarded two dispensary and cultivation licenses. Wright agreed that the social equity process in Illinois in 2021 was a terrible process and a failure in many ways. But with the advantage of that perspective, she also still believed it would kick the door open for Black and Brown applicants because she compared the recreational process to what it took to win a license during the medicinal pilot project, when applicants needed millions of dollars in the bank and had to own the property for the dispensary before they could even apply. In addition, her team needed architectural plans, so it hired an architect. It also hired an accountant and a lawyer and had to pay for lobbyists. It was, Wright realizes now, truly the Wild, Wild West.

Anyone familiar with the rhythm of the cannabis industry knows that where a medicinal regime is entrenched, the move to legal recreational cannabis is sure to follow. When people realized legal recreational cannabis was going to be enshrined in law in Illinois, Wright started getting calls. Some were from people she knew; some were from people she didn't know. But they were all asking for advice or to partner. These were owners and operators, all white, who were looking for an opportunity to participate in the market and realized that this was a social equity play and that there was really no way they could come away with the highest number of points without having a social equity partner: "Given my background and my skin and their assumptions about my connections in the community, those phone calls came in and they were saying 'Hey, do you want to join our team to build these programs?'" Wright recalled. "Some of those folks who called had great intentions and wanted to do work with integrity. But I doubted they knew what social equity meant. The others? It was clear there was no sense of integrity about what they wanted to do."

All her white callers were looking for her help in finding Black or Brown people who could be their 51 percent minority face so they could be most competitive in the application process. Some may have had the best of intentions and wanted to help Black people build wealth. But most wanted to have control over those businesses and did not have any goals beyond their own self-interest. "That's why I said 'No,' and hung up the phone and said, 'No, we're not doing this, it's bullshit. It pissed me off." She was not alone. That practice of putting Blacks or Browns in the window in pursuit of a license has a name in Illinois. They call it the "slave master clause" (so called because it allowed the use of employees hurt by the War on Drugs to benefit white dispensary owners who would be reaping the benefits).

Michigan-based Sozo Health tried to derail the long-delayed Illinois license lotteries with litigation in July 2021 but eventually withdrew a lawsuit challenging the constitutionality of the Illinois social equity legislation on the eve of the awarding of a first tranche of licenses. The state had previously allowed companies to qualify as social equity applicants if they had at least ten employees, at least half of whom came from communities most harmed by drug laws or had been convicted of cannabis-related offenses, even if the firm's ownership otherwise would not qualify. Sozo qualified under that provision because it hired eight employees from "disproportionately impacted" areas of Illinois, but the employees would remain at the bottom of the food chain. Under pressure, Illinois legislators excluded such companies from license lotteries, prompting Sozo to argue that the rules were changed in the middle of the game.

After Wright hung up the phone on her last white suitor, she decided she could put a team together to raise capital and train and support Black and female entrepreneurs who wanted to get into the cannabis business: "We looked at the War on Drugs and how it impacted Black and Brown communities and we looked at the wealth gap overall and we thought about the social determinants of wealth, and we knew we could use cannabis as a tool for change." And she did. She created Green Equity Collaborative. Wright never expected to be a social equity advocate, but she wanted to help those who may not have understood what they were getting into. Black and Brown people who may have been in prison for cannabis offenses and distrusted the government were now being asked to get deep into the bushes and work with an unyielding government bureaucracy.

She knows from her work that Black women make up the fastest growing sector of the US economy, yet they have the least access to capital. She wants to lend a hand because she also knows that Black women perform best with what is made available to them: "There is a wealth gap. This is the big picture, a ten-times gap between white and Black families." Wright cited statistics showing the average white family in the United States has a net worth of $170,000; the average Black family has a net worth of $17,600. She was quoting from an oft-cited Hamilton Project study from 2016 that showed that the gap has remained consistent dating to the days of slavery.[13] It has endured boom and bust periods and transcended generations through the values of real estate, economic opportunities, and inheritances passed down in families, among other factors.

An updated study in 2019 by the Federal Reserve Survey of Consumer Finances found that the gap had narrowed slightly to 7.8 times, but the Brookings Institute found that, by the end of the second quarter of 2020, white households, which accounted for 60 percent of the US population, held 84 percent of the wealth, while Black households, which comprised 13.4 percent of the American population, held only 4 percent of total household wealth.[14] Wright believes cannabis gives Black Americans the opportunity to create businesses and close the wage gap. If that happens, she believes $5 trillion could be added to the gross domestic product (GDP). Think about it—cannabis provides the opportunity for Black Americans to build a business from the ground floor, narrow the wage gap, and raise the GDP. There are signs that Illinois might finally get a social equity program right, but, in the meantime, many other jurisdictions are studying its experience to determine what not to do.

But, as Wright maintains, that is the goal, after all—to see what worked and what didn't and do better. All states should look at different methods, or tweak laws to create more transparency and accountability or provide earlier support to social equity applicants: "The whole point is that this must constantly evolve the way Illinois did. The states should be trying to outdo each other on social equity." And that is why, by the summer of 2021, all states would be looking to New York and its ambitious program, the product of the determination of a woman who kept telling Andrew Cuomo "No."

* * *

"It's a life experience that you lived," Crystal Peoples-Stokes said, explaining the roots of her passion for cannabis social equity legislation.[15] She saw the damage done to Black youth during the War on Drugs. That's just the way it was growing up Black in Buffalo. As a county legislator in New York state's second largest city, Peoples-Stokes watched family court in Erie County expand beyond its capacity. The county had to build a new courthouse to accommodate the crush of cases. The demand had become overwhelming.

It was common to see older women with children in tow, trying to talk to a lawyer in an overcrowded hallway: "That was because people were being incarcerated for drug charges, both men and women, and then their families had to go to family court to figure what to do with the children." She saw police officers stopping young Black and Brown boys, patting them down, asking to see what was in their pockets, and, when those pockets were emptied, the police had the power to arrest, often leading to conviction and incarceration.

Peoples-Stokes saw a failed policy that destroyed generations of Black people. Children were going to foster homes in her district, and she saw firsthand the impact the loss of parents had on the lives of children in the Buffalo area. She vowed change but came to her cannabis activism in an unorthodox fashion. Regardless, at the age of seventy, the first Black woman to ever be elected New York Assembly majority leader stood as the architect of cannabis legalization in the state that should not—will not, as she declared—leave victims of cannabis prohibition out in the cold. She does not champion the smoking of cannabis because she does not think people should smoke anything. But she knows they do, and she knows where that leads. There is one principle she holds above all others, one that transcends her belief that cannabis should not be smoked. She champions second chances.

She has long been an outspoken advocate for cannabis decriminalization and the expungement of records, but her journey to leader of legalization is a much shorter road, one that began around 2013 largely out of respect for a colleague from Rochester who had brought cannabis legalization to the New York Assembly but died before he could see support grow. Little by little, year by year, she grew support and picked up adherents in the Assembly where she is known as a tenacious fighter who will not bend on her beliefs. She certainly did not bend when the wealthy white men with dollar signs in their eyes flocked to her office from as far away as California. Everyone was looking for a piece of this action. She certainly was not cowed by Andrew Cuomo who liked the looks of the revenue from legalized cannabis but remained blind to the opportunities for Black and Brown people in his state. He did not want to be told how to spend the money coming into New York. He certainly did not want to be dictated by statute. In 2019, New York was on the verge of legalization, but Cuomo would not budge on social equity. So, Peoples-Stokes would not give him his cannabis revenues. She said "No."

She is a tough woman, a product of an upbringing wedged between an older and younger brother. That toughness was on display when she told her Democratic caucus in Albany (more than once) that, regardless of what the rigid governor might be saying, the equation was simple: no progressive social equity provisions, no legal cannabis in the New York market. It did not matter that the California crowd was outside her door salivating for a cut of the riches in the country's second largest market. She would not be moved. For two years, she did not budge. She continued to say "No."

Melissa Moore, New York director of the Drug Policy Alliance, which was pushing for legalization, credited Peoples-Stokes with convincing lawmakers that people of color in their state were victims of prohibition and that it was time to pay back. "She was deeply committed and would not accept the old deals that would not (recognize) social justice," Moore told the *Buffalo News*.[16] It was evident to Moore that Peoples-Stokes had the integrity needed to ensure that legalization would benefit the communities most affected by racist cannabis prosecutions. Others will tell you that Peoples-Stokes had the patience, the respect of her colleagues, the political savvy, and, yes, the right skin color to get this done.

Peoples-Stokes may have known of the social costs of cannabis convictions on people of color, but it was not until her fifth year pushing for legalization, around 2018–19, that she began to get a real handle on the value of that market in New York: "I started to be visited by very wealthy people from all over the country and Canada about our legislation. I began to realize how big it was in terms of the economic opportunity. . . . I was thinking, 'Wow, these people flew all the way from California to talk to me about this legislation? This is something they really want.' If they wanted it that badly, I didn't mind that they got access to it, but they couldn't get access to it until the people who had suffered the most had opportunity as well." All those people from California with all that money would still have an opportunity to get in, but so would those people who had been hurt by the War on Drugs and did not have a lot of money and the wherewithal to get into the business quickly. She did not care what the monied entrepreneurs thought. It was not about them. It was about the people hurting in those communities that she knows so well.

Politics often comes down to timing, and timing finally smiled on Peoples-Stokes. Cuomo was facing allegations of sexual harassment and widespread bipartisan calls to resign, something he ultimately did in August 2021. In the late winter of that year, with the allegations mounting and cannabis legislation stalled, the embattled governor had to change the channel. It was also a time of racial reckoning in America following the murder of George Floyd. And COVID was ravaging Black America. "It was a factor not just for the Governor but white people generally. It was pushed in your face vividly," Peoples-Stokes said. She said all of America was coming to the realization that there was something wrong with a country that would allow Derek Chauvin, a public servant, to commit homicide on an unarmed Black man in broad daylight.

Cuomo may have needed to try to salvage his political future, but the changed perceptions in his state and beyond, stemming from the Floyd murder, have pushed him in the right direction. On March 31, 2021, Cuomo signed into law the Marihuana Regulation and Taxation Act.[17] "This is a historic day in New York—one that rights the wrongs of the past by putting an end to harsh prison sentences, embraces an industry that will grow the Empire State's economy, and prioritizes marginalized communities so those that have suffered the most will be the first to reap the benefits," he said.[18] New York's legislation created the Office of Cannabis Management, an independent office operating as part of the New York State Liquor Authority. It would have five members, three appointed by the governor and, significantly, one by each house of the New York legislature.

The law would provide incentives for those "disproportionately" impacted by prohibition, expunge past cannabis convictions, and dedicate 40 percent of tax revenues to rebuilding New York communities damaged by the War on Drugs. It would also use those revenues for education and drug abuse treatment. Its stated goal was to set aside 50 percent of dispensary licenses for minorities, women, distressed farmers, or veterans disabled in service to their country. Those communities that had been "disproportionately" impacted by the War on Drugs were loosely defined as areas with histories of arrests, convictions, or other law enforcement activity that demonstrated a disparate, harsher enforcement of cannabis laws when compared to the rest of the state. Those areas were to be defined by a zip code, police precinct, or neighborhood, but the time frame on which these measurements were based remained undefined in the legislation and were to be determined under the ensuing regulations.

To qualify for a social equity license, the application must be at least 51 percent owned by a minority member or group, showing "real, substantial and continuing" control, and, to outlaw white enterprises putting a minority applicant in the window, the minority owner must show that they exercise day-to-day control of, and decision-making in, the enterprise. Priority is given to applicants who live in a community identified as one harmed by prohibition policies, have an income below 80 percent of the median income in the county in which the applicant lives, have been convicted of a cannabis-related offense, or have a parent, guardian, child, spouse, or dependent who has been convicted of a cannabis-related offense. "We know that you cannot overcome a problem without first admitting there is one," Cuomo has said. Beyond generating much-needed revenue for his state, the former governor vows that legalization "enables us to directly support the communities most impacted by the war on drugs by creating equity and jobs at every level, in every community in our great state."[19]

A quick look at the revenue projections explains why Peoples-Stokes had so many suitors sitting outside her office. The former governor's office estimated cannabis legalization would create more than 60,000 new jobs, spurring $3.5 billion in economic activity and generating an estimated $300 million in tax revenue when fully implemented. Another study prepared for the state's medicinal cannabis industry projected the market to be worth $1.2 billion in sales by 2023 and $4.2 billion by 2027 and stream about $350 million in annual tax revenue.[20] That is substantial revenue, but, for perspective, New York Governor Kathy Hochul unveiled plans for $216.3 billion in the fiscal year of 2022–2023.[21]

According to the Marijuana Policy Project, the five-state northeast region of New York, New Jersey, Connecticut, Massachusetts, and Vermont was expected to generate an estimated $8.7 billion in cannabis-related sales by 2027. All eyes were always going to be on New York, specifically New York City. It is home to the country's most lucrative, sophisticated, and deeply entrenched illicit market, where buyers have relationships with dealers reaching back decades, and home delivery is not only offered but expected. In New York City, according to one estimate, seventy-seven metric tons of cannabis are consumed each year, more than any other city in the world.[22] The same city where even in the fourth quarter of 2020, more than nine of out of every ten residents arrested for cannabis offenses were Brown or Black.[23]

Why will New York be different than other states that have suffered such early pitfalls? Many believe that it will be a huge challenge, and there have been predictions of failure. Peoples-Stokes, knowing the devil is in the details, is a believer. She really does believe New York will provide the social equity gold standard, but she is mindful of the challenge of those who moved before the Empire State. Those challenges have been experienced by a number of jurisdictions. Toi Hutchinson is a former Illinois State senator who took on the task of the governor's senior advisor on cannabis control in that state until late 2021.[24] She told an Ohio State University conference on social equity that there is no simple solution to ninety years of oppressive drug policy. "There's no one bill that's going to do it," she told the spring 2021 conference. "So just acknowledge that. This is an ongoing thing. They did it [to people of color] over time, decade after decade after decade, state by state, community by community, block by block, person by person. And that's how we have to come to all the fixes."

Illinois tried to do it all at once, she says. She talks about the expungement of some 500,000 arrest records and 20,000 felony pardons, the difficulty in working through convictions that are layered, and how difficult it is to expunge those types of records when cannabis convictions are embedded with other convictions and it is no longer the low-hanging fruit: "Breaking new ground, you need a jackhammer, and it's loud and messy and you have rock and debris thrown back at you, but you learn to deal with that because you are breaking new ground. . . . We're birthing a new industry and that means we're in labor and labor hurts, contractions are necessary and the only way through it is to push."

But Hutchinson also cautions that people would co-opt the term "equity" and try to interpret these programs as intended to help veterans or women. That is appropriation, she said. Social equity is for those who have suffered the most by the prohibition of the activity that we are now normalizing and legalizing. Hutchinson also knows there are plenty of people who will look to sabotage such programs and that they will fight for licenses with people who may be lacking business sense, capital, or certainly the savvy to navigate government. They will fight in the courts, and they cannot be stopped from doing that because it is part of the American system; so it takes time. "But you cannot waver," Hutchinson said. People of color fighting this cannabis war must realize they are in a system not created by them and are fighting in a system designed to keep them out: "This is real business, real life, real world, . . . And there are people who don't mean us well, no matter how hard we try. So chess, not checkers."

Shaleen Title is a veteran cannabis advocate who gained a passion for social equity while working on the pioneering Colorado legalization campaigns of a decade ago.[25] At the time, she said, there was little understanding of the need to enshrine social equity language specifically and deliberately in any legislation. Much had changed over that decade. The understanding of systemic racism in policing, the lack of equity in North American commerce, or the real costs to people of color from the War on Drugs percolated beneath the surface. Today, it is on boil and central to the political discussion. In Colorado, those pioneering legalization wanted to stay out of jail and keep any referendum question short and simple, devoid of any language that might spark a backlash or even give voters pause.

Title evolved into one of the leading social equity voices in America and today focuses her work on federal legalization. She was one of five commissioners on the Massachusetts Cannabis Control Commission, dubbed "the people's weed watchdog," and she worked tirelessly to make the state's legal cannabis market racially diverse. Her work on an embryonic social equity program in Massachusetts from 2017 to 2020 put her in a position to offer advice for others based on her experience steering that vessel through the uncharted shoals. Having been described as an activist in a risk-averse government agency, there were suspicions that Title may have been set up for failure as the only legalization activist on the five-member commission. There is no question that Title has dealt with frustrations, and she was quite public with them, once tweeting "Chill the Hell Out!" to critics who were pounding on the commission for the speed at which it was working. As an activist, she was comfortable with fiery calls to action but found herself having to work more collaboratively as part of government. And to get things done, she told the *Boston Globe*, she found she had to "suck up" to the key government players and found it distressing to have to spend years working through the system instead of just getting things done. Governments are simply not built for speed, Title knows.[26]

She shared three key takeaways with others crafting social equity initiatives, beginning with the nature of government itself: "In government, which has a very conservative top-down bureaucratic approach, typically everything is just done the way it was done before." As an activist, Title knew taking risks was essential, but, in government, risks can lead to mistakes and mistakes in government are not tolerated. Conversely, if mistakes are not made, expect no applause because that is just the way government is expected to operate. That means everything takes longer, is more difficult and has "more intense heat" on it. Second, she reminded others, one cannot lose sight that cannabis itself was new, it was a drug, it remained stigmatized in huge swaths of the population, and it remained illegal at the federal level. Cannabis legalization is complex, and it fires intense emotions on both sides of the divide.

Finally, Title and others working on equity were, by the very nature of the initiative, dealing with systemic racism and all the obstacles and prejudice laid at the feet of people of color every day. But if one tries to take the easy way out and opt for speed over diligence, the door is opened for the big corporations to bulldoze their way into the industry in your state, wiping out the very purpose of the equity program. Title summarized the difficult trajectory of social equity legislation this way: regulators listen to the community and make a sincere effort to implement an effective program and then a lack of capital, difficulty finding property that meets requirements in the legislation, and approval processes steeped in systemic racism at the local level conspire to set up roadblocks to the participation of those most harmed by the War on Drugs.

Title's successor as member of the commission in Massachusetts was Nurys Camargo, who formerly directed a youth violence protection program and founded a nonprofit to mentor Latinas. It was left to her to report on the obvious to state legislators—five years after Massachusetts voters chose legalization, social equity applicants were still being shut out. Massachusetts may have been the first US state to specifically mandate social equity as part of its legal cannabis framework, but Camargo testified at a legislative committee that only ten social equity licensees were up and running in the state by the summer of 2021. Her Cannabis Control Commission had provided technical or other types of support to about five hundred applicants, but the problem was simple. Applicants did not have the necessary capital to get started or the means to obtain that capital. One example crystallizes the difficulties that new businesses face: one team of minority investors spent more than $3.5 million in start-up costs before it sold its first edible.[27]

Because cannabis is still illegal at the federal level, dispensary aspirants have been unable to get bank loans to start their business. Had they been applying for a loan for any business other than cannabis, they would have been judged on their own merits, not on the hypocrisy of an antiquated federal law. The answer would appear to be a state-managed fund where entrepreneurs of color could access capital, and Massachusetts appeared to be—belatedly—headed in that direction. Peoples-Stokes is adamant that things will be different in New York where the legislation was written purposely to ensure inclusivity in the business. The Office of Cannabis Management will have a chief equity officer on staff, constantly monitoring equity progress, and the advisory committee, separate from the control board, will be monitoring how equity resources are expended: "You can try to put a Latina woman up, for example, and say she's the business owner but a white entrepreneur is putting the money up and scoring the benefits, . . . but there will be monitors checking on that and there will be a review every two years so if you are not running the business you said you were, that license will be revoked." The Office of Cannabis Management will have two members directly appointed by New York's two houses of its legislature, and the advisory board will have six appointees from the legislature. Both mark the first time such agencies were not comprised of members chosen by the governor.

Existing medicinal marijuana conglomerates in New York state are making a lot of money. They have been clamoring to get access to the adult dispensary business, and for three years in a row, Peoples-Stokes has kept them on the outside. If they want into the recreational market, it is going to cost them a lot of money because they are not allowed to jump the queue ahead of social equity applicants. Some of that money is going to be plowed back into social equity, providing incubator programs, technical training, or support to people who have a plan but need to renovate a building or hire legal counsel. There will be state officials dedicated to ensuring that happens. Social equity licenses cannot be sold or transferred for three years, meaning that big pharma or big tobacco could eventually get into the rich New York market; but, Peoples-Stokes said, "they're going have to buy it from Black folk. The government isn't going to just give it to them." And that money will stay in her community.

We see the potential in the New York plan, but we just as clearly see the potential pitfalls. The voices of minorities and those who have suffered under prohibition have to be heard right from the start of the conversation, and this had not happened by the time the bill was signed on March 31, 2021. Decisions were made by politicians behind closed doors, and those with the ability to lobby were, as always, those with the money. The bureaucracy moved slowly, and the program at its inception was already behind schedule. Where is the support for social equity applicants? You can move them to the head of the line, but then what? How do they build the business? We had already seen groups that were standing up real estate options, particularly in New York and Brooklyn, because they had the money for the leases. What happens to social equity applicants who do not have access to that kind of capital?

What we have seen in other states is that regulations require real estate to be locked in when you apply for a retail or cultivation license. That does not work for a social equity applicant, and the New York regulations will need a major push in that direction. A number of expensive pieces have to come together just to get the application in place. You could ask landlords, consultants, lawyers, and all the others with their hands out to agree that payment would be received once the license is granted and revenue began to flow, but that is a tall ask. Such a plan is a long shot at best, and it does not consider the ramifications of an unsuccessful application. That possibility simply lengthens the odds of contingency payments as a solution. New York has pledged to provide grants to the applicants—after the fact, as part of legalized tax revenues. Prior to that revenue flowing, what help is there for the social equity applicant?

Some creative short-term solutions are possible. The state could drop any requirement that a retail lease be in place, and successful applicants can be given six to twelve months to raise capital after the license has been granted. An investor will be far more interested in sinking some capital into a retail dispensary once revenue is flowing. These options would require some proactive movement from the Office of Cannabis Management. Others have suggested the state could sponsor programs to teach skills to new social equity applicants or partner with attorneys or accountants who will provide services without fees to the applicant. It could also provide low-interest loans itself or offer guarantees to private investors willing to take the gamble on social equity applicants.

Peoples-Stokes is not the type to take a victory lap, and she certainly is not taking credit for her cannabis triumph until regulations are rolled out according to plan. That is where other social equity efforts have skidded into the ditch, so she will remain vigilant. When the program really is the gold standard, the seventy-year-old may finally walk away, but not a minute before. "It's the work that keeps me going," she says, "because I'm not doing it for the four-hour drives to Albany." As states grapple with balky rollouts and false starts, the specter of federal legalization looms. But it is not on the immediate horizon, not with Olympic athletes still banned from competition, and White House employees fired for cannabis use—neither move condemned by US President Joe Biden. When Black American sprinter Sha'Carri Richardson was barred from the Tokyo Olympics for cannabis use, Biden responded: "Rules are rules." Five White House employees were terminated for past cannabis use, even though Biden's Vice President Kamala

Harris has used cannabis in the past and the Democratic leadership in Congress is seeking federal legalization.

Despite the apparent lack of White House buy-in, a legalization bill has been introduced by Democratic Majority leader Chuck Schumer. It focuses on record expungement and justice for people of color harmed by the War on Drugs. The bill acknowledges that communities most harmed by cannabis prohibition benefit the least from the legal market because a legacy of racial injustices, compounded by the disproportionate collateral consequence of more than eighty years of cannabis prohibition enforcement now limits their participation in the industry. There would be three grant programs established under the bill. One would fund nonprofits that provide services such as reentry help, job training, and legal aid to individuals adversely affected by cannabis prohibition. Another would provide funding to states and municipalities that provide loans to help small businesses in the cannabis industry owned by "socially and economically damaged" individuals; and, finally, the Equitable Licensing Grant Program would "provide funding to eligible states and localities to implement cannabis licensing programs that minimize barriers for individuals adversely affected by the War on Drugs."[28] Critics say this is too vague, however, and may offer less help to the "socially and economically damaged" than state initiatives. There is also a stick wielded by the Schumer bill. Want federal money? You will have to create an automatic process to expunge criminal records for cannabis offenses. If Schumer's bill ever becomes law, it will end any barriers for cannabis users seeking federal housing, food, or health benefits.

But federal legalization would bring with it peril for states' social equity programs. This peril comes in the form of the bulldozer that runs roughshod over small business owners—interstate commerce. Title, in her role as the director of the Parabola Center for Law and Policy, warns that opening the floodgates to interstate commerce will allow big tobacco and big alcohol to dominate the market at the expense of those who deserve a social equity boost. She has called for the federal regulations to slowly and incrementally create marketplaces while guaranteeing priority licensing and access to capital for those harmed by the War on Drugs. Parabola has called for pilot projects that would test regional marketplaces in New England or the

West Coast where the cannabis market is relatively mature. Alternatively, Title suggests only those with social equity licenses be allowed to engage in interstate commerce: "Handing control of a multibillion-dollar industry to major corporations and industries like Big Alcohol and Big Tobacco puts profit over people, especially when we know that many have records of advertising to children and lying about product safety."[29]

* * *

Maybe, just maybe, we are seeing the future of paying it back in a Chicago suburb of 75,000 hugging the shores of Lake Michigan. Evanston, Illinois, is home to Northwestern University and a populace that is keenly aware of a somewhat painful history. It is also home to the first reparations program in the United States, an initial step that has been funded by cannabis revenue that, on the surface, seems the perfect marriage of revenue from the new legal market and direct payment back to those most afflicted. Reparations, the name given to the effort to redress the historic costs of slavery, have been on the federal agenda for more than thirty years without any movement. In the wake of the 2020 summer of racial awakening, stoked by the Floyd murder, there was at last a stirring, with a House committee voting to establish a commission to study the question of reparations for Black Americans.

It marked the first advancement of HR 40, a bill that has lingered for three decades without ever advancing as far as a floor vote. The bill is named after the unrequited promise to make former slaves whole by giving them forty acres and a mule. Still, it faces solid Republican opposition and less than unanimous Democratic support. So, some municipalities have ignored Washington's inertia and are pledging to move on their own. Robin Rue Simmons believes HR 40 will eventually pass, but she also does not believe local municipalities should wait for that moment, whenever it may be.[30] As a one-term alderman in Evanston's largely Black Fifth Ward, she did not wait and has put the city—and possibly others beyond this suburb—on a remarkable path.

Simmons's family came to Evanston as part of the Great Migration, and she grew up in the city's Fifth Ward in her grandparents' home. They taught her about being Black in America and Black in Evanston and the challenges associated with both. She has always had an abiding interest in her African heritage, and, as a girl, she made beaded jewelry representing that heritage. She also learned of the history of Evanston and was taught to celebrate those titans of her neighborhood who stood tall and raised up their neighbors during a long history of disinvestment. People take care of each other in the Fifth Ward, and she never lost sight of this.

Successive policies of the local, white-led government created a segregated Evanston and ghettoized the Black population in the Fifth Ward. The city created segregated schools and cultural institutions. Black students at Northwestern were denied campus accommodation and told to billet with "nice" Black families in the Fifth Ward. Banks, under the policy known as redlining, refused to finance Black residents seeking home ownership. Redlining is the name given to racial discrimination in home financing derived from the 1930s policy of the Home Owners' Loan Corporation that would mark undesirable neighborhoods in red, signifying that providing federal mortgage insurance could be "hazardous" because of "undesirables" in the neighborhood. Real estate agents referred Blacks to the Fifth Ward, banks refused to loan to Blacks, and, in the early 1940s, Black-owned homes were razed to create space for a football field. White homeowners added riders to their deeds stipulating that their homes could not be sold to Black people.

Today, there is still a $46,000 wealth gap between white and Black families in Evanston, according to city data. Homes in the Fifth Ward today are still worth hundreds of thousands less than comparable homes in white neighborhoods. A 2018 study found that more than eighty years after this policy of redlining, which was responsible for segregating American cities, was instituted, three-quarters of those redlined neighborhoods were still suffering, and almost two-thirds of them were home to racialized populations.[31] Another study found that homes in Black neighborhoods are worth 23 percent less than homes in white neighborhoods, undervalued by $48,000 per home on average. Had those Black homeowners received market value for their homes, they would have realized $156 billion.[32]

Her grandparents did something else for Simmons. They indoctrinated her with the fear of using any illegal substance—she was taught she would not have the resources to rebound from any arrest. But she knew family members and others who were part of a history in Evanston in which Blacks made up a disproportionate percentage of cannabis arrests, right up until Illinois's legalization. In the thirty-six months leading up to November 2019, Black people in Evanston, who make up 17 percent of the population, made up 71 percent of all cannabis-related arrests.[33] As Simmons recounts, "As a member of the Black community, I knew I had very little room for error when it came to arrest." She was careful in her relationships, stayed on the straight and narrow, and largely stayed "safe" at home when she wasn't at school.

After she was elected in 2017, Simmons quickly realized that she likely only had a single four-year term in her. She is hardly wealthy, and, given the demands of her constituents in a ward that is historically marginalized and in need of greater social services and emergency help, she found herself working eighty hours per week and earning $15,000 per year. As a single mom, her work-life balance was badly skewed. But she also knew that she was not going to spend four years getting potholes filled: "I've always had to do the impossible without the resources. . . . That's often what we do as Black women in these communities." She had long explored ideas for racial equity in her hometown, an abiding interest that may have stemmed from a childhood experience. She was invited to a play date by a white friend as a little girl and remembers being dazzled by her friend's home. She wondered why her home and all the homes of her Black friends were so much smaller. That memory stayed with her.

When she began discussions about boosting racial equity in Evanston, she knew that a reparation effort had been mounted at city council years before, and she knew reparations did not merely right a historic wrong. Reparations could deal with the situation in 2019 when she began those meetings with a grand idea for a small community. Over the months, studies were commissioned and ideas were debated, but there was no significant pushback to the concept of reparations; and, in November 2019, by a vote of eight to one, the city council of Evanston approved a motion to divert cannabis tax revenue to a program of reparations, with an initial outlay of $10 million over ten years. It wasn't much. But it was a start, one that did not originally have any ties to cannabis.

Simmons knew she had to fund this initiative, and more than a dozen ideas of where the money might come from were floating around, but as she was advancing her plan in February 2019, Illinois was proceeding with a plan to legalize recreational cannabis. She struggled with various alternatives, including a real estate or amusement tax, but it was a colleague who suggested tapping cannabis funds. Simmons was hesitant to use revenue from the sales of a plant that had oppressed her people over the years, but when she received the report on cannabis arrests she had requested, the morality of the plan was apparent. So was its fiscal purity—this was restorative justice without a new tax that would burden anyone. "The timing was divine," she said.

There was little city council resistance, but despite the national media attention and adulation from equity advocates, Simmons had to overcome significant opposition within the community, and not just from the white trolls. Despite her support on council, some Black residents rejected this as a charitable handout. Others were offended that the reparations would be paid in housing grants that would create business for the same banks and real estate agents who helped create and foster racial disparity. Others felt that if this was to be an ongoing program it should not be dependent on the vagaries of cannabis revenues. In response, Simmons provided a list of Black banks and realtors for recipients, and she dismissed any thought that cannabis revenues would decline.

This is an example of a nimble local government doing what a rigid Congress cannot, but, for Simmons, it was really all about her village. She has been back in the Fifth Ward for twenty years, raising her children. While its heritage is undeniable, the neighborhood is gentrifying. She grew up in a neighborhood that was almost 100 percent Black; the neighborhood is now significantly whiter than it ever has been. "The Fifth Ward is always the Fifth Ward. It is the village that raised me up. It's prepared me well for life," she said. That life now includes leading a nonprofit that spreads the word about reparations across the country, and at least eleven mayors in medium and large US cities, including Chicago, Amherst, Massachusetts, Asheville, North Carolina, and Iowa City, have expressed interest. A case for reparations has been floated in Nashville. Discussions are underway in California,

Virginia, and Maryland about going in the same direction. Simmons is in direct contact with a reparations movement in Detroit.

The first $400,000 of Evanston's reparations fund was scheduled to be disbursed through a lottery system by the end of 2021. The money will fund home repairs or provide mortgage payments or other property costs. Payments of $25,000 were earmarked for sixteen Black residents (or their direct descendants) who lived in Evanston between 1919 and 1969, the period of greatest harm before federal fair housing laws ostensibly ended housing discrimination. They have been inevitably named the Evanston 16, in a nod to the Little Rock 9 who broke school segregation in Arkansas. And that sounds just fine to Simmons: "I was not thinking beyond my neighborhood when I introduced this. I was hyper-focused on my village. But I cannot deny the impact of what we have done in Evanston and how it has inspired other cities, community leaders, and institutions."

Others determined to start their own paths to reparation will choose their own routes, and these may or may not include legalized cannabis revenue. The Evanston experiment may have simply been a "divine" confluence of two events, but it is hard not to think of what could be. Simmons is now definitely thinking beyond her village: "I think we have already changed America."

8 ROOM AT THE TOP

TAHIRA

A relationship with cannabis often seems to have its roots in compassion. A need to lessen suffering, an effort to help a loved one, an attempt to offer something more substantive beyond a hug in someone's final days. Just as often, the passion for the plant blossoms from a fierce need to advocate for overturning a lifetime of wrongs in whatever form possible, big or small. For me, it was both. Cannabis was on my radar as a kid in small-town Ohio in the way cannabis often is—with friends while sitting around, staving off boredom, trying to figure out what to do with our angsty teenage years. It was not a party favor that followed me too far into adulthood, and it somewhat fell off my radar as I became a working professional. But cannabis forced itself into my consciousness with a curious text from my mother to my younger sister and me, simply asking: "Do you know where to get marijuana?" My grandfather's devastating cancer diagnosis left her in the unenviable position of caretaker, problem solver, and optimist, desperately searching for ways to ease his pain in hopes that he would recover or, at the absolute minimum, suffer a bit less and wake up another day.

As a family, we had never dealt with a loved one this close facing cancer. It is distressing, to say the least. And it just so happened that on the same day my maternal grandfather ("Nana") was diagnosed with cancer, my paternal grandfather ("Dada") passed away in Pakistan, and my parents had to face the reality of both. It was a shit day. I was somewhat shielded from the grief because I was away in business school and could find ways to distract myself. Still, I watched and listened as both my parents navigated the loss of my grandfather in Pakistan and as my mom ("Ami") tirelessly searched for solutions to try to save her father, turning to things I don't think anyone would have guessed she would consider—like cannabis.

I knew where to get the cannabis Ami asked about. From my fuzzy high school years, I knew who grew it in their basement and sold it, but I certainly was not going to send my mother there or have them deliver something to her. Plus, all I knew was flower, and with Nana facing lung cancer, he certainly was not going to smoke anything. In lieu of coursework, I unintentionally threw myself into cannabis with late-night Googling sessions. As a child of the 1980s and Nancy Reagan's "Just Say No" campaign, imagine my surprise when I learned that a plant that had prevented so many from reaching their potential had properties that could ease a range of suffering and become a tool of compassion. Had Nancy Reagan lied to me?

Ultimately, we could not find any form of cannabis that we needed in Ohio, and we lost my grandfather a few months later—a day before I received an unexpected text message from a former classmate who had joined a small, budding start-up (pun absolutely intended). "Do you have a job yet?" This was a sore subject; as a second-year MBA student, if you did not have a job by that time of year, inching closer to graduation and debt repayments, you were kind of freaking out. "How do you feel about Seattle and marijuana?" he then asked. He had joined the first cannabis-focused investment firm in Washington State, and he was reaching out at the moment I was immersed in learning about cannabis. Sometimes things just seem to converge in life, and there I was.

After graduation in 2014, with the surprise blessing of my parents, I was on my way to Seattle to legally work in cannabis, wondering whether I was signing up for a revolution or a short foray into something wild that would at least give me good stories to tell. At that time, the industry was hardly white guys in suits. It was legacy operators, who were some of the most fascinating characters I had ever met in my life. In fact, white guys in suits were seen as validation for the industry as it started to peek out from the shadows and lay the foundation for legitimate business. There were women and Black and Brown people, but not many. After all, it was risky to join cannabis at that time. There was no "industry." I had the benefit of being in a position of privilege, coming out of business school and ripe for an adventure. Had I stayed in my prior finance job or been in another stable role, I doubt I would have been willing to take the risk. I would have been worried about all the things we worry about—money, reputation, employability. At that stage, I had none of those things, so what the hell.

Looking back, I do not recall being constantly aware I was the only woman, or the only Brown person, or the only this or that. I was used to it. I had come from the world of finance and walking into a room of white men was not something that surprised me. It was status quo. As often the only woman in the room, I was sometimes invisible to the guys around the table. In meetings, I was sometimes not introduced and often not expected to speak. Being a minority woman with a name that is hard to pronounce, I am used to people not wanting to address me because that will then force them to have to say my name or try to recall it. These interactions often end with, "Ah! That's not so hard!" No, no it isn't.

Although I won't get into the nitty gritty of who hath scorned me most, or lay out vivid examples of my misgivings regarding the privileged I have encountered—I'll save that for the movie—I will share one narrative that perhaps personifies many. During an investment deal road show, I was at a pitch meeting sitting next to the founder of a high fashion brand who was contemplating investment. We were sitting around an oval table, and I was at his side for at least thirty minutes. I had also been introduced to him at the beginning of the meeting. As the meeting progressed, he asked a question of an associate of mine, and the associate replied: "Tahira can best answer that." "Who?" our would-be investor asked. "Me," I replied. "Who are you?" he asked. I told him I was the chief financial officer—hi, we met thirty minutes ago—and he offered a lazy shrug. I'm certain he didn't listen to my brilliant response. Somehow, I wasn't visible, yet there were only six of us in the room.

As I became more entrenched in the industry, I came to realize something was not right. I knew who had been hurt by cannabis prohibition, and I was seeing firsthand who was benefiting from its legalization. Not those who had been hurt. It was unfolding before my very eyes, and I was on the side of the "suits," which for me was a jarring disconnect. As I began to progress in the industry, landing in leadership positions where I was hiring people, I felt an obligation to try to change the dynamic in the industry, even as I was bumping up against my own ceiling. I had to decide what I wanted to represent in this industry. What did I want to represent in life? When I became a "voice" in the industry, that was when I realized I could use it and my network to help others learn and advance and find the right opportunities.

After a variety of roles—managing director of a venture capital fund, chief financial officer of a special purpose acquisition company, and sole proprietor of a little consulting business built on word-of-mouth references—I wanted to stop making things for others and start building something for myself and others who needed help. I partnered with an inspiring and talented woman, Jacqueline Bennett, who values what I do—people and helping others—and we started an investment and advisory firm focused on providing access to women and minorities who want to invest in emerging industries like cannabis. We also launched a brand with a mission to democratize access to health and wellness products and share the hemp and cannabis opportunity through a peer-to-peer model—because investing in and consuming cannabis should not just be for the white and wealthy.

In a world where alcoholism and opioid addiction are rampant, mental health issues are finally being properly recognized, and stress levels for everyone are through the roof, cannabis can help a huge array of communities have better days. Cannabis can also free communities from the prisons that we, through the actions of our societies and our government, have unjustly put them in. Those Black and Brown business leaders who have risen to the top of the industry have different stories to tell about how they got there. But they are all making a difference, and every story we share in this chapter is a compelling tale that often begins where mine began—rooted in care and the desire to help.

* * *

Her name is Viola, and she calls her grandson Baby Doll. She is the proper lady from the Deep South who loves her Bible and respects her God. He is a resilient and well-traveled National Basketball Association (NBA) star who endured the pain and strain of competition for sixteen seasons. He makes no apologies when he calls her his rock, nor does he shy from the Baby Doll name, despite his six-foot, nine-inch, 230-pound frame. When Viola came to visit her grandson, Al Harrington, in Denver, he was shocked to learn that his beloved grandmother was struggling with glaucoma, chronic pain, and futile efforts to control that pain.[1] It was a revelation for Harrington who had come face-to-face with his grandmother's declining health, and he had to find a way to provide some relief to the petite seventy-nine-year-old. Medicinal marijuana was legal in Colorado, and it seemed to Harrington that every day he was reading about the benefits of cannabis in the media. One article even claimed it could cure glaucoma.

Harrington did not use cannabis, but he took a brave step. He purchased some medicinal cannabis and offered it to his grandmother as a potential antidote to her agony. Just give it a try, he implored. He was met with a predictable response. "Boy, I ain't smokin' no reefer," she said, fixing her gaze on Baby Doll. Harrington understood. Growing up in East Orange, New Jersey, his single mother had told him to stay away from reefer. He was taught that it was a gateway drug, and soon he would be on heroin or crack and his life would be ruined if he started smoking. He was downright frightened of cannabis. This was the Reagan era, and there was a War on Drugs, but Harrington knew nothing of statistics showing the disproportionate number of young Black kids being busted for smoking cannabis. He just knew that in his neighborhood he would see the cops pull over and harass some of the older Black kids.

By the age of twelve, when even then he towered over his friends, Harrington was part of a group that would be hanging out on the street following an after-dinner game of hoops or kickball when the police would show up, sirens blaring, red lights flashing, asking him and his friends to empty their pockets. He remembers the cops showing up in school and searching the lockers of Black kids, remembers an uncle being locked up because he had a nickel bag. Those sirens, those flashing lights, they scared the hell out of a twelve-year-old kid who had done nothing wrong, and he remembers them to this day. Al Harrington spent sixteen years competing with the world's basketball elite, a remarkable record of longevity, followed by stops in China and Australia. No matter the acclaim, the success, or the lucrative paydays, he never really lost that fear of cannabis and how it could upend his life.

But Grandma Viola needed some help. Harrington would not give up and was shocked when his persistence paid off, and she finally agreed. So stunning was his grandmother's agreement that Harrington wondered whether this was God's work, though she needed some assurance from Baby Doll that the police were not going to swoop down and toss her in jail for this. After vaporizing some cannabis and giving it to his grandmother, Al took a pre-game nap before that night's Nuggets game, checking on her when he woke. She was in tears, but these were tears of joy. "I can read my Bible again," she told Harrington. Thus began a complete reappraisal of cannabis by Harrington, who at that point was in the twilight of a career that included stops in Indiana, Atlanta, New York, Golden State, Denver, Orlando, and Washington.

Harrington immersed himself in the restorative and medicinal properties of cannabis. He learned the statistics that tell how the lives of Black kids were interrupted or ruined by smoking a joint on the street, while the white kids did so with impunity in their rec rooms in the suburbs. And he saw a future after the relentless pain and post-game agony he so often felt over his basketball career. A man who had only one unhappy experience with cannabis himself before using it to give Grandma Viola saw a new lease on life when he started down a road that led to him becoming one of the most successful Black cannabis entrepreneurs in North America. Today, his Viola brand—yes, named for his grandma—is one of the leading wholesalers of premium cannabis products in the United States. It has operations in Colorado, Oregon, Michigan, California, Arizona, Nevada, and, through a licensing agreement, Canada. And he has welcomed former NBA icon Allen Iverson to Viola.

Harrington is giving back. He wants to help other Black and Brown kids make millions in this industry. He tells them that he has made it and they can too, and he is one of many successful Black entrepreneurs who are creating their own social equity programs. All of the individuals whose stories are chronicled in this chapter have reached the top of the heap, and they are embodiments of determination and self-belief. Some had advantages others could only dream of, but they want to give back through substantive programs and donations, through their pulpits that come with their stature, and through their example, their success, their very presence in an industry dominated by those who do not look like them.

Like so many others profiled in this book, Harrington's path to cannabis success began with a moment of empathy for a loved one. Yes, his basketball earnings put him on a track unknown to other kids on the street, looking for a way out by using the same flower that had halted their personal growth and blunted their dreams. Harrington had money, but there was a litany of other former players he approached for investment help who declined or ignored him, fearful of the stigma of cannabis and the lack of business background or expertise of a guy better versed on dunks and putbacks. Others followed a similar path.

Rob Sims was an offensive guard in the National Football League (NFL) and had the profile and finances that come with that position. He and former Detroit Lions teammate and Hall-of-Famer Charles Johnson partnered to form Primitiv, a cannabis company they hope might improve quality of life for those living with chronic pain and change the narrative around their product, which they call medicine.[2] For Sims, it took a football injury almost too gruesome to contemplate for him to turn his back on opioids for pain and search for a natural remedy, taking him to cannabis. Between them, Sims and Johnson were reported to have earned $130 million during their NFL careers, and they poured $5–6 million of it back into starting Primitiv.

Jay-Z, the world's first billionaire hip-hop artist, serves as chief visionary officer for California's The Parent Company (TPCO) and has his own cannabis brand, Monogram. Its wholesale distribution network reaches almost five hundred California dispensaries and reported $33.2 million in net sales for the first quarter of 2022.[3] TPCO is investing $10 million in social equity ventures, an initiative co-led by Jay-Z. He also hired Troy Datcher as the first Black chief executive officer of a publicly traded cannabis company in the United States. Datcher has promised TPCO will work to right the wrongs of prohibition, break down antiquated laws, and create a cannabis infrastructure rooted in diversity, equity, and justice for Black communities.

Others have more humble roots, but they still have scaled the cannabis heights. Jesce Horton, founder of Portland-based Love Our Weed Daily

(LOWD) sent out two thousand emails, texts, and decks looking for investors to get him started.[4] He did not get a single response. The son of a man who spent four years behind bars for a nonviolent cannabis offense parlayed his engineering skills, determination, and love of the flower into a company that projected $3.5 million in revenues and $1.5 million in profit by the close of 2021.

Ashley Athill gained a love of the land and what it can produce from her Jamaica-born mother and used to tend to her plants in the fields of the Toronto suburb of Scarborough. With her brother, Michael, Ashley cofounded HRVSTR, a premium cannabis cultivation facility that supplies the Canadian market. But to get to the point where she could chase a dream, she did not turn to a bank for help. She knew she would have been laughed out of the building. Instead, she sold her house to raise capital.

Wanda James was a navy lieutenant who became a highly sought-after political strategist before getting involved in cannabis legislation after her brother was sentenced to ten years in prison for possession.[5] She became the first Black person to own a cannabis dispensary when she opened Simply Pure Dispensary in Denver. She and her husband Scott Durrah became the first Black persons in America to be licensed to own a dispensary, a cultivation facility, and an edibles factory.

James and Sims have unique stories we will tell later in this chapter, but all of the others experienced the War on Drugs growing up and felt the oppression as young Black kids living in neighborhoods that were high on crime but low on hope. Their initial experiences with cannabis were quite different. In fact, the relationship between Harrington and cannabis was hardly love at first sight. It threatened to become a disastrous one-night stand. He was in Phoenix with the Golden State Warriors in the waning days of the 2007–2008 season, watching on television as the Denver Nuggets played the Los Angeles Clippers. A win by the Clippers would mean Harrington's Warriors would be in the playoffs with a win against the Suns the next night. But the Clippers did what the Clippers of that era did. They rolled over, and Harrington and his teammates sat at the bar watching a successful season go down the drain.

When they returned to the hotel, Harrington grabbed a drink, but his teammates were smoking. Harrington had bought into the scare propaganda machine, thinking teammates who smoked cannabis were not dedicated to their craft and were going to piss away lucrative careers. But he could not square that view with the fact that those who were smoking were often some of the best, hardest-working players in the NBA. That night would be different. "Al, tonight you're smoking, bro," said one teammate, and Harrington obliged. He almost immediately lapsed into a night of deep cannabis anxiety and paranoia. He retreated to his room. "I was in my room dealing with this all night long," he recalled. "The guys gave me some pretty good stuff." It was a long night. He thought he was hearing sirens in the room. His paranoia was going through the roof. But he wouldn't let that one night define his relationship with cannabis.

Jesce Horton cannot exactly remember when he learned that his father James had been sentenced to seven years in prison and had served four. It was never spoken of when he was growing up. His father had been convicted of intent to distribute because he had cannabis in a few bags, although he had less than an ounce when he was pulled over. He was also driving without a license. That night cost him his immediate future at the University of North Carolina (UNC), but his prison time could not break the man. After he was released, he went to UNC and earned a master's degree in business administration. He had to start his way back toiling as a janitor, but he worked his way up to become a vice president at State Farm Insurance.

It was only later in life, when the young Horton was involved in cannabis himself, that he learned that it had played a defining role in his father's life. The father is the hero to the son, and the son is still left to wonder at the heights his father would have scaled had he not been forced to start his way back pushing a broom. Still, his father's ordeal could not diminish Jesce's love of cannabis: "I was always told growing up that police targeted Black people and being Black you had to watch out." In Lakeland, Florida, where he spent part of his youth, it was just the way it was—when you were out with friends on the block, police would pull up wanting to search everyone, or, if you were in a car, you would be pulled over for no other reason than they wanted to smell something.

That systemic racism and oppression was just a day-to-day thing in the US South, something you had to deal with daily if you were Black, and a Black teen had to figure how to do things or avoid things to survive because there was no other way. Like Harrington, he never connected the dots as a youth. He just knew his Black friends were often busted for weed: "We had a lot of problems with cannabis and the police in Lakeland. But as it related to the use of cannabis to target Black kids and those disproportionate arrest rates, I probably didn't learn that until I got into the industry." That's because as a Black person from the South, you didn't have time or the inclination to dabble in ideals or injustice: "You were more rooted in the reality in doing what it took to get by and move on to the next phase in life. That's just the way it was."

Horton's father told him in no uncertain terms to stay the hell away from cannabis. He did more than preach. James Horton literally tested his son for cannabis use. And, like most teens, Jesce Horton ignored his dad, and he was arrested for cannabis use three times. Every time, it was for low-level possession under three grams. His father had no attorney in his day to fight for his rights, but it was James who ensured his son had an attorney. Jesce was pushed to diversion programs and never faced a penalty more severe than probation. Some of his friends got jail time. While he never questioned why more Black people were being arrested, he would occasionally question why he continually put himself in a position to hurt himself by continuing to use cannabis.

Horton knew cannabis was seen as wrong; there was not today's understanding of its benefits. At times he would think he was probably doing wrong, but he started smoking at fifteen and never really stopped, except to beat an occasional drug test. Even abstinence did not work when he was interning at General Electric, and they gave him a "hair test" in which hair follicles were tested instead of urine. Like father, like son. Jesce Horton persevered, gaining a degree in industrial engineering with a minor in science and physics. He turned that degree into a great position with engineering giant Siemens and a turn at its headquarters in Munich, where he would spend weekends in Amsterdam trying the local herb.

When he accepted a company transfer to Portland, Oregon, his life started down a different path. This was Horton's first exposure to life where cannabis was legal, and he started growing in his basement. He found the process of perfecting his consummate smoke to be empowering. He needed that sense of empowerment because he was becoming disillusioned with his path at Siemens, where he felt like a cog in a wheel. When he should have been making appointments for his Siemens work, he was tending to his plants. A change in direction came not only from his waning interest in engineering work but also because, as Horton only half-jokingly said, he was "terrible" at the job. He likes to think he quit before he was fired.

His parents had been out to Oregon for a visit, so they knew Jesce was growing. When he finally decided it was time to quit his job for a new direction growing his flowers, he called home to relay the news. His mom hung up on him. He phoned back, and she handed the phone to his father. James got it immediately. He never questioned his son's decision and knew Jesce had to escape the "golden handcuffs" that limit potential because one's path is ordained by a corporate master. Jesce immersed himself in honing his craft and learning from others, then dove into the politics of cannabis regulation in the state capital of Salem, learning the ins and outs of the regulatory framework, sitting in meetings, buttonholing key players, and making himself impossible to ignore. Just as his father had taught him: "I attacked it the way I was taught by my dad to attack everything. He always told me if you're going to do it you have to be better than everyone. You can't compare yourself to other Black persons or your peers. You must hold yourself to an absurdly high standard."

But that did not help him when he looked for investors. Two thousand pitches. Two thousand swings and misses. He had to realize that he had no experience; he was trying to play with the big boys, and he was Black. Like many Black entrepreneurs, he did not have the type of network that white guys had built and nurtured—the network that would be sorely needed if you needed someone to connect with you at a certain level and believe in you when you say you can get something done no matter how farfetched it might sound. You know, someone like your dad. The dad whose life was detoured by the same flower his son now wanted to turn into dollars. James anted up $30,000 to help his son get started. "The people who believe in you are really just friends and family and it's not just for Black people, but for white people too, so the money comes from your dad, or your dad's friends, or maybe your dad's friend has a warehouse," Jesce Horton said. Dad didn't have a warehouse, but he had a persuasive nature that went beyond charisma. People listened when he spoke. He made friends that became life-long alliances, and so James Horton somehow convinced a bunch of retired insurance guys to jump in. They delivered another $150,000 to a young man's cannabis industry dream. In all, Jesce came up with $300,000 to start LOWD. All the money came from fifteen Black investors.

For Sims, growing up in Ohio, just south of Cleveland, meant a single-minded pursuit of football. His father had been an NFLer and then became a police officer for Metro Parks in Ohio; his mother was a university profes-sor. Football and education ruled his early life in the Ohio community of Macedonia, and cannabis use was "very, very taboo." It was seen as some-thing that could kill his football aspirations. "My trajectory was all about football and getting to the next level," Sims recalled. Even in college, he was afraid that his football career would be punted if he had ever been caught smoking pot, so he stayed away. That discipline, and his talent, meant his trajectory was complete when, after completing his career at Ohio State, Sims was drafted as an offensive guard by the Seattle Seahawks. Two years later, a potentially career-threatening injury led him to a path of cannabis education and cannabis use.

During mid-week practice before that Sunday's Seahawks game in Buf-falo, Sims was running out to block on a screen play when another player ran right through his arm. He did not realize it at the time, but his pectoral muscle was probably partially torn at that moment. He should not have played in that game in Buffalo, but it was (and still is) the attitude of a NFL player that you just play through the pain: "When you have a chance to make millions of dollars and play in the best league, pain is way down the totem pole—way down the totem pole. You just do whatever you need to do to play through it." Before he hit the field that Sunday in Buffalo, he had to use special gear beneath his uniform to hold his arm in place. But during the third quarter, he was hit, and he recalled a "super sharp" pain shooting through his arm and up his back. He finished the game, but as he boarded the plane for the trip to the West Coast, he found he could not reach above to place his luggage in the overhead compartment. An older teammate came to him and said: "You probably shouldn't play in the NFL if you can't put your luggage in the overhead compartment."

Sims had torn his pectoral muscle right off the bone. After a visit to a radiologist—and a thought that perhaps he could still play through that injury—his coach at the time, Mike Holmgren, told him he had to have surgery and that he would miss the rest of the season. Otherwise, he might never play again. "I was thankful for that, because knucklehead that I was, I would have just kept playing," he said. When he came out of surgery, he was handed a bottle of opioids and was told to take one when he felt pain: "I was told to take as many as I needed, not the other way of 'Hey, be careful with this stuff.'" That took Sims on a search for a more natural way to deal with pain, which, of course, that led him to cannabis. It has been part of his life since 2008. Sims continued to play through pain when he came to the Lions, but, when he suffered another injury, he worried about gaining a reputation as "injury-prone," a stigma that fairly, or unfairly, can severely limit a career. Sims was determined to avoid that stigma, and he did. He played eighty consecutive games for the Lions and spent nine years in the NFL, almost three times the length of an average career in a league in which catastrophic injury is always waiting on the next play and chronic pain becomes a way of life, both during and after one's playing days.

Sims and Johnson formed Primitiv as a way of providing pain relief and improving quality of life. "When I got into this with Calvin," he said, "I thought our brand would just die if we talked about getting high. For us, it wasn't our authentic story. My authentic story was tearing my pec and playing eighty straight games. That was my truth, and if we were going to be faces of the brand, we had to tell our truth, not be the gorilla with the blunt in the mouth." As they embarked on this post-football phase as young men in their early thirties, Sims and Johnson had to concede that they really knew nothing about growing the cannabis plant. They knew how to use it and were well aware of its medicinal properties, but Sims spent hours research-ing, meeting people, and traveling to California and Colorado to learn this business. Johnson's fame opened doors for the two men.

Unlike Horton, an unknown who had to reach out to potential inves-tors, Johnson and Sims were targets. People saw bags of money coming their way, and they had consultants coming out of their ears. Three times they hired associates who they thought would be a good fit for the embryonic business, and three times it did not work, and they had to go back to the drawing board and spend more money before they finally established their cultivation facility in Webberville, Michigan. "People would look at us and say 'What do you know about business? What do you know about this industry?' And truth be told, they were right. Because of that we suffered," Sims said. "A lot of people out there were saying they were consultants and, oh yeah, they'll consult and consult and you'll pay them money, but that doesn't mean you'll get the outcome you're looking for. Anyone who tells you they just got into this business and hit the ground running and everything was good, they're just lying."

But here is where Sims and Johnson have carved out their own niche. They have teamed with the International Phytomedicines and Medical Can-nabis Institute at Harvard University. They are at the cutting edge of plant-based medicine, and the school is providing quality assurance for Primitiv products. A profile of each Primitiv strain will be clinically tested for its effec-tiveness, and its THC and CBD composition will be logged. In announcing the partnership with Harvard, any stigma attached to what they were doing melted away, Johnson said—a strong counterargument to Sims's mother's verdict when he had first launched with Sims: "Have you lost your mind?"

They also partnered with NESTRE Health and Performance, a company working with neuroplasticity to improve brain health. Now the two are in the quality-of-life business, hoping to use cannabis-based medicine to attack cancer cells and provide pain management to those who suffer from chronic traumatic encephalopathy, the brain-wasting injury endemic to former foot-ball player players. Their product can be used to not only manage the pain but also to reduce the anxiety that comes with the disease, allowing those with the condition to sleep. If cannabis can be used to ease the pain of former football pros, Sims said, it should be used to help little old ladies dependent on walkers with tennis ball handles: "Very quickly we went from being washed-up athletes and turned to something that will really help people."

James had a different upbringing. She was an air force brat and would split her youth between England, Germany, and Colorado, returning to the state every four years where her father was stationed at airbases. She grew up in white neighborhoods and went to white schools, so cannabis was never an issue, just something that was always around. She remembers sitting on the steps of her University of Colorado dorm with a pound of pot she and three friends were rolling for the weekend. The campus police came by and merely asked them to put it away. She smoked it with friends in front of Colorado's best hotels. She never knew anyone who had been busted for weed until she met her brother for the first time at her father's funeral. Darrick Barnes had been raised in inner-city Texas, and when he met his older sister at the funeral, he sheepishly told her he had just been released from prison. "My heart sank because in my world if you went to prison you did something really bad. You raped somebody or you killed somebody," James recalled. "He told me it was for four ounces of pot, and I didn't really believe him."

He gave her his court records and she showed them to an attorney friend who dumped a huge dose of reality on James, explaining that some 800,000 young men and women between the ages of seventeen and twenty-four, mainly Black and Brown youth, were arrested each year for nonviolent cannabis offenses. At the age of eighteen, Barnes had been sentenced to ten years of hard labor in a federal penitentiary in Texas. He was part of what James calls the slave class in the United States, made up largely of Black and Brown prisoners who clean litter from the highways, fight fires, or grow the flowers for big box plant stores. There is no point tapping white youth for this class. They get lawyers and challenge injustice, but many Black folks do not have the money or connections to do that, so they are effectively conscripted into this class.

Her brother had to pick one hundred pounds of cotton a day to purchase his freedom in 1992. When she found out that Black kids were picking cotton as part of a prison work program, her anger turned white hot: "That's when I became a warrior." James's background also differed from other Black North Americans who have punched through to the top of the cannabis heap. She was a US naval lieutenant and an influential political strategist, running Colorado Governor Jared Polis's successful campaign and serving on Barack Obama's 2008 finance committee. She was also a successful restaurateur with her chef husband, Durrah. She worked on the legalization campaign in Colorado with Mason Tvert, and she and Durrah helped craft the state's regulation on edibles, which was key to smoothing the unpredictability and potential danger of ingesting the wrong dose of edibles. But she remained a warrior.

When she and Durrah set out to open a dispensary in 2009, there were no social equity programs in place. They used credit cards and equity in their house, but at that point in cannabis history, there were really no rules or regulations, let alone license fees. You had to get a lease on a location, pay first and last month security deposit on the lease, find product, and open a store. Durrah made his own edibles in their restaurant, and they built out their garage by half to grow their inventory plants. "We were flying and building the plane at the same time," she recalled. It cost about $200,000 to get started. It was no different than opening a restaurant or a yoga studio. Today, if you want to open a dispensary in Colorado, you better have $2.5 million; if you want to buy one, you better have $5 million.

Even though they had become the first African Americans to be legally licensed to own a dispensary, a cultivation facility, and an edible company, they were not aware of the milestone until asked about it in a television interview. James got into the cannabis industry so she could raise awareness about the racial inequality associated with the plant during prohibition. She did it to become that warrior: "I'm sick and tired with the arguing about who was first. . . . I don't give a fuck who was the first, but if you were the first and you haven't spoken up about it then you are a lousy first. I don't care about being first, third or tenth. Our voice has always been out there since Day One." She is first and foremost a politician, and she has been talking about slave labor, pushing politicians to move, coming down hard on anti-cannabis politicians, and fighting the cops for years: "That to me is more important than being the first. First to me just means that I have knives and arrows in my back."

Ashley and Michael Athill were born in the Toronto suburb of Scarborough, but their family came from Jamaica.[6] It was a way of life for the family to grow and extract what was needed for health and well-being from the earth. Scarborough of the late 1980s and early 1990s was Crip territory. In their Birchmount and Finch neighborhood, there were guys on street corners chopping weed everyday just to make sure their kids were taken care of and the lights stayed on in their homes, and, as young teens, the Athills thought nothing of it. That was just the way it was at Birchmount and Finch. Weed was the fragrance of the neighborhood, and daily stresses were relieved with a spliff on the street. With the gang activity came a police presence, and any night was marked by the wail of sirens and people fighting with the police. Michael recalls people walking through the neighborhood and being harassed by cops for no other reason than the color of their skin.

Ashley remembers sitting in her classroom at Stephen Leacock Secondary as police came in and grabbed a student in the home economics class without even checking in at the principal's office. Leacock would have been about 40 percent Black at the time. The remainder were Asian, Middle Eastern, and white, but this melting pot had one thing in common—their families had arrived in Canada recently, and they did not have much; when you arrived with little, Scarborough was one place where you could afford shelter. "We became numb to it," Ashley recalled. "Seeing Black men always being picked up and sent to jail was just what happened. What we expected." As her brother Michael put it, "The War on Drugs did not need a passport to cross the border. The same mentality was happening here in Canada. For the police, as long as you had a skin tone with a little bit of pigmentation in it you were a target."

But while the Athills lived it, they did not become ensnared in it. A solid family structure, a mother who was a nurse and a father who was one of the few Black teachers in Scarborough in that era maintained a steady hand. They allowed the Athills to rise above what was happening on the street, while simultaneously giving them the skills to navigate those streets. They also gave them a love of the earth and growing and nurturing. One day, Ashley found a cannabis seed in a flower. Most kids would not have noticed or given it a second thought, but Ashley Athill could not help but wonder what might happen if she planted it: "I was one of those kids, we called them guerrilla growers. I would go into those hiking fields, and I would go deep into the bush with this Chinese kid Kenny and this Indian guy Rav, and we planted plants. We smoked weed, but we didn't do it on the road, we did it in the bush."

This was a burgeoning love affair with the growth and tender care of the plant: "I would grow these massive plants. People would pass right by them, and they wouldn't know they were there. It was mind blowing because every Thursday I would leave class with these big, distilled water bottles and pour water on them. Something called to me. It was something I found out I was good at. I learned how to nurture the plant from my mother. I just thought, let's see if we can grow something and then we'll share it among ourselves. And that's where it all started." But it was not a linear climb. Ashley worked in the mental health field, toiling at a call center counseling stressed employees of, among other organizations, the Toronto Police Service. Every day, she heard the anxiety that is part of policing, and barely a day passed when she didn't want to just tell the cop at the other end of the line to light a spliff, kick back, and chill. Eventually, this would take a toll on her as well.

Michael, meanwhile, was climbing the corporate ladder and was making a lot of money. He too was becoming exhausted on the nonstop treadmill despite his "cushy" lifestyle, paying his mortgage and keeping his two kids in expensive dance classes. His marketing executive position was losing its allure, and for the first time in his adult life he was not smoking cannabis. Ashley's restlessness led her to seek alternatives—maybe start a line of yoga apparel—until something took her to a government website. Health Canada was looking for suppliers of cannabis. She attended a $2,500 workshop on how to obtain a license, surrounded by white guys in suits and heavy watches. She became a teacher at cannabis activist Abi Roach's Ganja School, a "grow school" in Toronto's Kensington Market that saw enrollment sky-rocket after it was featured in a local television report. She could see her future, but first, she had to take a deep breath and knock at her brother Michael's door. "Do you want to start a cannabis farm with me?" she asked.

By the time the evening was over, Michael knew he had to do it. He had to scratch his entrepreneurial itch.

When they set out to finance their project, they knew that the nation's banking system was inherently racist. "No one would have been invested in us," Ashley says. "No one would fund a black female launching a cannabis cultivation business." She had done her homework. She had traveled to Oakland and Colorado and was told, largely by white entrepreneurs, not to get investors because she would get burned. "I didn't even go that route. I am open to taking risks. So, I sold my house." Today, HRVSTR is producing premium cannabis from cultivating facilities in Ontario's Durham region, home to almost 3,000 plants—craft product aimed at the cannabis connoisseur.

All those whose stories are told in this chapter have found success. They do, however, have differing views on social equity and what needs to be done, but they all believe that they can be models who can encourage other entrepreneurs of color to get their rightful share back. Harrington is working to raise awareness around the opportunities in the cannabis space, because prohibition "destroyed our communities." Some 85 percent of all drug arrests in African American communities have always been cannabis related. Black people represent only 4–6 percent of the entire legal cannabis industry, Harrington says, but Black people never owned the farms that grew the plant or the trucks that got it into our communities: "Hopefully we can inspire other people of color to realize that cannabis is the opportunity to rebuild our community, . . . Generational wealth is at risk if we don't do it. Black people started rice, sugar, cotton, alcohol, the lottery. These are all industries that we helped pioneer and we have no ownership stake. In those days, we didn't have the resources that we have now. Now, we should be able to own a part of this industry."

Harrington has created a coalition of people of color as investors in Viola, and he has committed more than $500,000 to partner with young Black and Brown prospective entrepreneurs as part of his social equity program, Viola Care, in Los Angeles. He is aiming to create one hundred Black millionaires. "That's bigger than Viola," he says. "This is our opportunity to help liberate our people." Harrington believes politicians do not really know how to institute social equity. They are trying to give licenses to people who have no resources or experience dealing with the bureaucracy. Harrington is active in the Minority Cannabis Business Association, which is working to simplify access to the industry for marginalized Americans: "The only way this is going to work is to put people like me in the room when they're crafting legislation so we can tell our stories. . . . Even me, a guy who played sixteen years in the NBA and had all kinds of friends, it was difficult." As he puts it, who is going to invest in a guy making $50,000 who may have recently been in prison: "[Social equity] is not set up to be successful. We need more programs to coach these people up for these opportunities. It is difficult to start up a business and keep it intact. It's all about having a seat at the table. If we're going to wait for the lawmakers or government to save us and create the opportunities, it'll never happen. We'll be customers for all these industries that we've pioneered."

Harrington is creating opportunities to create wealth: "If not us, I don't know who will do it. We have to have a real effect and real change and real impact on people who look like us." He has seen the pitfalls of social equity programs. He knows people in California who sold their homes trying to get into this business, and the bureaucracy moved at such a glacial pace it denied them any revenue for so long they had to give up, their homes lost: "You are asking people to take on a lot of risk. I know they are looking at this as a once-in-a-lifetime opportunity for them and their families, but it is a fact they swing for the fences for these licenses, and if they lose, they don't get a second chance. . . . It's a vicious cycle. A lot of that risk can be reduced by using tax revenue to help these people. It's one thing to say Black people can do this, that, and the other thing. But without the capital we are left behind again."

The Athills did not set out to break down doors, but they are mindful of their responsibility as pioneers. When they began, they didn't even know if other Black or Brown entrepreneurs were licensed: "All I knew was we were going to grow weed and sell it to the government." But when they realized they were game changers, their perspectives changed: "We had to process what this really means to each of us. People have called us pioneers. . . . We actually had to sit down and deal with that. After so many people of color had been persecuted, incarcerated, or killed over that plant, that was something for us to deal with. We do not take this lightly. We are focused on getting other people through this door."

The Athills are working to transform Canada from laggard to leader when it comes to diversity in the industry. Health Canada reached out to the Athills about creating more diversity in the cannabis space, and Ashley hit on the idea that the cannabis licensing infrastructure program be integrated into an existing government program, the Black Entrepreneurship Program, a Justin Trudeau initiative in which the government partnered with banks on a fund of $350 million over four years to help Black Canadians grow their businesses. It provided technical support and programs aimed at helping Black Canadians overcome barriers to their entry into business. It also offered loans from $25,000 up to $250,000.

Ashley pitched her idea to the government and found a receptive audience. The infrastructure was already in place, and it would not have to reinvent the wheel. The government embarked on consultations, but the Athills wanted more momentum behind the plan so they went to cannabis regulators in Ontario and other established BIPOC (Black, Indigenous, and people of color) businesses. With a bit more muscle added to their pitch, the Canadian government accepted it and said that it planned to roll out a program that would run until 2022–2023. But, first, there would be more consultations, this time outside the government. Those consultations were set to begin in the autumn of 2021, following a Canadian election that returned Trudeau to Ottawa. When the government opened the program to loan applications—without the cannabis component championed by the Athills—it received 12,000 applications in the first forty-eight hours. That showed Ashley that people in her community were willing to bet on themselves. Adding cannabis to the process would be like adding rocket fuel.

Ashley knew that $250,000 was not going to start HRVSTR, and few loans of that size would be available under the program. But a $50,000 loan could start a Black entrepreneur on the way to a partnership with established licensees to provide ancillary products such as essential oils, body care products, or CBD products for therapists. There is cannabis tourism. Perhaps they could open a Bud B&B. It could lead to a pathway to ownership of a retail store. On their own, the Athills have created the SEED initiative, in which they will provide resources and expertise to help entrepreneurs get on their feet through incubator programs. "Canada can be one of the global leaders in diversity and it should be a leader," Ashley says. "We are leading this, but we are very much a part of this." There is likely a circuitous path ahead, and they cannot do it on their own, but the Athills believe cannabis can change not only minds and bodies but also the economy and the very shape of Canada. The goals are lofty, but Ashley is still very much the girl who headed out after school with Kenny and Rav. Her torrid love affair with the plant has not cooled.

Jesce Horton has a different take on social equity. He does not believe any people of color should be waiting for a government program to get them started. For Horton, the keys are unlimited licenses, regional markets, and friendly environments for Black people starting a business, something he found in Portland. He also benefited from the policy of unlimited licenses in Oregon. "Unlimited licenses—if we could export that concept across the country, you would see far more Black and Brown entrepreneurs in this industry," he said. "'Unlimited' engenders fear in some," he acknowledged. "Oh my God, what would happen if cannabis licenses were unlimited? . . . But we've got unlimited fast-food restaurants, we've got unlimited liquor outlets, unlimited places where you can buy sugar. The market will shake out. The people who provide the best value to the marketplace will win out." But we are dealing with a fear-based policy because of the stigma that still surrounds cannabis—hence, the move to limit. There is still a taboo: "It's the thing that made my mother hang up on me, or drove away potential investors from me, where I could have raised $1 million instead of the $300,000 without this fear factor." When licenses are limited, Horton said, even with social equity points or mandates, you are still largely benefiting those with political connections and a deep well of funds. Unlimited licenses will lead to greater diversity in the market. But liberalized retail and cultivation cannabis licensing in Oregon, believed to be home to the country's cheapest legal cannabis, has had another, somewhat counterintuitive effect. The state is grappling with an abundance of illegal cannabis farms, mainly exporting to large East Coast states, where retail cannabis outlets still do not exist, or undercutting the cost of legal cannabis in other states. They are also meeting demand outside the state (Oregon is believed to have a six-year inventory of legal cannabis) created by years of legalization that other licensed markets have trouble meeting. These illicit farms are also supplying a market caught between legalization in some states but federal illegality fueling an illegal market elsewhere.[7] Another license liberalized state, Oklahoma, is dealing with the same issue. Illegal operations are also degrading the environment and posing a threat to local residents.

But Horton says licensing rules that remove barriers are more effective than legislated social equity programs: "If you have ten licenses and you say they are all going to social equity applicants, well, congratulations, you made ten millionaires. But what about people like me who added a lot of value to the market and to patients, consumers and the community, who are not politically or financially well-connected? We still don't get in." There are other, well-known, barriers identified by Horton. There is the question of capital—a $20,000 license fee can still grow to a $1 million commitment when all requirements are tallied. Those numbers are astronomical and well beyond the grasp of those with no access to financial markets. It all adds up to fear—fear of making it in the capital market, fear of reengaging with a system that has screwed them, fear (for some) of going back to jail. As Horton explains, "We have been criminalized and harassed and blocked from licenses. This stops so many people of our communities from not only getting into this market or even taking advantage of the health benefits of this product. They don't want to go to jail. They have PTSD when it relates to law enforcement. That hurts people of color from benefiting in a multitude of ways."

Horton founded the Minority Cannabis Business Association (MCBA) in Oregon in 2015 and oversees the NuLeaf Project incubator program, which provides funding for cannabis business and a mentoring program for racialized persons seeking to enter the industry. NuLeaf is dedicated to helping others because, as Horton puts it, "I've been able to develop resources that put me in a position to help others." Like Harrington, he believes that he has a responsibility to inspire others merely by being seen as someone who broke into the industry and thrived: "A lot of people are doing a lot of good.

There is a lot of low-hanging fruit lying around, things that can be done that create ripples that turn into waves and help inspire a lot of people. That's one of the main reasons I started MCBA. Just the ability to see and hear from people who have been successful is extremely important."

Be aware of your region, Horton advises, because Florida, for example, is different in every respect from Oregon. Know what is doable in your region: "Just dive all the way in, headfirst. If you want to be a cultivator, move to a legal state and get involved with cannabis organizations, go to the meetings, talk to the people who are deciding things, spend as much time as you can diving all the way in and don't worry about anything else." A lack of capital need not be intimidating, Horton says. He tells people they would be surprised how many aunts and uncles have $10,000 in 401(k)s or IRAs: "Plunge into that network of people who know you, believe in you, trust you, who love you, because you're not going to have everything right. But if they believe in you, you can get those small amounts and it will add up." Most importantly, he says there are a lot of people who are Black and Brown who are starting up and see people like him and recognize their goal isn't so far-fetched.

Sims is straight with others trying to enter this space: "It is the toughest thing you'll ever do, way tougher than the NFL. . . . It'll cost money, and doors will be slammed in your face." He has seen Black youth being shut out of that space, not only in North America but also in Jamaica and South Africa. Primitiv is providing grants to the Detroit Homegrown Fund, which offers an incubation program and financial help for racialized citizens looking to enter the industry. Sims and Johnson are offering internships to those who can learn from their growing expertise. The duo has also been enlisted as ambassadors at the Last Prisoner Project, which aims to free those still behind bars for nonviolent cannabis convictions. "It's our mission to be a light for these people. As visible as we are, we have to make sure we carry the torch appropriately with a certain amount of grace and class so those folks can believe, because it's going to be hard for them," Sims says.

James puts much of the difficulty in enacting sound social equity regulations at the feet of Ward Connerly and his 1996 Proposition 209 in California. Connerly, now eighty-two, is no historical footnote. This man, born in a segregated Black community in Louisiana before coming to California in the Great Migration, has transformed the journey to racial equity in the United States. He rose in the world of academia and was appointed a regent at the University of California by Governor Pete Wilson, whom Connerly had befriended years earlier. Connerly had worked on a campaign to end housing discrimination in the state, but while at the University of California he developed an interest in race-based admissions and concluded that white and Asian students were being discriminated against because affirmative action was favoring Black and Latino applicants.

It was the early 1990s, another tumultuous time in US racial history, and a move to end affirmative action failed in the California legislature. Along came Connerly, who sought to put the question to voters. He gained enough signatures to put Proposition 209 on the ballot for the 1996 elections, one of California's omnipresent voters' propositions, and then won with 54.5 percent of the vote despite high-profile opposition. California Constitution's Declaration of Rights had Section 31 added, declaring that the state could not discriminate against, or grant preferential treatment, on the basis of race, sex, color, ethnicity, or national origin in the operation of public employment, public education, and public contracting.

When Michigan instituted a similar policy years later, it was challenged in the courts and went all the way to the US Supreme Court, which ruled in 2014 that states had the right to limit affirmative action through legislative action. But, in 2020, in the year of racial reckoning following the murder of George Floyd and the prominence of the Black Lives Matter movement, California voters were given a chance to finally repeal Connerly's proposition, twenty-four years later. Proposition 16, overturning Connerly's work, was on the ballot, and eighty-one-year-old Connerly, then living in Idaho, returned to California to protect his original proposition. "Every time you give someone affirmative action, you're discriminating against somebody else," he said, holding firm to his long-held belief. "In order to build a civil society, everyone needs to believe they will be treated equally and fairly by their government."

This time, his opponents raised nearly twenty times more money than those who backed the original proposition. Proposition 16, repealing the

1996 constitutional amendment had the backing of virtually every prominent Democrat at the state and local level. Regardless, California voters rejected the move to repeal, this time with 56 percent of the vote, making Connerly's proposition more popular than in 1996. James believes this has allowed endless moves to circumvent the goals of social equity throughout the country. "We essentially can't put a law on the books anywhere that says we are going to put Brown and Black people harmed by the War on Drugs first in line for these licenses," James said. Laws have to be written with ridiculous workarounds including limiting social equity to certain zip codes or people living in certain communities defined by statistics during certain years or specifying incarceration for certain offenses.

This is what we are left with, according to James: white firms find a social equity applicant who has never earned more than $30,000 a year in their lifetime and pays them $100,000 to go get a social equity license. The firm then milks that license for all it is worth, and although the social equity applicant owns 51 percent of the operation, they end up paying a management fee to a big multistate operator, so the social equity applicant ends up owning only 1 or 2 percent of the business. Then rounds of litigation begin, and everyone sues because the rich white operators didn't get a license. This puts a chill on everything for two, four, or five years, a period during which the social equity applicant is holding an empty space they can no longer afford while the courts decide their future: "So they end up selling the space and lo and behold, we have an all-white industry." A complex issue oversimplified? No; what she describes is in fact happening.

Black investors, who, if they are fortunate, may have had that wealth for a single generation, are risk averse with that wealth, certainly more so than a white investor who has had financial comfort for generations, James says. And there is still a stigma to the industry—family members in Texas told her she was going to go to jail if she opened a dispensary. James thinks that is changing. Most of the opposition to dispensaries is now limited to conservative suburban moms "who are thrilled to be interviewed between glasses of wine and a Valium and don't think their kids should have to walk past a dispensary. That stigma is fading. But it's still okay for Black mothers to mourn the deaths of their children over possession of a joint. It is Catch-22 for us at every turn." James has a five-step prescription for any social equity ills:

- Make it illegal to arrest anyone for cannabis.
- Expunge every record of everybody who had a criminal record for a nonviolent cannabis offense across the United States.
- Remove anyone from prison who is there for a nonviolent cannabis offense—immediately.
- Legalize at the federal level so we could have interstate commerce and have cannabis move across the United States as the agricultural product it is.
- License dispensaries the way restaurants are licensed.

James wants to create a cross-country awareness program with Black entrepreneurs explaining why they are in the business. She remains that self-described warrior, and she will continue to use her voice when she sees injustice.

These are some of the leaders who will fill the voids where governments fail. They are the leaders whose voices will be regarded, who will lend the helping hands, and who will provide the inspiration. They are the ones whom others can see and think, "Why not me?" There is much work to be done, but if you believe in happy endings, these people are so far crafting nothing but good vibes. Harrington's grandma Viola just celebrated her ninetieth birthday in Fayetteville, North Carolina. She still uses cannabis edibles. Horton's dad not only got his investment money back, but Horton helped his proud parents with their home renovations. James has employed her brother in her restaurant and her cultivation facility. And Ashley Athill? "I'm still a person who goes into the woods and pours water on the plants."

9 THE WAY FORWARD

The way forward first involves looking back. It requires us to acknowledge and understand the history that led us to where we are today. It allows us to always be aware of the weight of that history—a century of racism and injustice. That oppression was inflicted on communities day by day, year by year, neighborhood by neighborhood with one heavy-handed tactic after another. That legacy will not be overturned in a handful of years. Harry Anslinger and his kind laid the framework for a War on Drugs that persists to this day. They set in motion the development of laws and policies that would elevate drug possession, cultivation, and trafficking to the same level as murder or rape. They oversaw the establishment of specialized enforcement teams that were the precursor to the highly militarized police we have today. They scooped up Black and Brown youths in unprecedented numbers, leading to what we now call mass incarceration. They left generations to deal with the consequences of this mass incarceration, leaving children without parents, parents without hope, and communities without prosperity.

As we unwind these laws, dismantle these structures, and legalize cannabis (and, eventually, other drugs), we must keep the harms of the War on Drugs in the front of our mind. We must remember that Michael Thompson, Corvain Cooper, and Evelyn LaChapelle are among millions whose lives have been derailed and their futures clouded by unfair prohibition laws. They are the casualties of an offensive that has lasted more than a hundred years and cost us tens of billions of dollars. If a racist history isn't enough to get you to question the merits of drug prohibition, consider this: for most—scratch that, for almost all—of human history, drugs were not illegal. There were no laws dictating their sale or consumption and no penalties attached to their possession. Drug prohibition is a recent phenomenon and a dangerous anomaly.

We are not suggesting everyone embrace drugs and their use but, rather, to recognize their normality in society, their therapeutic benefits, and their often-sacred status in some cultures. We subscribe to the views of Carl Hart, the Columbia University psychology professor and author of *Drug Use for Grown-Ups*, who has built a huge following by persuasively arguing for the legalization of drugs and against government efforts to legislate against adults who choose to alter their consciousness. He has argued, as we have, that the War on Drugs is about social control, boosting prison populations and police budgets in the process. Dr. Hart's views on the effects of cannabis are really not much different from those of Lester Grinspoon some fifty years ago.

We need a full understanding of what we are dealing with so that we can move forward to where we need to go. In this book, we have laid out a three-part framework for cannabis equality and fairness: first, there is amnesty, the clearing of those unnecessary and ever so damaging cannabis-related criminal records; second, there is the redistribution of a portion of the financial gains of legalized cannabis back into the communities most harmed by its criminalization; and third, there is inclusion in the legal industry for those most harmed by prohibition.

AMNESTY

People, families, and communities cannot move forward without a clearing or downgrading of these sentences and records. Canada ignored this imperative, but San Francisco, and later Illinois and New York, are on the right track. The onus must be on the state to clear these records—the process should be comprehensive, automatic, and free. Where the use of novel technology—such as Clear My Record—is feasible, great. Whatever we can do to clear these records quickly and efficiently, we should do.

If records are not so easy to access, or novel technological approaches cannot be used for any other reason, old-fashioned hard work should be employed. We have noted the great effort that local, state, and federal law enforcement agencies have used to criminalize people for cannabis and the costs associated with those efforts. We shouldn't think twice before going to equal or greater lengths to see these records erased—society will be better for it. At the state level, Illinois provides an excellent example of the work to be done here—state and local law enforcement agencies had cleared several hundred cannabis-related records in the year following the onset of legalization, and a deadline for all counties to have expunged arrest records between 2013 and 2019 was set for January 1, 2021. All eligible records are to be expunged by January 1, 2025.[1]

We should also consider being bolder in our amnesty efforts and seek to clear the records of any offenses linked to an initial cannabis offense. This would include offenses such as breach of conditions or failure to comply with a court order—offenses that would not have been possible to commit had it not been for the cannabis offense in the first place. Starting over with a clear record is one thing. Coming back from a period of incarceration is another. Anyone who understands the challenges of "reentry," the process of assimilating back into society after a period of incarceration, will know of the difficulties faced by ex-prisoners as they try to find housing, secure employment or other sources of money, access health services, reconnect with family and satisfy the conditions of their release, typically with very little or no support. The Last Prisoner Project (LPP), for example, provides reentry grants to ex-prisoners to help ease the transition from incarceration back into the community. Such programs could be greatly expanded with the involvement of state governments.

REDISTRIBUTION OF REVENUE FROM LEGAL SALES INTO THE COMMUNITIES MOST HARMED

We need to press our governments to reinvest some of the tax revenue they are getting from legal cannabis sales back into the communities that have been harmed by prohibition. In doing so, jurisdictions explicitly acknowledge the devastation caused by the War on Drugs and the burden shouldered by the individuals and communities most harmed. They also recognize that the billions of dollars spent on the police, court systems, and correctional institutions as part of this war took money from the schools, hospitals, and community centers that form the backbones of healthy communities. It is no coincidence the American neighborhoods with the worst-performing schools, poorest health outcomes, and most meager public services also have the highest levels of police activity and greatest numbers of incarcerated residents.[2] As established in California, Massachusetts, Illinois, and now New York, tax reinvestment funds must be set up to do the hard work of rebuilding families, communities, and social infrastructure. Although there are questions about the success of early reinvestment programs, Illinois announced the distribution of $31.5 million in grants funded by cannabis tax dollars to communities disproportionately affected by the War on Drugs. Included in the allocation was $3.5 million for street intervention programs aimed at reducing violence.[3]

New York's Marihuana Regulation and Taxation Act aspires to ensure members of minority communities who have been negatively and disproportionately impacted by cannabis prohibition would benefit from legalization by creating a social and economic equity program to encourage those individuals to participate in the adult-use market.[4] The primary social equity components of the new law include expanding eligibility of social equity applicants, creation of a community reinvestment fund supported by cannabis tax revenue, and automatic expungement of past criminal cannabis convictions. The New York model should set the standard for all states that follow, and could set the standard for federal legalization if it is successful. If carried out as intended, New York's program will have a genuine impact on individuals, families, and communities harmed by prohibition or disregarded by the emerging industry for years to come.

INCLUSION IN THE INDUSTRY

Diversity is good for business. Companies with diverse workforces, leadership teams, and corporate boards outperform their peers whose workforce and leadership does not reflect the market they seek or the community they serve. Governments should be pressed to ensure the nascent cannabis industry does not unfairly exclude the casualties of cannabis prohibition. Laws that exclude those with a cannabis criminal record from working in weed pour salt on a festering wound. Access to the industry should be open, and it should be encouraged. Encouragement can come in the form of dedicated avenues for entry into the industry through the points systems and other models that we have laid out, but they must be adequately developed and regulated. The New York model, dedicating the first one hundred cannabis retail licenses to individuals or family members of people who have been convicted of cannabis offenses, is an excellent example.[5] This industry cannot remain the domain of elite white entrepreneurs.

The reinvestment detailed above can come into play as governments use money from legal sales to provide grants or loans to social equity applicants or establish mentoring and incubation programs to aid Black and Brown applicants who lack the natural advantage of white applicants in their communities. The industry itself needs to take note. Reinvestment and engagement with communities that have been left out of the industry is an effort that transcends politics. Diversity and inclusion in hiring practices should be table stakes at this point, but for cannabis businesses, it is an absolute must with a focus on impacted communities and mentorship opportunities.

Businesses should also put their money where their mouths are and fund programs that are having a direct impact in significant ways, like Cannabis Amnesty and LPP. They can look to Ascend Wellness Holdings (AWH), a multistate cannabis operator that pledged to raise $500,000 by July 2022 through a customer donation program at all AWH retail locations. Previously, AWH raised $250,000 through a similar customer donation program with the company matching customer donations. The chief executive officer has personally pledged to donate to LPP to start the organization's Freedom Circle, which provides an opportunity for cannabis industry leaders and criminal justice reform-focused philanthropists to make sizable donations that support LPP's direct service, public education, and scholastic initiatives.

Some final thoughts. In order to really achieve cannabis justice, we need to make like Spike Lee and do the right thing. We need to apply pressure on our governments to do the right thing. We need to put pressure on the industry to do the right thing. We need to do the right thing ourselves, by voting in elections for candidates who understand the need for equitable legalization. We also need to do the right thing by voting with our wallets. Businesses will take notice if customers demand justice and inclusion. In the age of conscious consumerism, people are increasingly aligning themselves with brands and businesses that share their values and ethics. Industry will want a part of this, and it is on the people who purchase cannabis to create the incentive for businesses.

After almost one hundred years of cannabis prohibition and a mere ten years since the first legal recreational cannabis was consumed in North America, we still have a long way to go to find justice. This book is our call to collectively make that happen. Progress has been slow, but momentum is building. There were no measures for redress built into legalization in early states such as Colorado and Washington. Things began to change in California and then in Massachusetts, Illinois, and now New York. Momentum is also building at the federal level with the Marijuana Opportunity, Reinvestment and Expungement Act and strong statements in support of cannabis justice from the likes of Cory Booker, Bernie Sanders, Elizabeth Warren, Alexandria Ocasio-Cortez, and Chuck Schumer.[6]

We do not believe fairness stops at cannabis. It may have been the most widely used illegal drug under prohibition, but it is certainly not the only one. As calls grow louder for the decriminalization and legalization of psychedelics and other mind-altering substances, we must remember those who have been unjustly persecuted for using those drugs. Legalization is happening fast, but it has not done enough to reduce the racial disparities in cannabis that have existed for generations. The reality is that all current and future legalization efforts must have equity at their heart or else we will end up right back where we are today, with a system of legalization again rigged against those who suffered under prohibition. The history of cannabis is undeniably racist, and it's time to not only confront this intolerable contradiction within our industry but change it for good. The fight for racial justice in cannabis will be long and complicated, just like its past. We hope this book can provide more awareness and a set of resources to help us along this journey.

Acknowledgments

This book draws on the individual and collective experiences of those whose lives have been impacted and irreparably damaged by the War on Drugs. We extend our profound thanks to the courageous people who shared their stories and experiences with us and whose stories we have retold. We are grateful for the tireless efforts of the individuals working to make our society a better place and who are using cannabis legalization as a tool to do so. We owe much to our friends and colleagues who have accompanied us on our journeys, both personal and professional. We are greatly indebted to Tim Harper, Ron Eckel, and Matt Browne for seeing this book to fruition. We also owe our deepest gratitude and love to our families and partners for inspiring us to do the work that we do and supporting us in the process.

Notes

CHAPTER 1

1. "No Vote for Cannabis Legalisation Shrinks to 50.7 Percent after Final Vote," *Radio New Zealand*, November 6, 2020, https://www.rnz.co.nz/news/national/430007/no-vote-for -cannabis-legalisation-shrinks-to-50-point-7-percent-after-final-votes.

2. The *Report of the Indian Hemp Drugs Commission* (1894–1895), as cited by David Bewley-Taylor, Tom Blickman, and Martin Jelsma, *The Rise and Decline of Cannabis Prohibition* (Amsterdam: Transnational Institute, 2014), minimized the dangers of cannabis use; but *The LaGuardia Committee Report: The Marihuana Problem in the City of New York*, begun in 1939 and released in 1944, specifically refuted the theory, promulgated by Anslinger, that cannabis was a gateway drug: https://www.druglibrary.net/schaffer/Library/studies/lag/lagmenu.htm.

3. American Civil Liberties Union (ACLU), *The War on Marijuana in Black and White* (New York: ACLU, 2013), 4, https://www.aclu.org/sites/default/files/field_document/1114413 -mj-report-rfs-rel1.pdf.

4. ACLU, *War on Marijuana*, 4.

5. ACLU, *War on Marijuana*, 16.

6. Single Convention on Narcotic Drugs, 1961, https://www.google.com/url?sa=t&rct =j&q=&esrc=s&source=web&cd=&cad=rja&uact=8&ved=2ahUKEwjUlaeehPP2AhXYG cOKHVOtD0UQFnoECA4QAQ&url=https%3A%2F%2Fwww.unodc.org%2Fpdf%2F convention_1961_en.pdf&usg=AOvVaw02YN2ZzdHDxw9UCixna6L-.

7. Wendy Sawyer and Peter Wagner, *Mass Incarceration the Whole Pie 2020*, March 24, 2020, https://www.prisonpolicy.org/reports/pie2020.html.

8. ACLU, "Mass Incarceration," https://www.aclu.org/issues/smart-justice/mass-incarceration, accessed June 7, 2022.

9. *Thompson v. Bock*, United States District Court, Eastern District of Michigan, Northern Division, February 11, 2004, http://www.michbar.org/file/opinions/district/2004/021104/ 22178.pdf.

10. Letter from Dana Nessel to Michigan Governor Gretchen Whitmer, August 5, 2020.

11. John Simerman and Jeff Adelson, " A Life Sentence for $20 of Weed? Louisiana Stands Out for Its Unequal Use of Repeat Offender Laws," NOLA.com, December 20, 2021, citing statistics from Louisiana Department of Public Safety and Correction, https://www.nola .com/news/courts/article_5f7931ca-5d17-11ec-bcd7-730a4fb99798.html; "Incarceration Trends in Louisiana," Vera.org, https://www.vera.org/downloads/pdfdownloads/state-incar ceration-trends-louisiana.pdf (accessed July 6, 2022).

12. Simerman and Adelson, "Incarceration Trends in Louisiana."

13. *State of Louisiana v. Derrick L. Harris, Court of Appeal of Louisiana*, Third Circuit, January 22, 2014.

14. N'dea Yancey-Bragg, "Black Veteran Serving Life for $30 Marijuana Sale Set Free after Nearly a Decade in Prison," *USA Today*, August 20, 2020, https://www.usatoday.com /story/news/nation/2020/08/20/black-veteran-serving-life-selling-30-worth-marijuana-set -free/5615148002/.

15. Defense Logistics Agency, "Then and Now: A 2020 Look into Leso," June 10, 2020, https:// www.dla.mil/AboutDLA/News/NewsArticleView/Article/2214350/then-and-now-a-2020 -look-into-leso/.

16. Philip M. Bailey and Tessa Duvall, "Breonna Taylor Warrant Connected to Louisville Gentrification Plan, Lawyers Say," *Louisville Courier-Journal*, July 5, 2020, https://www .courier-journal.com/story/news/crime/2020/07/05/lawyers-breonna-taylor-case-connect ed-gentrification-plan/5381352002/.

17. Ontario Human Rights Commission, *A Disparate Impact*, August 10, 2020, 8.

18. Ontario Human Rights Commission, *A Disparate Impact*, 12.

19. A. Owusu-Bempah and S. Gabbidon, *Race, Ethnicity, Crime, and Justice: An International Dilemma* (New York: Routledge, 2020).

20. ACLU, *War on Marijuana*, 19.

21. A. Owusu-Bempah and A. Luscombe, "Race, Cannabis and the Canadian War on Drugs: An Examination of Cannabis Arrest Data by Race in Five Cities," *International Journal of Drug Policy* 91 (2021): 102937.

22. Kanika Samuels-Wortley, "Youthful Discretion: Police Selection Bias in Access to Pre-Charge Diversion Programs in Canada," *Race and Justice* 12, no. 2 (2019): 387–410; Jim Rankin, "Black Youth More Likely to Be Charged and Less Likely to Be Cautioned for Minor Crimes," *Toronto Star*, January 6, 2020, https://www.thestar.com/news/gta/2020/01/06 /black-youth-more-likely-to-be-charged-and-less-likely-to-be-cautioned-for-minor-crimes -study-of-durham-police-data-finds.html.

23. Rachel Browne, "Black and Indigenous People Are Overrepresented in Canada's Weed Arrests," *Vice News*, April 18, 2018, https://www.vice.com/en_ca/article/d35eyq/black-and-indige nous-people-are-overrepresented-in-canadas-weed-arrests.

24. Browne, "Black and Indigenous People."

25. Akwasi Owusu-Bempah, "Where Is the Fairness in Canadian Cannabis Legalization? Lessons to Be Learned from the American Experience," *Journal of Canadian Studies* 55, no. 2 (2021): 395–418.

26. ACLU, *War on Marijuana*, 7.

27. Jimmy Carter, "Call Off the Global Drug War," *New York Times*, June 17, 2011, https://www.nytimes.com/2011/06/17/opinion/17carter.html.

28. Cameron Joseph, "AG Jeff Sessions Calls for Return to 'Just Say No' Policies, Slams Marijuana Use," *New York Daily News*, March 15, 2017, https://www.nydailynews.com/news/politics/sessions-calls-return-no-policies-slams-pot-article-1.2999149.

29. H.R. 3884 Marijuana Opportunity, Reinvestment and Expungement Act, 2019, https://www.congress.gov/bill/116th-congress/house-bill/3884.

30. Natalie Fertig, "House Votes to Legalize Weed," *Politico*, December 4, 2020, https://www.politico.com/news/2020/12/04/house-votes-to-legalize-weed-442903.

31. "Seeds of Change," *Leafly*, June 2021, https://leafly-cms-production.imgix.net/wp-content/uploads/2021/06/25091621/Leafly-2021-white-paper-Seeds-Of-Change-by-Janessa-Bailey-1.pdf.

32. Jeff Smith, "Rhode Island, Mississippi, Maryland Lead 2022 Marijuana Legalization via Legislatures," *MJBizDaily*, June 28, 2022, https://mjbizdaily.com/rhode-island-mississippi-maryland-lead-2022-cannabis-legalization-efforts-via-legislatures/.

33. "Cannabis Taxes Could Generate $132 Billion, Create 1.1 Million Jobs by 2025," *New Frontier Data*, January 10, 2018, https://www.globenewswire.com/news-release/2018/01/10/1286558/0/en/Cannabis-Taxes-Could-Generate-132-Billion-Create-1-1-Million-Jobs-by-2025.html.

34. "New York State Potential Legal Adult-Use Cannabis Sales," *New Frontier Data*, January 26, 2020, https://newfrontierdata.com/cannabis-insights/new-york-state-potential-legal-adult-use-cannabis-sales/.

CHAPTER 2

1. Michael Weinrub, "The Complicated Legacy of Harry Anslinger," *Penn Stater Magazine*, January–February 2018, https://www.case.org/system/files/media/file/Penn%20Stater%20Harry%20Anslinger.pdf.

2. Much of the biographical data on Harry Anslinger was gleaned from Michael Weinreb, "Complicated Legacy"; Harry Anslinger, *The Murderers: The Shocking Stories of the Narcotics Gangs* (New York, Farrar, Straus and Cudahy, 1961); John C. McWilliams, *The Protectors: Harry J. Anslinger and the Federal Bureau of Narcotics* (Newark: University of Delaware Press, 1990); as well as contemporary newspaper reports.

3. *Report of the Indian Hemp Drugs Commission*, 11.

4. Emily Dufton, *The Rise and Fall and Rise of Marijuana in America* (New York: Basic Books, 2017), 3.

5. Harrison Narcotics Tax Act, 1914, https://www.druglibrary.org/schaffer/history/e1910/harrisonact.htm.

6. Second International Opium Convention, 1925, https://treaties.un.org/pages/ViewDetails.aspx?src=TREATY&mtdsg_no=VI-6-a&chapter=6&clang=_en.

7. Haggai Ram, *Cannabis: Global Histories*, ed. Lucas Richert and James Mills (Cambridge, MA: MIT Press, 2021), 111.

8. Rudolph Joseph Gerber, *Legalizing Marijuana: Drug Policy Reform and Prohibition Politics* (Westport, CT: Greenwood Publishing, 2004), 9, citing Statement of Harry J. Anslinger, Commissioner of Narcotics, Treasury Department to the Congressional Ways and Means Committee, 1937, https://www.druglibrary.org/schaffer/hemp/taxact/anslng1.htm.

9. Harry Anslinger, "Marijuana: Assassin of Youth," *Reader's Digest*, February 1938, https://www.druglibrary.org/schaffer/history/e1930/mjassassinrd.htm.

10. Timmen L. Cermak, "The History and Art of Marijuana Policy," in *From Bud to Brain: A Psychiatrist's View of Marijuana*, ed. T. Cermak (Cambridge: Cambridge University Press, 2020), 199.

11. Roman King, "The Resurgence of American Nativism in the Early-Twentieth Century and Its Effects on Industrial Hemp Production in the United States" (Master's thesis, Fort Hayes State University, 2018), 3121, citing "Delirium or Death: Terrible Effects Caused by Weeds and Plants Grown in Mexico," *Los Angeles Times*, March 12, 1905, 56.

12. "Mexican Family Go Insane: Five Said to Have Been Stricken by Eating Marihuana," *New York Times*, July 6, 1927, https://www.nytimes.com/1927/07/06/archives/mexican-family-go-insane-five-said-to-have-been-stricken-by-eating.html.

13. Haggai Ram, *Intoxicating Zion: A Social History of Hashish in Mandatory Palestine and Israel* (Stanford, CA: Stanford University Press, 2020), 120.

14. Marihuana Tax Act, 1937, https://www.druglibrary.org/schaffer/hemp/taxact/mjtaxact.htm.

15. Steve D'Angelo, *The Cannabis Manifesto* (Berkeley, CA: North Atlantic Books, 2015), 27.

16. Anslinger, "Marijuana."

17. Statement of Anslinger to Congressional Committee, 1937.

18. Statement of Anslinger to Congressional Committee, 1937.

19. Richard J. Bonnie and Charles H. Whitebread II, *The Marijuana Conviction* (New York: Lindesmith Center, 1999), citing "Prof Flies High and Crashes, All on the Wings of Marihuana," *New York Post*, April 7, 1938.

20. Dale H. Gieringer, "The Forgotten Origins of Cannabis Prohibition in California," *Contemporary Drug Problems* 26, no. 2 (1999): 237–288, 262.

21. Eric Schlosser, "Reefer Madness," *Atlantic*, August 1994, https://www.theatlantic.com/mag azine/archive/1994/08/reefer-madness/303476/.

22. McWilliams, *The Protectors*, 104.

23. Marihuana Conference, United States Bureau of Internal Revenue, Washington, DC, December 5, 1938.

24. US Commission on Marihuana and Drug Abuse, *Marihuana: A Signal of Misunderstanding*, 1972, citing Harry Anslinger testimony to Congress on Boggs Act, 1951, 493.

25. Kate Allen, "Why Canada Banned Pot (Science Had Nothing to Do with It)," *Toronto Star*, December 1, 2013, https://www.thestar.com/news/canada/2013/12/01/why_canada _banned_pot_science_had_nothing_to_do_with_it.html.

26. Allen, "Why Canada Banned Pot."

27. British North America Act (UK), 1867, 30–31 Vict., c. 3.

28. Emily Murphy, *The Black Candle* (Toronto: Thomas Allen, 1922), 332.

29. Murphy, *Black Candle*, 333.

30. Emily F. Murphy, "The Grave Drug Menace," *Maclean's Magazine*, February 15, 1920.

31. Catherine Carstairs, "How Pot Smoking Became Illegal in Canada," *LawNow*, November 2, 2018, https://www.lawnow.org/how-pot-smoking-became-illegal-in-canada/.

32. P. J. Giffen, Shirley Endicott, and Sylvia Boorman, *Panic and Indifference: The Politics of Canada's Drug Laws* (Ottawa: Canadian Centre on Substance Abuse, 1991), 178.

33. Giffen, Endicott, and Boorman, *Panic and Indifference*, 182.

34. Single Convention on Narcotic Drugs, March 30, 1961, https://www.unodc.org/unodc/en /treaties/single-convention.html?ref=menuside.

35. Dan Baum, "Legalize It All," *Harper's Magazine*, April 2016, https://harpers.org/archive /2016/04/legalize-it-all/.

36. Akwasi Owusu-Bempah, "Race and Policing in Historical Context: Dehumanization and the Policing of Black People in the 21st Century," *Theoretical Criminology* 21, no. 1 (2017): 23–34.

37. Comprehensive Drug Abuse and Prevention Act, 1970, https://www.govinfo.gov/app /details/STATUTE-84/STATUTE-84-Pg1236.

38. Transcript of Richard Nixon's War on Drugs speech, June 17, 1971, http://media.avvosites .com/upload/sites/396/2019/07/Transcript-of-Richard-Nixon's-War-on-Drugs-Speech-on -June-17-1971-Google-Docs.pdf.

39. "US Drug Enforcement Administration, Staffing and Budget," 2021, https://www.dea.gov /data-and-statistics/staffing-and-budget.

40. Mario Parker and Josh Wingrove, "Trump Reboots Rallies in Tulsa wWith Smaller Crowd Than Promised," *Financial Post*, June 21, 2020.

41. Richard Sandomir, "Lester Grinspoon, Influential Marijuana Scholar, Dead at 92," *New York Times*, July 2, 2020, https://www.nytimes.com/2020/07/02/science/lester-grinspoon-dead.html.

42. Lester Grinspoon, *Marihuna Reconsidered* (New York: Bantam Books, 1971), 412.

43. Interview with Peter Grinspoon, August 31, 2020.

44. James L. Goddard, "The Best Dope on Pot So Far," *New York Times*, June 27, 1971.

45. Dan Adams, "At 89, Legendary Psychiatrist and Marijuana Advocate Still Wonders about Harvard Professorship," *Boston Globe*, April 28, 2018, https://www.bostonglobe.com/metro/2018/04/28/legendary-psychiatrist-and-marijuana-advocate-still-wonders-about-harvard-professorship/7UBEbWBedoW44gKHpFhLGI/story.html.

46. *The Report of the National Commission on Marihuana and Drug Abuse: Marihuana: A Signal of Misunderstanding* (Section III: Social Impact of Marihuana Use), March 1972 https://www.druglibrary.org/schaffer/library/studies/nc/ncmenu.htm.

47. US National Commission on Marihuana and Drug Abuse, *Marihuana: A Signal of Misunderstanding* (Washington, DC: National Commission on Marihuana and Drug Abuse, 1972).

48. Emily Dufton, *Grassroots: The Rise and Fall and Rise of Marijuana in America* (New York: Basic Books, 2017), 11, citing California National Organization for the Reform of Marijuana Laws, *Fiftieth Anniversary of the First Pot Protest*, August 16, 2014.

49. Jack Healy, "Voters Ease Marijuana Laws in 2 States, but Legal Questions Remain," *New York Times*, November 7, 2012, https://www.nytimes.com/2012/11/08/us/politics/marijuana-laws-eased-in-colorado-and-washington.html.

50. Colorado Division of Criminal Justice, "Impacts of Marijuana Legalization in Colorado," July 2021, https://cdpsdocs.state.co.us/ors/docs/reports/2021-SB13-283_Rpt.pdf.

51. Weinrub, "The Complicated Legacy."

52. John Halpern and David Blistein, *Opium: How and Ancient Flower Shaped and Poisoned Our World* (New York: Hachette Books, 2019).

CHAPTER 3

1. John Griswold, "Running for Sheriff in Aspen," *Common Reader*, March 30, 2021, https://commonreader.wustl.edu/c/running-for-sheriff-in-aspen/.

2. *Cultural Baggage*, August 4, 2013, transcript, https://www.bakerinstitute.org/media/files/page/41c5f904/FDBCB_080413.txt; Kevin E. G. Perry, "'Freak Power': What Hunter S. Thompson's Fight to Fix America Can Teach Us in 2020," *NME*, November 2, 2020, https://www.nme.com/features/hunter-s-thompson-freak-power-documentary-2807295.

3. Daniel Joseph Watkins, *Freak Power: Hunter S. Thompson's Campaign for Sheriff* (Aspen, CO: Meat Possum Press, 2015).

4.   Sophie Gilbert, "When Hunter S. Thompson Ran for Sheriff of Aspen," *Atlantic*, June 26, 2014, https://www.theatlantic.com/national/archive/2014/06/when-hunter-s-thompson -ran-for-sheriff-of-aspen/372949/.

5.   Sean D. Hamill, "Raymond P. Shafer, 89, Governor of Pennsylvania, Dies," *New York Times*, December 14, 2006, https://www.nytimes.com/2006/12/14/obituaries/14shafer.html.

6.   Richard J. Bonnie and Charles H. Whitebread II, *The Marijuana Conviction* (New York: Lindesmith Center, 1999), 274.

7.   Bonnie and Whitebread, *Marijuana Conviction*, 274, citing *Birmingham News*, March 23, 1972.

8.   Bonnie and Whitebread, *Marijuana Conviction*.

9.   All quotes from Mason Tvert come from interviews he did for the Colorado State University's history of the state's cannabis legalization, September 16, 2015; October 2, 2015; October 23, 2015; December 7, 2015; and an interview with the authors on September 23, 2020.

10. Associated Press, "Legalize Marijuana Adverts Target Bush," *Sydney Morning Herald*, November 6, 2006, https://www.smh.com.au/world/legalise-marijuana-adverts-target -bush-20061106-gdorgq.html.

11. Kris Kane, "The Cannabis Industry Remembers Steve Fox," *Forbes Magazine*, April 15, 2021, https://www.forbes.com/sites/kriskrane/2021/04/15/the-cannabis-industry-remem bers-steve-fox/?sh=70c6efd12685.

12. Curtis Hubbard, "Let's Have a Real Pot Debate," *Denver Post*, September 14, 2012, https:// www.denverpost.com/2012/09/14/hubbard-lets-have-a-real-pot-debate/.

13. Thomas Mitchell, "Vying for White House, Hickenlooper Looks Back on Marijuana Policy," *Westword*, April, 22, 2019, https://www.westword.com/marijuana/john-hickenlooper-looks -back-on-colorados-marijuana-policy-as-he-aims-for-white-house-11316932.

14. Mitchell, "Vying for White House."

15. Nicole Brodeur, "Alison Holcomb, Waging Weed-Rights War with Grit, Heart," *Seattle Times*, July 20, 2014, https://www.seattletimes.com/entertainment/alison-holcomb-waging-weed -rights-war-with-grit-heart/.

16. Melissa Santos, "Washington Lawmakers Accused of Breaking Promise to Expand Marijuana Licensing to Address Equity Concerns," *Marijuana Moment*, February 14, 2022, https:// www.marijuanamoment.net/washington-lawmakers-accused-of-breaking-promise-to -expand-marijuana-licensing-to-address-equity-concerns/.

17. Kyle Jaeger, "New Jersey Governor Works to Get Out the Vote for Marijuana Legalization Referendum," *Marijuana Moment*, September 30, 2020, https://www.marijuanamoment. net/new-jersey-governor-works-to-get-out-the-vote-for-marijuana-legalization-referendum/.

18. ACLU, *A Tale of Two Countries: Racially Targeted Arrests in the Era of Marijuana Reform* (New York: ACLU, 2020).

19. ACLU, *War on Marijuana*.

20. Alexander Kirk, "Here's How Much Money Was Spent on Marijuana in Colorado Last Year, 9News, February 18, 2022, https://www.9news.com/article/money/colorado-sets-record -marijuana-sales/73-ea670635-1add-46de-b595-cfa57dededa6.

21. Robert Davis, "Colorado Earned $423 Million in Marijuana Tax Revenue Last Year, *Marijuana Moment*, January 14, 2022, https://www.marijuanamoment.net/colorado-earned-423 -million-in-marijuana-tax-revenue-last-year/; "Marijuana Sales Reports," *Colorado Department of Revenue*, https://www.colorado.gov/pacific/revenue/colorado-marijuana-sales -reports.

22. "MED Resources and Statistics," *Colorado Department of Revenue*, October 1, 2020, https:// www.colorado.gov/pacific/enforcement/med-resources-and-statistics.

23. "Public Information," *Colorado Department of Public Health and Environment*, https://www .colorado.gov/pacific/cdphe/news/cdphe-releases-latest-healthy-kids-colorado-survey-data.

CHAPTER 4

1. "An Industry Makes It Mark, The Economic and Social Impact of Canada' Cannabis Sector," *Deloitte*, February 1, 2022, http://ca-en-consumer-business-cannabis-annual-report -2021-AODA.pdf.

2. This and all comments from Gerald Butts come from an interview, January 8, 2021.

3. This and all comments from Anne McLellan come from an interview, December 17, 2020.

4. This and all comments from Nathaniel Erskine-Smith come from an interview, January 7, 2021.

5. This and all comments from Murray Rankin come from an interview, January 28, 2021, and from email exchanges, February 5, 2021.

6. Senate of Canada debates, 1st Session, 42nd Parliament, Volume 150, Issue 271, March 19, 2019.

7. "Proportion of Indigenous Women Nears 50%: Correctional Investigator Issues Statement," *Office of the Correctional Investigator*, December 17, 2021, https://www.oci-bec.gc.ca/cnt /comm/press/press20211217-eng.aspx.

8. "Office of the Correctional Investigator Annual Report 2020–2021," *Office of the Correctional Investigator*, June 30, 2021, https://www.oci-bec.gc.ca/cnt/rpt/annrpt/annrpt20202021 -eng.aspx.

9. Celina Caesar-Chavannes, Twitter, December 4, 2019, https://twitter.com/iamcelinacc /status/1202404035736850433?s=21; Celina Caesar-Chavannes, "If Black Lives Matter, It's Time for True Policy Action and Accountability," *Policy Options*, June 4, 2020, https:// policyoptions.irpp.org/magazines/june-2020/if-black-lives-matter-its-time-for-true-policy -action-and-accountability/.

10. This and all comments from Melvyn Green come from an interview, January 20, 2021.

11. Controlled Drugs and Substances Act, SC 1996, c. 17.

12. Samantha McAleese, "Suspension, Not Expungement: Rationalizing Misguided Policy Decisions around Cannabis Amnesty in Canada," *Canadian Publicd Administration* 62, no. 2 (2019): 612–33.

13. This and all comments from Ralph Goodale come from email exchanges, February 1 and 4, 2021.

14. Criminal Code, RSC 1985, c. C-46.

15. Centre for Addiction and Mental Health, *Cannabis Policy Framework*, October 2014, https://www.camh.ca/-/media/files/pdfs---public-policy-submissions/camhcannabispolicyframework-pdf.pdf.

16. Akwasi Owusu-Bempah, "Canada's Legalization of Cannabis a Success Story Despite a Shaky Start," *Globe and Mail*, January 15, 2022, https://www.theglobeandmail.com/opinion/article-canadas-legalization-of-cannabis-is-a-success-story-despite-a-shaky/.

17. "80% of Canadians Unaware of Pot Pardon Program: Survey," *Mugglehead*, September 4, 2020, https://mugglehead.com/80-of-canadians-unaware-of-pot-pardon-program-survey/.

18. "Cannabis Pardons," *Public Safety Canada*, August 12, 2020, https://www.publicsafety.gc.ca/cnt/trnsprnc/brfng-mtrls/prlmntry-bndrs/20201201/001/index-en.aspx.

19. H.R. 3884 Marijuana Opportunity, Reinvestment and Expungement Act.

20. Nazlee Maghsoudi, Indhu Rammohan, Andrea Bowra, Ruby Sniderman, Justine Tanguay, Zachary Bouck, et al., "How Diverse Is Canada's Legal Cannabis Industry?" *Centre on Drug Policy Evaluation*, October 14, 2020, https://cdpe.org/wp-content/uploads/dlm_uploads/2020/10/How-Diverse-is-Canada's-Legal-Cannabis-Industry_CDPE-UofT-Policy-Brief_Final.pdf.

21. Figures provided by email by Tammy Jarbeau, Health Canada, in response to authors' request, January 27, 2022.

CHAPTER 5

1. All comments by Evelyn Lachapelle come from an interview with the authors, September 28, 2020 and June 23, 2021.

2. All comments by Corvain Cooper come from an interview with the authors, May 4, 2021.

3. All comments by Michael Thompson come from an interview with the authors, April 22, 2021.

4. Javier Hasse, "40k People Are in Prison for Cannabis in the US: Here's How Steve DeAngelo, Damian Marley and Stephen Marley Are Helping Them," *Forbes*, September 26, 2019, https://www.forbes.com/sites/javierhasse/2019/09/26/last-prisoner-project/?sh=6a2ad0c979d8.

5. Mississippi Department of Health, *Annual Bulletin of Vital Statistics*, vol. 1 (1955), 3, https://msdh.ms.gov/phs/old_bulletins/bul1955.pdf.

6. D. Mark Anderson, Kerwin Kofi Charles, and Daniel I. Rees, *The Federal Efforts to Desegregate Southern Hospitals and the Black-White Infant Mortality Gap* (Bonn: IZA Institute of Labor Economics, December 2020), 1, https://docs.iza.org/dp13920.pdf.

7. Tana Ganeva, "Pot Prisoners: Meet Five Victims of the War on Drugs," *Rolling Stone*, September 13, 2017, https://www.rollingstone.com/culture/culture-lists/pot-prisoners-meet-five-victims-of-the-war-on-drugs-200055. Ganeva later met him for his first meal after his release, tweeting that he was "one of the best people on earth." Tana Ganeva, Twitter, February 15, 2021, https://twitter.com/tanaganeva/status/1361453630340149251.

8. Gersten interview with ABC12 News, Flint, Michigan, February 2021, https://drive.google.com/file/d/17fd0vosHddQ7P5opQ8KhD7Hw8bELgKFg/view.

9. Letter from Attorney-General Dana Nessel to Governor Gretchen Whitmer, August 5, 2020, https://www.michigan.gov/-/media/Project/Websites/AG/marijuana/Ltr_to_Gov_Reg_Thompson_08052020.pdf?rev=3420cb3c5c2a4486831181b117877003.

CHAPTER 6

1. James Queally, "San Franciscans Question George Gascón's Legacy as 'the Godfather of Progressive Prosecutors,'" *Los Angeles Times*, October 17, 2020, https://www.latimes.com/california/story/2020-10-17/some-san-franciscans-question-george-gascons-legacy-as-the-godfather-of-progressive-prosecutors.

2. Yiren Lu, "Code Cracking: Why Is It So Hard to Make a Website for the Government?" *New York Times*, November 10, 2016, https://www.nytimes.com/interactive/2016/11/13/magazine/design-issue-code-for-america.html.

3. Jennifer Pahlka, "Coding a Better Government," February 2012, https://www.ted.com/talks/jennifer_pahlka_coding_a_better_government?language=en.

4. ACLU, *War on Marijuana*, 139.

5. US Drug Enforcement Administration, *Get Smart About Drugs*, November 4, 2021, https://www.getsmartaboutdrugs.gov/consequences/federal-student-aid-and-drug-use.

6. Jesse Wegman, "The Injustice of Marijuana Arrests," *New York Times*, July 28, 2014, https://www.nytimes.com/2014/07/29/opinion/high-time-the-injustice-of-marijuana-arrests.html.

7. Bruce Western, *Punishment and Inequality in America* (New York: Russell Sage Foundation, 2006).

8. Pew Charitable Trusts, *Collateral Costs: Incarceration's Effect on Economic Mobility* (Philadelphia: Pew Charitable Trusts, 2010).

9. Bruce Western and Becky Pettit, "Incarceration and Social Inequality," *Daedalus*, Summer 2010, https://www.amacad.org/publication/incarceration-social-inequality.

10. Western and Pettit, "Incarceration."

11. International Covenant on Civil and Political Rights, 1966, 999 UNTS 171.

12. "50-State Comparison: Marijuana Legalization, Decriminalization, Expungement, and Clemency," *Collateral Consequences Resource Center*, June 2021, https://ccresourcecenter .org/state-restoration-profiles/50-state-comparison-marijuana-legalization-expungement/.

13. "RCU Partners with Cannabis Amnesty to Bring Awareness to Bill C-93," *Responsible Cannabis Use*, September 3, 2020, https://thercu.org/blogs/blog/rcu-partners-with-cannabis -amnesty-to-bring-awareness-to-bill-c-93.

14. All comments by Cristine Soto DeBerry come from an interview with the authors, October 5, 2020.

15. Chicago High Intensity Drug Trafficking Areas, "The Impact of Legalization of Marijuana in Illinois," fall 2021, https://static1.squarespace.com/static/57839de5c534a5d68f2bc36e /t/61844300952c2571c7457546/1636057857820/Chicago+HIDTA+2021+Marijuana +Legalization+Impact+Report+for+Illinois.pdf.

16. Code for America, *Partnership Report: Results from Code for America's Automatic Record Clearance Pilot with the San Francisco District Attorney's Office*, February 2019, http://s3-us-west-1 .amazonaws.com/codeforamerica-cms1/documents/Partnership-Report_Clear-My-Record -SFDA_Code-for-America_February-2019.pdf.

17. H.R. 3884 Marijuana Opportunity, Reinvestment and Expungement Act.

18. Controlled Substances Act, 1971, https://www.dea.gov/drug-information/csa.

19. Joe Biden campaign speech, Wilmington, Delaware, July 28, 2020, https://youtu.be/SYs 14l0cIQ0.

CHAPTER 7

1. All comments by Mon-Cheri Robinson come from an interview with the authors, July 23, 2021.

2. "Social Equity Project," *The Initiative*, 11, https://intheinitiative.com/social-equity.

3. "Disproportionately Impacted Areas," *CT Data*, https://data.ct.gov/stories/s/Disproportion ately-Impacted-Areas-Identified-for-P/8nin-pkqb/.

4. "Social Equity Project."

5. Oklahoma Medical Marijuana Authority, *Twitter*, June 1, 2021, https://twitter.com /OMMAOK/status/1400481435149012995/photo/1; "Oklahoma Is the New 'Wild West of Weed'—Colorado Marijuana Entrepreneurs Are Helping Fuel the Green Rush," *Denver Post*, August 9, 2021, https://www.denverpost.com/2021/08/09/oklahoma-marijuana -boom-colorado-cannabis-companies/.

6. Jeremy Berke, Shayanne Gal, and Yeji Jesse Lee, "Marijuana Legalization Is Sweeping the US: See Every State Where Cannabis Is Legal," *Business Insider*, May 27, 2022, https:// www.businessinsider.com/legal-marijuana-states-2018-1; Minority Cannabis Business

Association, *National Cannabis Equity Report*, 2022, https://minoritycannabis.org/equitymap/equity-download/.

7. Eli McVey, "Chart: Percentage of Cannabis Business Owners and Founders by Race," *mjbizdaily*, September 11, 2017, https://mjbizdaily.com/chart-19-cannabis-businesses-owned-founded-racial-minorities/.

8. Maghsoudi et al., "How Diverse."

9. US Treasury Department, "Marijuana Banking Update," *Financial Crimes Enforcement Network*, https://www.fincen.gov/sites/default/files/shared/508_299423_MJ%20Banking%20Update%201st%20QTR%20FY2021_Public_Final.pdf.

10. 1595 Secure and Fair Enforcement Act, 2019, https://www.congress.gov/bill/116th-congress/house-bill/1595/all-actions.

11. "Illinois Adult Use Cannabis Monthly Sales Figures," *Illinois Department of Financial and Professional Regulation*, August 3, 2021, https://idfpr.com/Forms/AUC/2021%2008%2003%20IDFPR%20monthly%20adult%20use%20cannabis%20sales.pdf.

12. All comments by Kara Wright come from an interview with the authors, July 22, 2021.

13. "Examining the Black-White Wealth Gap," *Hamilton Project*, February 26, 2020, https://www.hamiltonproject.org/blog/examining_the_black_white_wealth_gap?_ga=2.22568 2010.1163852746.1628093306-1248450630.1628093306.

14. Emily Moss, Kriston McIntosh, Wendy Edelberg, and Kristen Broady, "The Black-White Wealth Gap Left Black Households More Vulnerable," *Brookings Institute*, December 8, 2020, https://www.brookings.edu/blog/up-front/2020/12/08/the-black-white-wealth-gap-left-black-households-more-vulnerable/.

15. All comments by Crystal Peoples-Stokes come from an interview with the authors, August 4, 2021.

16. Robert J. McCarthy, "New York Legalized Pot: You Can Thank Crystal Peoples-Stokes," *Buffalo News*, April 11, 2021, https://buffalonews.com/news/local/new-york-legalized-pot-you-can-thank-crystal-peoples-stokes/article_1de9c4fa-97af-11eb-859b-b3f835f26ef1.html.

17. Marihuana Regulation and Taxation Act, 2021, https://legislation.nysenate.gov/pdf/bills/2021/s854a.

18. Luis Ferré-Sadurní, "New York Legalizes Recreational Marijuana, Tying Move to Racial Equity," *New York Times*, March 31, 2021, https://www.nytimes.com/2021/03/31/nyregion/cuomo-ny-legal-weed.html.

19. Addison Herron-Wheeler, "New York Governor Rolls Out 30-Day Cannabis Amendments," *High Times*, February 17, 2021, https://hightimes.com/news/new-york-governor-rolls-out-30-day-cannabis-amendments/.

20. "2021 New York Cannabis Legalization Market Opportunity Analysis," https://static1 .squarespace.com/static/5c3630d5af2096f093e42993/t/604a8b9c1afc951ce792762f/16 15498140904/MPG+NY+Market+Opportunity+Analysis+3-11-2021+Exec+Summ.pdf.

21. "New York State Fiscal Year 2022–23 Executive Budget Review," February 2022, https:// www.osc.state.ny.us/files/reports/budget/pdf/executive-budget-review-2022-23.pdf.

22. Timothy Seymour and Jeff Schultz, "Op-ed: Recreational Pot Is Legal in New York: Four Factors That Could Strengthen the Cannabis Sector," *CNBC*, July 7, 2021, https://www .cnbc.com/2021/07/07/these-four-factors-could-strengthen-the-recreational-marijuana -sector.html.

23. "Marijuana Arrests and Summonses," *New York Police Department*, 2021, https://www1.nyc .gov/site/nypd/stats/reports-analysis/marijuana.page.

24. All quotes from Hutchinson taken from Toi Hutchinson, presentation at The Ohio State University symposium, April 28, 2021.

25. All quotes from Title from Shaleen Title, presentation at The Ohio State University symposium, April 28, 2021, unless otherwise noted.

26. Dan Adams, "Q&A with outgoing cannabis commissioner Shaleen Title," *Boston Globe*, December 29, 2020, https://www.bostonglobe.com/2020/12/29/marijuana/qa-with-out going-cannabis-commissioner-shaleen-title/.

27. Marcela García, "For a More Equitable Marijuana Industry, the State Should Bankroll Loans," *Boston Globe*, June 21, 2021, https://www.bostonglobe.com/2021/06/21/opinion/more -equitable-marijuana-industry-state-should-bankroll-loans/.

28. MORE Act of 2021, https://www.govinfo.gov/content/pkg/BILLS-117hr2649ih/html /BILLS-117hr2649ih.htm.

29. Parabola Center, "Policy to Support People Not Corporate Profits," https://www.parabola center.com.

30. All comments by Robin Rue Simmons come from an interview with the authors, August 24, 2021.

31. Bruce Mitchell and Juan Franco, "HOLC 'Redlining Maps': The Persistent Structure of Segregation and Economic Inequality," *National Community Reinvestment Coalition*, March 20, 2018, https://ncrc.org/holc/.

32. Andre M. Perry, Jonathan Rothwell, and David Harshbarger, "The Devaluation of Assets in Black Neighborhoods," *Brookings Institute*, November 27, 2018, https://www.brookings .edu/research/devaluation-of-assets-in-black-neighborhoods/.

33. City of Evanston memorandum report to Alderman Rue-Simmons, November 20, 2019 (on file with author).

CHAPTER 8

1. All comments by Al Harrington come from an interview with the authors, July 26, 2021.

2. All comments by Rob Sims come from an interview with the authors, September 16, 2021.

3. The Parent Company, "The Parent Company Reports First Quarter 2022 Financial Results," May 16, 2022, https://www.newswire.ca/news-releases/the-parent-company-reports-first -quarter-2022-financial-results-802287497.html.

4. All comments by Jesce Horton come from an interview with the authors, August 16, 2021.

5. All comments by Wanda James come from an interview with the authors, September 3, 2021.

6. All comments by Ashley Athill come from an interview with the authors, July 27, 2021 and August 31, 2021; all comments by Michael Athill come from an interview with the authors, July 27, 2021.

7. Natalie Fertig, "Talk About Clusterf—k: Why Legal Weed Didn't Kill Oregon's Black Market," *Politico*, January 14, 2022, https://www.politico.com/news/magazine/2022/01/14 /oregon-marijuana-legalization-black-market-enforcement-527012.

CHAPTER 9

1. Raymon Troncoso, "Illinois State Police Clear Nearly 500,000 Marijuana Arrest Records," *Journal Star*, January 4, 2021, https://www.pjstar.com/story/news/2021/01/04/illinois-state -police-expunge-almost-500-000-marijuana-arrest-records/4135803001/.

2. Ruth D. Peterson and Lauren J. Krivo, *Divergent Social Worlds: Neighborhood Crime and the Racial-Spatial Divide* (New York: Russell Sage Foundation, 2010).

3. Kyle Jaeger, "Illinois Adult-Use Marijuana Sales Exceed $100 Million for Sixth Month in a Row, State Data Shows," *Marijuana Moment*, September 2, 2021, https://www.marijuana moment.net/illinois-adult-use-marijuana-sales-exceed-100-million-for-sixth-month-in-a -row-state-data-shows/.

4. Marihuana Regulation and Taxation Act.

5. Jesse McKinley and Grace Ashford, "New Yorkers with Marijuana Convictions Will Get First Retail Licenses," *New York Times*, March 9, 2022, https://www.nytimes.com/2022/03/09 /nyregion/marijuana-sellers-licenses-hochul.html.

6. H.R. 3884 Marijuana Opportunity, Reinvestment and Expungement Act.

Index